Early Advaita Vedanta Philosophy, Volume 2

Other Books

by

Richard H. Jones

———

Science and Mysticism

Mysticism Examined

Reductionism

Analysis and the Fullness of Reality

Mysticism and Morality

Curing the Philosopher's Disease

Time Travel and Harry Potter

Piercing the Veil

The Heart of Buddhism Wisdom

Nagarjuna: Buddhism's Most Important Philosopher

*For The Glory of God: Christianity's Role
in the Rise and Development of Modern Science*

Indian Madhyamaka Buddhist Philosophy After Nagarjuna

Early Indian Philosophy

Early Advaita Vedanta Philosophy, Vol. 1

One Nation Under God?

Philosophy of Mysticism

Mystery 101

Introduction to the Study of Mysticism

Early Advaita Vedanta Philosophy

Volume 2

_____

Shankara's Commentary

on the Brahma Sutra

in Plain English

_____

Richard H. Jones

Jackson Square Books

2022

Printed and distributed by www.createspace.com

Printed in the United States of America

Copyright © 2022 Richard H. Jones

Library of Congress Cataloging-in-Publication Data

Early Advaita Vedanta Philosophy, Volume 2 / translations with notes and essays by Richard H. Jones.
Includes bibliographical references.
ISBN: 9798812487331
1. Religion (Asian). 2. Hinduism. 3. Sacred books. 4. Jones, Richard H. 1951-

~ Contents ~

I. Translation and Summary

II. Essays

~ Abbreviations ~

BG	The *Bhagavad-gita*
BGB	Shankara's Commentary on the *Bhagavad-gita*
BS	*Brahma Sutra*
BSB	Shankara's Commentary on the *Brahma Sutra*
BSR	Ramanuja's Commentary on the *Brahma Sutra*
BU	*Brihadaranyaka Upanishad*
BUB	Shankara's Commentary on the *Brihadaranyaka Upanishad*
CU	*Chandogya Upanishad*
GK	*Gaudapada-karikas*
GKS	Shankara's Commentary on the *Gaudapada-karikas*
IU	*Isha Upanishad*
KaU	*Katha Upanishad*
KeU	*Kena Upanishad*
KsU	*Kaushitaki Upanishad*
ManU	*Mandukya Upanishad*
MunU	*Mundaka Upanishad*
RV	*Rig Veda*
SU	*Shvetashvatara Upanishad*
TU	*Taittiriya Upanishad*
TUB	Shanakara's Commentary on the *Taittiriya Upanishad*
Upad	*Upadeshasahasri*

~ *Preface* ~

Volume 1 of *Early Advaita Vedanta Philosophy* covered Gaudapada's *Gaudapada-karikas* and Shankara's commentary upon it. The *Brahma Sutra* is *not* a work of Advaita nondualism, but it is translated here into readable English as the platform for the most important work in all of Advaita — Shankara's commentary on it. The portions of the commentary that are important for their philosophical claims or reasoning are translated or summarized. Explanatory essays on both texts are also included.

The aphorisms of the *Brahma Sutra* are very terse and require interpretation. The first aphorism literally translates as simply: "Now Brahman inquiry." Material must be added to any translation to make intelligible sentences. But this process is often very much a matter of a translator's *interpretation*. I have added material in parentheses to indicate my understanding. But there are disputes between the various schools of Vedanta over virtually every aphorism — beginning with what the word "now" indicates in the first line! The text of Shankara's commentary is much more complete, but I have added material without parentheses when what is indicated is fairly clear and added material in parentheses in other places to indicate my interpretation.

I have not attempted to translate Shankara's entire commentary — English translations are usually 800 to 900 pages long with small print. Instead, I have relied mainly upon others' translation to guide me to the philosophical material in his commentary and have translated or summarized the philosophical portions that may remain of interest today. In order to make it more readable, I often changed the grammar, skipped some words, or paraphrased passages, but I retained the meaning (I hope), if not the literary feel of the work.

And it should be noted that I am departing from convention in a major way for one of the two central terms: I am not translating "*atman*" as "self" when it is related to Brahman. For clarity, I distinguish three senses of "*atman*" in the *Brahma Sutra* and in Shankara's commentary: "Atman" as Brahman (i.e., the ontic essence of everything), as the "essence" (atman) of a transmigrating individual (*jiva*), and as a reflexive reference to oneself without any metaphysical implications. As explained in the essays, the term "self" psychologizes the concept too much — "atman" rather is a matter of the *ontic essence* of any phenomenon and will be left untranslated when translating it as "self" would be susceptible to too much misunderstanding.

I. Translation and Summary

~ *The Brahma Sutra* ~

Book 1: The Nature of Brahman
Chapter 1

[1] After (the ritual portion of the Vedas),[1] there is then the inquiry into (the nature of) Brahman (in the knowledge portion of scripture [*shruti*], i.e., the Upanishads).[2]

[2] Brahman is that from which proceeds the origin, existence, and dissolution of this (world). [3] (Brahman) is the source of scripture, i.e., the Vedas (or scripture is the source of knowledge). [4] But (Brahman is known from scripture) because (knowing Brahman) is the aim (of scripture).

[5] (The Samkhyas think nonconscious primal matter [*pradhana*] is the origin of the world), but since (the Upanishads state that the cause of the world) sees, (an unconscious cause) cannot be founded on scripture.

[6] The word "Atman" is used to refer to the cause of the world, and so the word "sees" is not being used in a figurative sense (to refer to a nonconscious beingness). [7] Also because liberation is declared to be for one who holds tight to that one (i.e., Brahman). [8] Also because scripture does not declare that (the world) should be abandoned (but Samkhya declares that liberation involves a separation of the person from matter). [9] And because of the merger (of the world) into the Atman.

[10] (Brahman is considered the cause of the world) because of the uniformity of this teaching (in scripture). [11] And also because that is the

---

[1] The material in parentheses is added to the translated material to indicate my interpretation. I have not followed the traditional grouping of aphorisms within each chapter into different sections.

[2] This is one of only three occurrences of the word "Brahman" in the text (4.1.5, 4.4.5), along with a few references to the "world of Brahman" (*brahma-loka*). The text prefers "Atman." I supply it elsewhere without parentheses when it clearly appears to be the subject because the text is an "inquiry into Brahman." I do this sometimes even when the Atman may be the subject because they are equivalent.

(direct, final) teaching of scripture (on the cause of the world). (That is, the language is meant literally and is not indirectly leading the mind to something else.)

[12] Brahman consists only of bliss, as repeatedly stated (in scripture).

[13] *Objection*: Bliss is a modification (and so is not Brahman).

Response: No. The word you think means "modification" actually means "abundance." (So Brahman is an abundance of bliss.) [14] Also because Brahman is indicated to be the source of bliss. [15] Also because Brahman is referred to in the aphorism on bliss from the Brahmanas that is sung.

(*Objection*: The individual person is the source of his or her own bliss.)

Response: [16] Brahman and not (the individual person) is meant because the claim that the latter is the source of bliss cannot be justified. [17] And because of the declaration (in scripture) of the difference (between Brahman and the individual person). [18] And because desire (propels creation requires consciousness), there is no need to infer (a nonconscious primal matter as the cause as Samkhyas do). [19] In addition, scripture teaches the joining (*yoga*) of this (the individual person) with that (bliss of Brahman).

[20] The one that is within (an individual person is Brahman) since the properties of Brahman are declared to be so (by scripture). [21] (But they are) also different (in some properties) because scripture declares (Brahman to be) different from (the individual person).

[22] Space (*akasha*) is Brahman since Brahman's characteristic marks are mentioned (with regard to it). [23] Life-breath (*prana*) also indicates Brahman for the same reason. [24] Light too indicates Brahman because all four quarters of the world are mentioned with regard to it.

[25] *Objection*: Because quarters are mentioned, light cannot be Brahman (since Brahman is partless).

Response: Scripture declares that the mention of the quarters is to direct the mind toward Brahman. This is also seen in other passages. [26] This also makes possible the representation of beings as the feet, and so forth (of Brahman).

[27] *Objection*: This is not so because of the differences from the earlier specifications (concerning space and light).

Response: There is no contradiction between the two (depictions).

[28] Life-breath is Brahman. This is so understood (in many scriptural passages).

[29] *Objection*: It is not so because the passages (about life-breath) only refer to the speakers themselves (i.e., individuals and not Brahman).

Response: There are abundant references (in these passages) to the innermost atman (as the speaker). [30] The instruction proceeds from the sage's vision that agrees with scripture, as in the case of Vamadeva (the seer of the fourth book of the Rig Veda).

[31] *Objection*: (Brahman is not being spoken of here) because the characteristics of the individual person and the life-breath (are mentioned).

Response: That would lead to a threefold meditation (on Brahman, life-breath, and the individual person as different, which they are not). Also because elsewhere life-breath is accepted as meaning Brahman. Moreover, the characteristics (of Brahman) are mentioned in these passages.

Chapter 1.2

[1] (Brahman is consciousness) because of the teaching that is well-known everywhere. [2] Also because the properties intended to be expressed are fitting for Brahman and [3] are not fitting for the embodied individual person (*sharira*). [4] Also because of the reference of the actor separate from the actions. [5] And because the words denoting them are grammatically different. [6] And because the traditional texts (*smriti*) (agree).

[7] *Objection*: (The supreme Atman is not taught in these passages) because of the smallness of the abode (e.g., the space within the heart is too small to contain it), and because what is discussed is designated (as atomic in size).

Response: (Brahman is referred to as such only) for the sake of contemplation. And (in these passages Brahman) is said to be analogous to (infinitely large) space.

[8] *Objection*: (If Brahman and the embodied individual person are one, then) Brahman would feel the results of the person's experiences.

Response: There is a difference (in the properties of Brahman and an individual person). [9] (The Atman) is the eater, and all movable and immovable (things) are what is eaten (i.e., destroys all of creation at the end of each world-cycle). [10] Also because (the Atman) is the subject of this passage. [11] Both (the Atman and the individual's atman) enter the cavity (of the heart and so are not identical), for that is seen (by other authorities). [12] Also because the distinct properties of the two (are specified in scripture).

[13] The claim that the inner person (*antara*) is Brahman is justified because of the agreement (between its properties and properties appropriate only to Brahman). [14] Also because of its (inner) location (within the body) and so forth attributed to it. [15] Also because the texts attribute bliss to it

(and only Brahman is bliss). [16] And because of the practices to be followed by those who have heard the Upanishadic teaching. [17] Nothing else (but Brahman can be the inner person) because (all other things are) impermanent, and because it is not possible (to attribute the characteristics of the inner person to anything other than Brahman).

[18] Brahman is the inner ruler of the gods and all other beings because of the characteristics that are mentioned. [19] And the inner ruler (is not Samkhya's primal matter) since the scriptural passages mention properties not applying (to matter but only to consciousness). [20] So too (the individual person cannot be the inner ruler) since both recensions (of the Brihadaranyaka Upanishad) speak of it as different from (the inner ruler). [21] The possessor of invisibility and so forth is (Brahman, not the person), because of the characteristics mentioned concerning it. [22] And (primal matter and the individual person) are not mentioned (in these passages) because the distinctive characteristics (of Brahman) are mentioned, as is its difference from these two. [23] And because the form (of Brahman as Lord) is mentioned.

[24] The Cosmic Person (of the Chandogya Upanishad is Brahman) since words denoting the same properties specifically (characterize both). [25] Also because what is stated in the traditional texts (*smriti*) is (only) an inference.

[26] *Objection*: (The Cosmic Person is not Brahman) because words are used (that refer to a specific deity that are not applicable to Brahman) and other reasons, and because the Cosmic Person abides (within the person).

Response: No — the instruction is to conceive (Brahman as inner) and (its properties) are not attributed to anything else, and because Brahman is referred to as a person. [27] For the same reason, the Cosmic Person is not a divinity nor the great element (*bhuta*) (of Samkhya theory).

[28] According to Jaimini, there is no contradiction here even if (Brahman) is directly (meditated upon as the Cosmic Person).[3] [29] The teacher Ashmarathya says that this is so from the point of view of (Brahman's) manifestation (as space). [30] The teacher Badari says that this (form with a size) is only for the sake of constant remembrance (in meditation). [31] Based on scripture, Jaimini says that it is because of an imaginative identification (of Brahman as only what is in the space in the heart for purposes of meditation only). [32] The wandering ascetics of the Jabala school teach that Brahman is inside (the space within the head).

---

[3] Jaimini is said to have been a student of this text's author, Badarayana. He is the author of the *Mimamsa Sutra* that discusses the ritual portion of the Vedas.

Chapter 1.3

[1] Brahman is the underlying support (*ayatana*, "repository") of heaven, earth, and the rest of the world since scripture uses the word "own" (that denotes Brahman). [2] Also because of the teaching that this is (the reality) attained by the liberated. [3] This support cannot be inferred (to be the primal matter of Samkhya theory) since there are no terms indicating (non-conscious matter). [4] So too with any living creature. [5] And because the difference (between the knower and the object to be known) is mentioned. [6] And because Brahman is the subject of the passage. [7] And because of the difference between observing with detachment and eating (MunU 3.1.1). (Brahman does the former and an individual person does the latter.)

[8] The abundance of reality (*bhuman*) is Brahman since the instruction about it is additional to the instruction about serenity (*samprasada*). [9] Also the characteristics of "abundance" fit (only Brahman).

[10] Brahman is the imperishable (*akshara*) since it supports space and all other things. [11] Such support is possible only by Brahman's command. [12] Also because of the exclusion (in scripture) of all things (from it) whose nature (*bhava*) is other than Brahman's.

[13] Brahman is mentioned (in scripture) to be the object of the act of (meditative) perceiving (*ikshati*).

[14] The small space (within the heart) is Brahman for the following reasons: [15] the action of going (into Brahman is through the space in the heart); that space is described as the phrase ("world of Brahman"); it is seen (to be so in other Upanishadic passages); ("small space within the heart") is a characteristic mark indirectly indicating Brahman. [16] Also because the property "supports the world" is (attributed to the small space). Its greatness is seen in that. [17] And the familiar use (of the term "space" also indicates that it is Brahman).

[18] *Objection*: (The essence of an embodied person [atman]) is referred to (as the space within the heart) in other passages, and so (the individual person is meant here).

Response: It is impossible (for a person to reside in that space).

[19] *Objection*: But (a person) is so referred to in subsequent passages.

Response: It is referred to as such only to reveal its real nature (as Brahman). [20] And the reference (to the individual) is for a different purpose.

[21] *Objection*: But scripture declares that this space is limited.

Response: This has already been explained. [22] (The space within the heart) also attains the likeness of Brahman and is referred to as "his." [23] The traditional texts also state this. [24] Brahman is said to be measured by the size of the thumb, [25] but (scripture) speaks of this only concerning Brahman within human beings.

[26] According to Badarayana, gods (are also capable of studying the Vedas and meditating on Brahman) since that is possible. [27] Ascribing corporeality to the gods does not contradict this since it is seen (in scripture) that (the gods) can assume many different bodies. [28] Nor does (the corporeality of the gods) contradict the words of scripture since (the world) arises from the words of scripture, as is known by direct perception and inference. [29] For that reason, the eternity (of the Vedas follows). [30] Nor is there a contradiction since the same names and forms (appear) in each world-cycle, as is seen (from scripture) and the traditional texts.

[31] *Objection*: According to Jaimini, (the gods are not qualified to attain knowledge of Brahman) because they are not qualified (for the preparatory Vedic knowledge, being themselves the objects of meditation and ritual). [32] Also because (their meditation is limited to only) the realm of light.

[33] *Response*: But according to Badarayana, (the gods are qualified for Brahman knowledge) because (their competence for this) exists.

[34] Grief arose (in King Janashruti when he heard a god in the form of a swan) disparage him (as being of the lowest class [a Shudra] and thus not qualified to receive this knowledge). [35] But his being a member of the warrior class is known (from scripture) and from characteristics indicating that he is a descendant of Chitraratha (a known warrior). [36] Also because of the mention of the purificatory ceremonies (that he performed) and the impossibility of that (by a Shudra). [37] Also because the inclination (of teachers to impart knowledge to him) could arise only after ascertaining that he is not (a Shudra). [38] And because the traditional texts prohibit (Shudras) hearing, studying, and acquiring the meaning of the Vedas.

[39] The life-breath is Brahman because (the entire world) trembles (from the breath that is Brahman).

[40] Light also is Brahman because scripture declares it.

[41] Space also is Brahman because (scripture declares space to be) different from (objects in space, i.e., names-and-forms).

[42] Brahman is different (from the individual person) because of the difference between the two in deep dreamless sleep and at death. [43] And because Brahman is described as "the Ruler" (i.e., Lord of the universe).

Chapter 1.4

[1] *Objection*: (The Samkhyas) can infer (from Kaushitaki Upanishad 3.11 that unconscious primal matter is the cause of the world).

Response: The passage shows that (the word "unmanifest" in this passage) is used in a simile concerning (what is contained in) the body and refers to the body itself.

[2] *Objection*: (The "unmanifest" is) the subtle (unseen) body since it deserves that label.

[3] *Response*: (But the unmanifest cannot be the cause of the world) because it is dependent (on Brahman). It serves a purpose (only of being a subtle cause). [4] It is not Brahman also because it is not mentioned in scripture as something that should be known.

[5] *Objection*: The Upanishads do refer to nonconscious primal matter (as an object of knowledge) when they say "unmanifest."

Response: From the context, it is the atman of insight (*prajna*) (that is being referred to). [6] And the question and answer (in the passage) relate to only three things (i.e., fire, the individual person, and the Atman, not primal matter). [7] Just as *"mahat"* (the "great one" that is the first evolute of matter in Samkhya metaphysics) does not refer to (Brahman), neither does *"avyakta"* (the unmanifest or unevolved). [8] So too, *"aja"* (unborn) cannot refer to (matter) since no special characteristics are mentioned, just as we cannot identify which bowl (is being referred in BU 2.2.3) because no special characteristics are specified there.

[9] *Objection*: But some (recensions of the Vedas) consider the three elements beginning with light (to be unborn) — (i.e., fire, earth, and water).

[10] *Response*: There is no contradiction since this is an instruction based on imagery, as with honey (denoting the sun). [11] Even the mention of the number (of Samkhya categories, i.e., 25) cannot be cited for support (for matter as the primal cause) since the categories are different and there is an excess (number of Samkhya categories). [12] So too with life-breath and the breaths (are the origins [*janas*], not Samkhya categories), as is seen in a complementary passage. [13] (In one recension), food is omitted and light is included instead in order to reach the number five (given in the Samkhya system of categories). [14] (Nor is there a conflict between the recensions as to the items created but only with their order of creation) because Brahman is spoken of as the cause of space and everything else.

[15] (Nor does nonbeing mean literal nonexistence) because of the connection (of the passages to Brahman). [16] Because (the word "work" in

Kaushitaki Upanishad 4.19) indicates the world, (the world is the work of Brahman).

[17] *Objection*: (Brahman is not meant here) because characteristics of the individual person and the primary life-breath are mentioned.

Response: This has already been explained (above at 1.1.31). [18] But Jaimini asserts that (the reference to the individual person) is for a different purpose, as the question and answer of the passage indicates. In addition, some (mention this in their recension). [19] (The essence that is to be seen, heard, studied, and meditated upon is Brahman) because of the correlation (of the Upanishadic passages). [20] The teacher Ashmarathya asserts (that the individual person is taught to be the object of realization only as) an indirect indication, and this proves the declaration (that the individual person's essence is Brahman). [21] The teacher Audulomi asserts that (the person's essence becomes one with Brahman) when it departs the body at death (after liberation) because such is its nature. [22] The teacher Kasha-kritsna thinks it is because (Brahman) exists (in the person as the essence).

[23] (Brahman is) also the material cause (*prakriti*) (of the phenomenal world). Thus, there is no contradictions in the declarations and illustrations in scripture. [24] Also because of the teaching on the will (to create). [25] Also because scripture directly teaches that (Brahman) is both (the efficient and material cause of the worlds). [26] (Brahman is the matter) because it transforms itself (*parinama*) by its own action. [27] And because scripture declares (Brahman) to be the source.

[28] Thereby, all (doctrines of the cause of the world) are explained. Indeed, they are explained.

Book 2: Refutations and Defenses
Chapter 1

[1] *Objection*: (If Brahman is the cause of the world), then doctrines from some traditional texts have no scope (to elucidate scriptural teachings).

Response: (If we reject Brahman as the cause of the world), other traditional texts would have no scope (to elucidate scriptural teachings). [2] Also because (the truth of the Samkhya doctrine) is not seen (by other authorities). [3] By this, (the doctrines of the) Yoga school are also refuted.

[4] *Objection*: Brahman cannot be the cause of the world because the world is dissimilar in nature (from Brahman). That (is known) from scripture.

[5] *Another opponent's response*: The dissimilarity is only between the world and the presiding gods based on the special characteristics (of the conscious gods) and (of them) entering (nonconscious matter).

[6] *Vedanta's Response*: (Things in this world with contrary natures) are observed (e.g., persons having conscious and nonconscious parts).

[7] *Objection*: (Effects) do not exist (in their causes before their creation).

Response: Then this is a denial (without an existing object to negate).

[8] *Objection*: With the dissolution of the world at the end of a world-cycle, the cause becomes like the effect (i.e., will have the same nature). Thus, (the doctrine that Brahman is the cause of the world) is unacceptable.

[9] *Response*: There are instances (of reabsorption without the retention of the properties of the effect in the cause, e.g., the Atman embodied in a person retains no effects of the individual person). [10] And also because the defects that you assert apply also to (your own Samkhya) doctrines.

[11] *Objection*: Reasoning is inconclusive, but (doctrines) can be inferred in a different way (that avoids the defects).

Response: There is no escape (from the defects) that way. [12] By this (reasoning), the doctrines (of the other schools) that praiseworthy sages do not accept are also explained.

[13] *Objection*: When the objects to be enjoyed merges into the enjoyer, there is no distinction between the two.

Response: The distinction is well seen in common experience.

[14] The nondifference of (Brahman and the world as cause and effect) is (shown by scriptural texts) with words like "origin" and so forth. [15] Also because (the cause) is seen when (the effect) is present. [16] And because a later (effect) has its existence due to the existence of a prior (cause).

[17] *Objection*: (Scripture sometimes) declares that the effect is nonexistent (in the cause prior to its production since we do see it there).

Response: In complementary parts of the passages (the word "nonexistent") is used to designate a difference in characteristics. [18] (The pre-existence of an effect in a cause and hence nondifference is established) by reasoning and by other scriptural passages. [19] Also from the analogy of the piece of cloth (and the threads it is made from). [20] And as with the different vital organs (*pranas*) (which all exist in the same chief life-breath but appear in different forms as effects).[4]

[21] *Objection*: (If the individual person is not different from Brahman), then faults arise (in Brahman) from (the individual) not doing what is beneficial (for others) and so forth.

[22] *Response*: Brahman is something greater (than the individual person) because of the declarations in scripture of the difference (between Brahman and the individual person). [23] So too, (your position is) unjustified because (the difference) is the same as with a stone (which does not share the same nature with the earth it come from), and so forth.

[24] *Objection*: (Brahman cannot be the cause because we notice that) we need instruments (to make effects and Brahman has none).

Response: It is like milk making itself sour. [25] Also (Brahman creates without instruments) like the gods and others creating in this world.

[26] *Objection*: (Brahman as the material cause of the world involves) the possibility of the transformation of the whole (of Brahman). Otherwise, (Brahman must have parts, some of which transform, but then) scriptural passages about Brahman being partless are violated.

[27] *Response*: (That Brahman is the material cause) must be accepted on scriptural authority because Brahman is known from scripture (*shabda*) alone. [28] And thus it is also in the case of the individual person (in dreams) and of (the gods) that various creations occur (in one substance). [29] Also your position is subject to these same faults (that you allege ours have). [30] And because Brahman is endowed with all (powers), as is revealed in scripture.

[31] *Objection*: Brahman cannot act because it lacks organs.

Response: This was explained earlier (in v. 24 concerning instruments).

[32] *Objection*: Brahman is not the creator because he has no motive to create.

[33] *Response*: But (creation) is a mere pastime (*lila*) for Brahman, like recreation (for us) in this world.

[34] Partiality and cruelty cannot (be attributed to the Lord, i.e., Brahman) because the Lord takes other factors (the karmic acts of individual persons) into consideration (when creating). That (scripture) shows.

---

[4] "*Prana*" in the singular is the life-breath animating a body. In the plural, the "*pranas*" are the vital organs of the body, but their functions and the physical organs (*indriya*) are not always clearly distinguished. "*Prana*" (*life-breath*) is sometimes the chief of the *pranas*.

[35] *Objection*: Brahman cannot take (karmic merit and demerit into consideration from the beginning) because the fruits of actions had no distinctions (before creation to distribute among different actors).

Response: But the (world and the cycle of rebirths) have no beginning (and so there is always some prior actions that generated karmic effects). [36] This is also justified (by reason) (*upapatti*) and comports (with scripture).

[37] (Brahman is the cause of the world) also because all the properties (necessary to create) are present (in Brahman).

Chapter 2.2

[1] (The primal matter) that is inferred (by the Samkhya school cannot be the creator of the world) because (nonconscious matter) cannot explain the orderly arrangement of the world. [2] Also (nonconscious matter) cannot have a tendency (to act).

[3] *Objection*: (Primal matter can undergo transformations without conscious agents), as with milk (into curds) and water (into ice).

Response: But even there (conscious agents are involved in arranging those transformations). [4] Also because there is nothing extraneous (to primal matter), there is nothing for it to rely upon (to cause it to act). [5] Nor can it be like grass (transforming into milk in a cow) since (such a transformation) does not occur elsewhere (i.e., transformations occur only in specific order, and nonconscious matter could not decide which transformations should occur where). [6] Even if we admit (that it is possible that primal matter could transform itself without outside aid), it still could not do so because of the absence of any purpose (to change since it is nonconscious).

[7] *Objection*: The soul (*purusha*) can move primal matter like a lodestone (can move iron) or a lame man (with sight can guide the blind).

Response: Even if that were so, the same defect still exists (since matter would not create by itself). [8] And because of the relation of a principal (to subordinates) is impossible here (since there are only different forms of matter, and matter cannot act to make matter act). [9] Even if (the existence of primal matter could be established) by inference in another way, (it still could not act) due to the absence of the power of a knower. [10] And because of the contradictions involved, (the Samkhya doctrine) is untenable.

[11] So too (the nonconscious could arise from a conscious Brahman just as you claim that) the big and the long are produced from the short and spherical (i.e., infinitely small atoms). [12] From either (the Vaisheshika or

Samkhya) point of view, no (conscious) action is possible. Thus, there would be an absence (of creation). [13] And because (Vaisheshikas accept) the inherence of properties in a substance, this leads by the same reasoning to an infinite regress (of substances and inherences, and so creation could not occur). [14] And also because (either the activity or inactivity of atoms) would persist eternally (since inherence prevents any changes). [15] And because we see that things have color, (the doctrine of invisible atoms) is refuted. [16] Either way (i.e., either atoms are invisible and so we cannot account for color, or they have color), (this doctrine) is defective (and thus untenable). [17] It is also be to disregarded because it is not accepted (by those who are praiseworthy).

[18] Creation of aggregates would not occur even from a combination (of primal matter and atomism).

[19] (Against the Buddhist doctrine of "dependent co-arising"): causes cannot be the cause of one another. Rather, (each cause can only cause the next item in a series — causation is linear, not mutual). [20] Nor (can a momentary earlier element cause a later one) because of the cessation of the prior when the later one arises (and so there is no contact of the elements and so no causal relation). [21] When there is no cause, there can be no claim of causation. (But if the cause does not cease), then there is the contradiction of the cause and effect existing simultaneously. [22] (In the latter case), neither an observable nor unobservable destruction (of the cause) is possible since there is no interruption (of the cause). [23] (Thus, the Buddhist position is untenable) either way due to these defects. [24] The case of space does not differ (i.e., it cannot be treated as going out of existence).

[25] (An enduring entity has to be admitted also) because of our ability to remember. (Memory would not be possible if everything arose and vanished each moment.)

[26] Nor (does something ever arise) from nothing, since that is never observed. [27] If something did come from nothing, people could attain a goal without effort.

[28] (Against Buddhist Yogachara idealism): The doctrine of the non-existence (of external objects) is not true because (such objects) are perceived. [29] Also because (experience in the waking state) is different in nature from a dream. [30] There would also be no existence (of sense-impressions) since (sense-objects would) not be perceived. [31] And (there cannot be a permanent "storehouse consciousness") due to momentariness of everything.

[32] And (Buddhism in general) is unjustified from every point of view (raised above and more).

[33] (The Jaina doctrine of multiple points of view) is not tenable because of the impossibility of contrary properties existing in the same thing (at the same time). [34] Also because the transcendent Atman would then not be all-pervasive. [35] Nor can the contradictions be removed by assuming a succession (of changing particles of the Atman) since this involves the defect of the changeability (of the Atman) and so forth. [36] And since the size (of the Atman) is permanent (in the state of liberation), the size (of the atman prior to liberation also) must be permanent because there is no difference between them (at any time).

[37] (Against a creator god:) (The universe is eternal, and so) a god (cannot be its creator) for that would be impossible. (The god could not be either the efficient or the material cause of the universe.) [38] And (if the god and matter are distinct), they could never be connected, [39] and (thus the universe) could not be supported (or directed by him).

[40] *Objection*: (God directs the universe) like a person directs his or her organs.

Response: Then (God would have) experiences and so forth (associated with organs and leading to rebirth). [41] (God would then last only) a finite time and not be omniscient.

[42] (Against the Bhagavatas): (Individual persons [*jivas*] are not real or created, nor is their cycle of rebirths.) Because of the impossibility of being created, (individual persons cannot emerge from God). [43] And because an instrument cannot (be produced) from the agent (who wields it). [44] Even if (God) possesses knowledge and so forth, this defect is not remedied. [45] In addition, (the Bhagavatas' doctrines) have many contradictions.

Chapter 2.3

[1] Space is not (created) since that is not stated in scripture.

[2] *Objection*: But scripture does state (that space sprang from the Atman [TU 2.1]).

[3] *Response*: (Any scriptural passages on the origin of space are to be taken) in a figurative sense, (not the final truth), since it is impossible (for space to be created). [4] Other scriptural also passages state (that space is eternal). [5] And it is possible for the same word (here, "sprang") (to have both direct and indirect meanings), as with the word "Brahman." [6] The

declaration (that space is not created) stands unaffected because of the nondifference (of all effects from Brahman). This is confirmed in scripture. [7] But division persists wherever there is a modification, as is seen in the world. [8] In the same way, air (as an effect of Brahman) is explained. [9] But (there is no origin to) reality (*sat*), since that is impossible.

[10] Fire is produced from (air), for scripture says so. [11] And water (is produced from fire). [12] (And earth is produced from water.) (The word "food" means) earth because of the topic and color, and other scriptural passages say so. [13] But Brahman as the Lord alone (is the creator) through deep meditation. This is confirmed by his indicatory marks.

[14] The order (of dissolution at the end of a world-cycle) proceeds in reverse of the order of creation. That is the only possibility.

[15] *Objection*: Scripture indicates that the intellect (*vijnana*) and mind (*manas*) are in between (Brahman and the elements) in the order of creation and dissolution.[5]

Response: This is not so because there is no difference (between the intellect and mind and the elements — i.e., they are material). [16] Rather, the mention (of creation and dissolution) is meant (in the direct, literal sense) in relation to what moves and what does not move (i.e., all things). In relation to the individual person's atman, it is meant in an indirect sense since it is applicable (only) when (a body) is present.

[17] The individual's atman is not (created) because scripture states that, and because from scripture the atman is known to be eternal. [18] Based on (scripture), (the atman is known to be) conscious (*jnah*, a "knower"). [19] Because (scripture mentions atmans) departing (the body), going (to a new realm), and returning (in a new rebirth), (the individual's atman is not identical to Brahman but must be atomic in size). [20] (The relation of) one's own atman to these two events (confirms this size).

[21] *Objection*: (The individual's atman is) not atomic in size because it is heard (from scripture) to be otherwise (i.e., that is all-pervading).

Response: Those passages relate to the other (atman, i.e., the Highest Atman — Brahman — not an individual's atman). [22] (Scripture) directly states the atomic size (of an individual's atman).

[23] There is no contradiction (between an individual's atman being atomic in size and the sense that it pervades the entire body): it is like

---

[5] The "*vijnana*" as a mental function is not the same as the mind (*manas*): the latter involves what is seen through the senses and the former "sees" only Brahman.

sandalwood paste (where one drop contacting any part of the body gives pleasure to the entire body).

[24] *Objection*: (That is true for sandalwood paste) because of its particular property (but it does not apply to an individual's atman).

Response: (Scripture states that the atman lies) in the heart.

[25] Or (another analogy): (an individual's atman pervades the body) like (consciousness) pervades the world. [26] (Consciousness) extends beyond (the body) like the sense of smell (extends beyond the object giving rise to the smell).[27] Scripture declares that.

[28] *Objection*: (The atman and consciousness are distinguishable) because they are taught separately (in scripture).

[29] *Response*: But (the individual's atman) is said to be (consciousness) because of the dominance of that mode (i.e., the intellect), just as in the case (of Brahman). [30] And because (consciousness) persists (within the individual) as long the individual's atman continues to be reborn, there is no fault in this claim for that is observed (in scripture).

[31] (Consciousness is not always manifested in the individual,) but the manifestation (of consciousness in the waking and dream states) is possible only because (consciousness) already exists (within a person), (just as with) virility (which is not constantly manifest in all states either) and so on. [32] Otherwise, there is either perpetual perception or perpetual nonperception, or thus one or the other (i.e., the atman or consciousness) would be limited.

[33] (The individual person who is limited by the mind) must be the active agent. Otherwise, scriptural (injunctions about an agent) would have no purpose. [34] Also scripture teaches about (an individual person) roaming. [35] Also because (the individual person) takes up (its sense-organs). [36] And because of the mention (of the person as an agent) concerning action. If it were not so, there would be an indication to the contrary.

[37] (Just as there is no restriction) in the case of individuals' perception, so there is no restriction (in the case of their actions). [38] (The individual person with adjuncts must be the agent) because (if the mind were the agent) there would be a reversal of power. (That is, the mind would control the atman and not vice versa.) [39] And because (if the mind were the agent), meditative concentration (*samadhi*) would be impossible.

(*Objection*: if the individual person is the agent and the organs of action are in the individual, then there would be perpetual action.)

[40] *Response*: It is like a carpenter: he exists under both conditions (of having a mind and having working tools, but he is not perpetually working).

[41] *Objection*: But (the agency of the atman comes) from the highest (i.e., Brahman) as stated in scripture.

[42] *Response*: But the highest (Lord as the common cause makes the person act) according to the efforts made (by that person). Thus, the injunctions and prohibitions (of the ritual part of the Vedas) are not meaningless.

[43] (An individual person) is a part of Brahman because (the person) is mentioned in scripture as different. Also some (passages) tell otherwise (of Brahman's) identity with fishermen, gamblers, slaves, and others. [44] This follows from the words of the mantras. [45] And it is also stated in the traditional texts: ("An eternal part of myself became a living individual person" [BG 15.7]).

(*Objection*: If the individual person is part of Brahman, then Brahman experiences pains, and one who attains Brahman will then feel greater pain.)

[46] *Response*: The highest (Atman) is not so (i.e., it is not touched by the sufferings of individuals), just as light is not (affected by what it illuminates). [47] That is stated in traditional texts. [48] Scriptural injunctions and prohibitions are possible because of the association (of the Atman) with the body, just in the case of light (being associated with the fires that burn good and bad things) and so forth.

[49] And because (the individual person) does not extend beyond the body, there is no confusion (of the karmic effects of one person's actions with those of another). [50] (And the individual person is) certainly only a mere reflection (of Brahman). [51] The unseen principle (of Samkhya theory) does not allocate (karmic) effects of works (to individuals since that would lead to a confusion of the results of different persons' actions since each conscious soul for Samkhyas and Vaisheshikas is all-pervading). [52] And the same (problem) would occur for (mental acts) such as resolutions (to act).

[53] *Objection from the Vaisheshikas*: (Even though atmans are each all-pervasive, there is a distinction of results) from the difference of the (limited) place (within each atman where contact is made with a body).

Response: Since (according to the Vaisheshikas) all souls are infinite, each individual's atman would be in all bodies.

Chapter 2.4: The Vital Organs

[1] The same arguments (given above concerning space arising from Brahman apply to the arising of) the vital organ in a person. [2] (The creation of the organs must be accepted) because of the impossibility of the (scriptural

passages about origins) having an indirect meaning (rather than of a direct, literal meaning). [3] Also because the word "created" is used in its literal sense earlier in scripture (in connection to the life-breaths). [4] And because speech is preceded by (the creation of the elements).

[5] (The organs) are seven in number both because they go (with the person in rebirth) and are specified in scripture. [6] The hands and so forth (are also called "breaths," since they assist an individual while the atman) abides (in a body), and so the number of organs varies (in scripture).

[7] And (the organs' functions) are atomic in size. [8] And (Prana, the chief life-breath is) the foremost. [9] Prana is neither air nor the power of a sense-organ since it is mentioned separately (from those). [10] But (Prana is subordinate to the Atman). The organs are like the senses since they are taught together, and for other reasons. [11] But scripture shows that they are not senses, (and so) no fault (arises here in not calling them) "instruments."

[12] (Scripture) teaches that the life-breath is of five types like the mind and [13] is atomic in size. [14] But (scripture) also teaches that Agni and other gods guide the life-breaths [15] and that (the life-breaths are connected) to the body possessing it. [16] This is so also because of the (permanence of the embodied transmigrating self).

[17] Scripture designates the "breaths" as organs, as distinguished from Prana. [18] This distinction is mentioned in scripture. [19] And (the senses and organs are) dissimilar in characteristics (from Prana).

[20] But scripture teaches that the creation of conceptions and shapes (*samjna-murtis*) is by the maker who made the three types of elements (i.e., fire, water, and earth). [21] According to scripture, the body is created from the earth and from the other two elements as well (e.g., blood from water). [22] But because of their distinctive nature, (the organs) have a distinctive designation.

Book 3
Chapter 1: The Path of Rebirth

[1] (An individual's atman) at death leaves the body still enveloped (by the subtle elements) to attain another body. This is known from the question and answer (in scripture). [2] An (individual's atman is not enveloped solely by water), since the envelop has three components (i.e., fire, water, and earth), but (water alone is mentioned) because of its predominance. [3] And because the vital organs go forth (to the next rebirth with the atman).

[4] *Objection*: (The organs do not go forth) because scripture states that they enter the deities such as Agni.

Response: Such statements are only meant in an indirect sense.

[5] *Objection*: (Water) is not mentioned in the first instance (concerning a certain ritual and water taking the shape of a man).

Response: The word "water" (must be meant) because it is the only word that makes sense.

[6] *Objection*: (The individual's atman does not depart enveloped in water) since that is not stated in scripture.

Response: It is understood that those who perform the ritual (go to a heaven). [7] Or (alternatively), the statement is figurative because (the speakers) have not yet come to know Brahman, for so scripture declares.

[8] After the exhaustion of (the karmic effects of good) actions (that lead to a rebirth in a heaven), (an individual person's atman) follows the path dictated by other karmic effects (to rebirth on earth or elsewhere). This is known through scripture and the traditional texts.

[9] *Objection*: (The individual's atman gets a rebirth) due to the person's ritual action (alone, not due to the residual effect of earlier actions).

Response: Scriptural passages suggest that (the word "action") is used indirectly (to indicate the karmic effects). So says the teacher Karshnajini.

[10] *Objection*: (Unless conduct alone is the cause rebirths rather than the effects of prior conduct), then conduct is valueless.

Response: (Karmic effects) depend upon (conduct). [11] The teacher Badari states that nothing but good and bad acts themselves (are meant).

[12] *Objection*: Scripture declares that (the path of rebirth is through the moon) even for those who do not perform the sacrifices, and so forth.

[13] *Response*: But scripture declares that those who have suffered in the abode of Yama (Death) also ascend and descend (from the moon). [14] The traditional texts also declare this. [15] In addition, there are seven (hells for the evil-doers mentioned in the Puranas). [16] Since Yama's control extends (over all of them), there is no contradiction (in texts mentioning different overseers of the hells). [17] Rather, the path of knowledge (*vidya*) and the path of action (*karma*) are (the "two paths" meant here) since that is the topic under discussion.

[18] (Authorities) see that (going to the moon) is not to be applicable (to a person) in a third state (i.e., a hell and not in a heaven or this world). [19] In addition, this is observed in the world as well in the traditional texts (where Drona and a few others are observed to have been born without

parents when the rituals were not performed). [20] So too, it is seen (that some creatures are born without mating), [21] including the third class (of animals and plants) born from heat or moisture.

[22] (The person descending from the moon) attains a similarity of nature (with space and air). Only) that (claim) is justified. [23] Based on the authority of scripture, (this descent) does not take a long time. [24] Scripture also declares that the descending person (before being born) enters into what is already ruled by another (i.e., plants), as seen in prior cases. [25] (Sacrificing animals) is not unclean, as it is stated in scripture. [26] Next (the person) is connected with the one who inseminates, and then [27] from the womb a new body (is born).

Chapter 3.2

[1] According to scripture, creation (by a person) occurs in the intermediate state (i.e., in the dream state between waking and dreamless sleep). [2] According to some (interpreters of scripture), (Brahman) is the creator and sons and other (desired things) are the created. [3] But (creation in the dream state) is mere illusion (*maya*) since the true nature (of the entities) is not fully manifested. [4] Yet (a dream) is an omen (of future events), as both scripture and experts in reading dreams state. [5] From deep meditation (*parabhidhyana*) on the highest (Lord), what is covered up (about the relation of the individual's atman to Brahman becomes uncovered), since bondage and liberation are from the Lord (i.e., "Brahman with attributes"). [6] Or (the covering) occurs because of (Brahman's) connection with a body.

[7] (The atman in the state of) dreamless sleep (resides) in the nerves and in Brahman, as is known from scripture. [8] Thus, awakening from dreamless sleep is (waking) from (the highest Atman). [9] But it is the same (person who returns from dreamless sleep). This is based on action, memory, scriptural authority, and Vedic injunctions.

[10] A person who is senseless in a swoon attains only a partial state of (sleep), since that is only alternative (to the waking and sleeping states).

[11] Brahman is without a twofold characteristic even in different places because scripture teaches throughout that it is (without any differences).

[12] *Objection*: (Scripture teaches that) Brahman has differences.

Response: (Scripture negates) each of the differences individually. [13] Also some schools teach this. [14] Brahman is indeed formless (*arupa*) since that is the dominant theme (in the Upanishads). [15] Like light (assuming the

form of things that it contacts, Brahman appears to have different forms).
Otherwise, scriptural passages (about Brahman having form) would be
without meaning. [16] And the passages (declare Brahman) to be that much
(i.e., consciousness) and no more. [17] In addition, (other scriptural passages)
reveal this, as do the traditional texts. [18] Thus, illustrations such as the sun's
reflection (appearing multiple on the waves of water are appropriate).

[19] *Objection*: There is no similarity (and thus no basis for comparison)
since nothing is perceived that is similar to the water (in the illustration since
Brahman alone is real and so there is no duality of two realities).

[20] *Response*: Brahman participates in the increase and decrease (of the
things it has entered) since it abides within (those things). Thus, since both
(the illustration and Brahman have the same features), the illustration thus
is applicable. [21] And scripture also declares this. [22] (Scripture) indeed
denies the limitation [of the forms] being discussed and then speaks of
something more after that: [23] Brahman is not manifested (and thus not
perceivable by the senses). [24] In addition, (Brahman is realized) by the
complete meditative concentration of the mind (*samradhana*), as is known
by both scripture and traditional texts.

[25] And Brahman (appears dual), like light during activity (appears
diffuse from the objects illuminated), yet it is nondifferentiated according to
repeated declarations in scripture. [26] Thus, (the individual person enters
into the oneness of) the nonfinite, as (scripture) indicates.

[27] *Objection*: Both difference and nondifference (between Brahman
and the individual person or the world) are mentioned.

Response: It is like the relation between a snake and its coils. [28] Or it
is like the relation between light and its source — both are luminous. [29] So
too, (the relation between Brahman and the individual person) has already
been given earlier. [30] And because of the denial (of difference given in
scripture).

[31] *Objection*: There must be some other (reality) superior to Brahman
since scripture mentions a bridge, limitation, connection, and difference.

[32] *Response*: (The Atman is referred as a bridge and so forth) because
of the similarity (between speaking of ordinary crossings and attaining
Brahman). [33] So too, (Brahman is described as) having four quarters in
order to make it easier grasp by the intellect (*buddhi*). [34] So too (statements
about connection and difference) are made concerning particular places (i.e.,
embodiment), as in the case of light (illuminating an object) and so forth. [35]

Also because (this position alone) is justified. [36] So too from the denial (of the reality) of everything else.

[37] Thereby, the all-pervasiveness (of Brahman is established) in accordance with scriptural statements about (its) extent and so forth.

[38] The (karmic) fruit of action comes from the Lord of the universe because (this position alone) is justified, and [39] also because scripture teaches that. [40] For those reasons, Jaimini asserts that religious conduct (*dharma*) (is what produces the positive fruits of actions). [41] But Badarayana asserts the former (i.e., the Lord himself bestows the fruits of actions) since he is mentioned as the cause (of the fruit).

Chapter 3.3

[1] What is understood by all Vedantic texts (is identical) since there can be no difference in the injunctions and so forth.

[2] *Objection*: (Meditative cognition) is not all the same because of the difference (in meditative practices).

Response: Not so. There may be differences (in practices) for even the same (cognition). [3] For example, rituals: in one school, (carrying fire on one's head) is part of the study of the Vedas based on the authority of their text. Variations are analogous to (various) offerings. (But such variations do not change Vedic knowledge. So too with different meditative practices.) [4] And scripture declares that (Brahman knowledge is one). [5] (Meditative cognition) being one and the same, all the properties (from different practices) should be combined because of the unity of purpose, like the subsidiary practices of an injunction or sacrifice.

[6] *Objection*: (The knowledge) is different (in BU 1.3.7 and CU 1.2.7) because the texts are different.

Response: (The resulting knowledge) is not different. [7] Rather, there is difference here due to the difference in subject-matter — one subject is "great" and the other is the "greater than great."

[8] *Objection*: Yet the names (are the same).

Response: That has already been explained. And the same name is found (where the practices are obviously different). [9] And since (meditating on Brahman) pervades (all Vedic practices), this differentiation (of different practices) is appropriate.

[10] Since all (cognition of Prana) is not different, these (characteristics) found in one place (can be asserted) elsewhere. [11] Bliss and other properties

of the principal subject (Brahman) are to be combined (in all mentions of Brahman). [12] (But some) properties, such as joy being the head (of Brahman), are not to be added everywhere since (they vary and their) increase and decrease occur in (the realm) of differentiations (but Brahman does not change). [13] But other properties (apply in all contexts) since their purpose is the same (in every context). [14] (Properties mentioned in Katha Upanishad 3.10 and elsewhere) are for the purpose of deep meditation (on the Atman) since they have no other purpose. [15] (This is so) because of the use of the word "Atman" (in these passages).

[16] (The word "Atman" in the Aitareya Aranyaka 2.4.1) is to be understood as referring to the highest Atman, as in the other texts (about creation), because of the subsequent (specifications).

[17] *Objection*: From the context of the passage as a whole (the highest Atman is not meant but only the individual person's atman).

Response: There is the clear statement (that only the highest Atman existed in the beginning).

[18] Since (the ritual of rinsing the mouth) is mentioned as a recognized duty (in one context), it can occur (in another context) in connection to a new injunction (i.e., to meditate on the vital organs). [19] And (the cognition) is the same since (the object of meditation) is not different. [20] So too, (the meditative cognitions) are the same because of the connection in different contexts (of the same reality in meditation).

[21] (The applicable "secret names" are different) because of the differences (of the objects) that are meditated upon (e.g., Brahman located the sun or in the eye). [22] Scripture also declares that. [23] For the same reason, (different properties of Brahman such as) possession of the sole power of supporting or pervading the heavens (are not to be combined with other meditations). [24] So too, (the properties of "knowledge of the Cosmic Person" meditations of the Chandogya Upanishad) are not mentioned (in the meditation of the same name in the Taittiriya Upanishad and so are not to be combined). [25] The "piercing (the heart)" (meditation) and so forth (are not to be combined with other meditations) because they have different purposes.

[26] When shaking off good and bad karmic acts (by the enlightened) is mentioned, that (the unenlightened) receive good and bad karmic effects is also implied since it is connected with the related term, as in the case of related ritual terms. This has been stated by Jaimini.

[27] At the time of (the enlightened) departing (from the body at death), (all action is left behind) since there remains nothing to be attained. Followers of other schools (also) declare that. [28] Since there is no contradiction (in nature) between the two (i.e., good and bad karmic effects), (all karmic effects are destroyed) by voluntary practices.

[29] The objective (of the individual person's) path (at death) is in two different ways: (the unenlightened travel one path to the world of the gods and the enlightened another). Otherwise, there would be a contradiction. [30] This (position on a twofold path) is justified because of indications (of the difference) are met with (in scripture), as well as in the world. [31] (There are no restrictions on the path of the enlightened). This involves no contradiction since it is known from both scripture and traditional texts.

[32] For people with a special mission (from the Lord for something in this world), the cycle of rebirths continues as long as the mission requires it.

[33] But conceptions of the imperishable must be included (in meditative practices) because of the similarity (of conceptions), and because the object is the same (in all practices). It is just as with the mantras of the Upasad sacrifice, as has already been stated (by Jaimini). [34] (The conceptions) are the same (in different Upanishads despite differences in wording) because of the mention of the same limit (in the different passages).

(*Objection*: These passages are about the individual's atman currently possessing a body that is an aggregate of elements.)

[35] *Response*: One's own atman is the innermost Atman (of everything) since the aggregate of all elements (has one Atman hidden in it).

[36] *Objection*: However, (unless the conceptions are different), the scriptural passages cannot be justified.

Response: The different instructions (lead to the same knowledge). [37] (There is) reciprocity (between conceptions in different meditations) since (scripture does this) in other cases. [38] The very same truth/reality (*satya*) and so forth is (present in both cognitions). [39] (Effective) desires and other (properties) (are to be combined) in other practices and vice versa because the support (of the properties) (*ayatana*) and so forth (are the same).

[40] Because of the respect (given to it in scripture), (the Agnihotra ritual) cannot be omitted. [41] It is to be performed from (the food) that is present, since scripture declares it. [42] There is no restriction about that (i.e., that all meditations must be connected to rituals) since it is seen in scripture that there is separate fruit (from the rituals and from meditation)

resulting in (meditation) not hindering (the rituals). [43] This is indeed so for offerings to the gods. That has been stated (by Jaimini).

[44] Because of the abundance of characteristic marks (lingas), such an indication is more powerful for establishing a meaning than the context (of a discussion of the ritual). This also has been stated by Jaimini.[45] But because of context, (mental fires) are an alternative to (ritual) fires. They constitute a ritual like the mental (imaginary drinking of Soma). [46] And (this position is supported) by the extended (similarities seen between the mind and fire). [47] But (mental fires) indeed constitute cognition (*vidya*) as is seen from scripture [48] and the indicating marks (in aphorism 44). [49] Because of the greater authority of express statements in scripture, this cannot be refuted.

[50] (The mental fires are independent of the ritual fires) because they are connected (with the mind) and for other reasons, in the same way that other cognitions are separate. And it is also seen (as another instance of a withdrawal from general matters). This too has been stated (by Jaimini). [51] (The mental fires are not connected to the ritual fires) even on the grounds of similarity, for they are learned (only on the grounds of scripture), and (they serve a different function) at the time of death. Nor does the world become (fire based on some similarities to fire). [52] And from the subsequent (Brahmana text), it follows that scripture has an injunction (to meditate) in view, and the connection of fire occurs because of the abundance (of parallels to fire in the mental state).

[53] *Materialist objection*: We deny the existence of a self (independent of the body) — for a self exists (only) where the body does.

[54] *Response*: (The self [atman]) is separate from the body) because (consciousness) may exist when (the body) does not, as with attaining Brahman.

[55] The (meditations) connected with the limbs (of rituals) are not (confined) to particular Vedic schools but (are common) to all (the schools), [56] as in the case of mantras and so forth. Thus, there is no contradiction.

[57] (Meditation) on the abundance of reality (*bhuman*) is superior (to meditation on lesser objects), just as with sacrifices. So scripture declares.

[58] (The meditations) differ because of differences in words, and so forth. [59] There are options (to choose among meditations on Brahman) because their results are indistinguishable. [60] But (meditations) connected to fulfilling worldly desires may be combined or not, as one wishes, because they have distinguishable results.

[61] *Mimamsa objection*: (Meditations) connected to the parts (of rituals) are as important as the parts themselves. [62] (The meditations can be combined) also because they are enjoined (by scripture). [63] And because (some meditations) rectify (deficiencies in other meditations, just as some rituals rectify deficiencies in other rituals). [64] And also because scripture declares a property (of cognition) to be common to all (the Vedas).

[65] *Response*: (The meditations connected to parts of a ritual) are not to be combined because scripture does not mention this [66] and in fact shows (the opposite).

Chapter 3.4: Knowledge

[1] Badarayana claims that scripture states that the highest purpose of man (*purusha-artha*) is achieved by this (knowledge of Brahman).

[2] *Objection*: But Jaimini claims that since (knowledge) is subordinate to (the ritual action), the statements about the end of man are merely to praise the person (acting in the ritual), as in other cases (of praise). [3] (This is confirmed) by what is seen in the actions (of the enlightened in scripture). [4] Also because scripture declares this, [5] the two (knowledge and ritual action) work together, [6] scripture enjoins rituals for one (who has Vedic knowledge), [7] and because of the required rules in the texts.

[8] *Response*: But scripture teaches that there is one greater (than the individual agent of the ritual, i.e., Brahman). Thus, Badarayana's position stands as it is, for this is revealed in scripture. [9] There are scriptural declarations equally supporting (our position) (contra aphorism 3). [10] The scriptural declaration (in support of aphorism 4) is not universally applicable. [11] (Knowledge and ritual actions) are to be divided like dividing one hundred (coins into two lots) (contra aphorism 5). [12] (Ritual actions are required) for one who has merely read (and recited) the Vedas, (not the enlightened) (contra aphorism 6). [13] And (the restrictive rules do not apply to the enlightened) since the restrictions do not explicitly say so (contra aphorism 7). [14] Rather, the permission (for the enlightened to perform ritual acts) is for the praise of knowledge (contra aphorism 2). [15] Some prefer (to refrain from ritual acts).

[16] In addition, the destruction (of all karmic effects comes from knowledge). [17] And scripture declares that (knowledge belongs) to those in the celibate (renouncer stage of life).

[18] *Objection*: According to Jaimini, scripture merely alludes to (the stages of life involving renunciation) and there are no injunctions (to lead that life) because (the scripture in other passages) condemns (renunciation).

[19] *Response*: But according to Badarayana, (the renouncer stage of life) is also be practiced because scripture treats all (stages) equally. [20] Or (reference to that stage) is an injunction, like holding (fuel for a ritual).

[21] *Objection*: The reference (to parts of the ritual) is only praise since (the parts have only a supporting role).

Response: Because of the unprecedented nature (of what is being taught, it must be a genuine injunction). [22] In addition, (they are injunctions) because they are expressed as injunctions.

[23] *Objection*: (Certain stories in the Upanishads) are meant only for ritual purposes (not to imply that the renouncer stage is to be followed).

Response: (That is so only for the stories) specified (and not for the Upanishads as a whole). [24] And because (the stories) are connected (with meditations) and so are (part of) one idea in that way. [25] For that very reason, (the renouncer) has no need to light the ritual fire and so forth.

[26] But (for the unenlightened,) all (religious actions) are necessary, as prescribed by scripture, just as a horse (requires a harness and so forth). [27] But one (intent on attaining enlightenment) possesses calmness, control of the senses, and so forth, since these are enjoined as subsidiaries for attaining that (knowledge) and thus necessarily must be practiced.

[28] Scripture declares that it is permissible to eat any type of food when one's life is in danger. [29] In this way, scripture (on restrictions of types of food) are not contradicted. [30] The traditional texts also agree. [31] (This is also consistent) with the scriptural passage prohibiting acting as one wishes.

[32] The duties of the stages of life are also to be performed (even by those not seeking enlightenment) since they are enjoined by scripture. [33] And because (their performance) is a co-generator of knowledge (along with meditation). [34] In either case, the same duties are to be performed both (to fulfill the duties of the three earlier stages of life and to aid in attaining knowledge in the renouncer stage). [35] In addition, scripture declares that (one leading the renouncer life) is not overpowered (by passions and other afflictions). [36] But even one standing between two stages of life (is qualified for knowledge of Brahman) since such cases are encountered (in scripture). [37] Traditional texts also record instances. [38] Special acts (e.g., fasting, repetition of mantras, or veneration of gods) favor (knowledge). [39] But scripture indicates that being in a stage of life is better than that.

[40] But Jaimini states that for one who has become (a renouncer), there is no return from it (to the other stages of life) because of scriptural restrictions and the absence of scriptural sanction for such a return and the absence (of precedence). [41] In addition, even (a lapse from celibacy) is not available for (the renouncer) since his fall is inferred (from traditional texts to be without remedy), and thus he must have no connection with (any expiatory ritual available to others). [42] But some consider this to be a minor transgression and claim that it can be (expiated), as in the case of eating (forbidden food). So it is explained by Jaimini. [43] But (whether it is a major or minor transgression), those (who violate celibacy are to be kept) outside (of a monastic community) in accordance with traditional texts and customary rules of good conduct.

[44] The teacher Atreya states that meditation on parts of a ritual is to be practiced only by the sponsor of a sacrifice who meditates, not the priest who performs it, because scripture speaks of the fruits of that meditation (and so the sponsor should get both. [45] But the teacher Audulomi states that it is the duty of the priest of the sacrifice (to engage in meditation) because he is paid for that (work). [46] And scripture also (confirms this).

[47] An injunction is implied to (practice) other auxiliary activity (of meditation as a third activity) in addition (to learning and being child-like) for one who seeks knowledge, just as when a principal injunction (requires the practice's subsidiary actions). [48] But since (knowledge) is included (in all stages of life), scripture ends with the householder life (in some passages). [49] Thus, there is an injunction to practice the other stages of life in addition to the stage of the silent one. [50] (Being child-like [BU 3.5.1]) means not displaying one's (knowledge) since that fits the context (of the entire passage).

[51] (The fruit from the arising of knowledge may occur) even in this life if there is no obstruction to the means adopted (for attaining knowledge). That is seen in scripture. [52] There is no rule concerning the fruit of final liberation because that state has been definitely ascertained (to be the same as knowledge itself).

Book 4: The Fruits of Meditation
Chapter 1

[1] Repetition (of the Vedantic teaching "You are that" is required) because the teaching is repeated in scripture and [2] because there are indications (in scripture of the need for repetition for the teaching to sink in).

[3] But (scripture) acknowledges (Brahman) as the Atman (i.e., the one universal ontic essence) and causes this (identity) to be understood.

[4] (A meditator should) not (project himself) into a symbol (meditated upon as Brahman) because the symbol is not Brahman. [5] (But the symbol) should be looked upon as Brahman because of the exaltation (of the symbol). [6] And (symbols) as a subsidiary part (of a ritual) are to be (looked upon as Brahman) since this is the only way to make (scripture) consistent.

[7] (One should meditate) in a sitting posture since (meditation) is possible (in that position). [8] Also because of the (possibility of) deep meditation (*dhyana*) (in that position). [9] And for (maintaining) motionlessness. [10] This is also mentioned in traditional texts.

[11] (One should meditate) wherever (attaining) one-pointed concentration (*ekagrata*) (is possible) since (scripture) specifies no particular place.

[12] (Such concentration should be maintained) even up to the moment of death, for this is seen (in scripture and traditional texts).

[13] (Scripture) declares that (the karmic effects of all) future and past transgressions are destroyed upon attaining (knowledge of Brahman) and no longer cling (to the enlightened). [14] In the same way, (meritorious deeds) do not cling. But (liberation from rebirth comes only) when (the body) falls (away at death). [15] But only those (deeds committed) prior to (enlightenment) that have not yet begun to bear fruit (are destroyed upon attaining knowledge), for (deeds that have begun to bear fruit) last until the limit of death.

[16] But scripture shows that performing the fire ritual and so forth surely (leads) toward the effect (of enlightenment). [17] According to both (Badarayana and Jaimini) and others, there are actions other than these that certainly also (have this result). [18] For (scripture) indeed (states that) whatever is done with knowledge (outside of rituals is free of karmic effects).

[19] But having exhausted (the good and bad karmic effects) by experiencing (their fruit in this life), one becomes one (with Brahman at death).

Chapter 4.2

[1] (In the process of rebirth,) speech (merges) with the mind (at death). This is observed, and also scripture declares it. [2] And for the same reason, all (the senses) follow (speech into the mind). [3] That mind (then merges) with the life-breath, as declared in scripture. [4] That life-breath (then

merges) with the ruler (i.e., the individual's atman) because it approaches it and so on.

[5] Scripture declares that the (individual's atman with the life-breath and senses) (abides) among the elements. [6] (The atman does not join only) one element. Both (scripture and traditional texts) show that.

[7] (The departure from the body for both the enlightened and unenlightened begins) the same way up to the beginning of the path (to the moon). (Embodied) immortality (from knowing the Lord, i.e., "Brahman with attributes") is attained while (all root-ignorance) is not burned up. [8] That (aggregate of elements constituting a body continues) until the liberation (from the cycle of rebirths). Scripture declares that rebirth continues until then. [9] The subtle (body) (that emerges at death) is minute in size. That is grasped in experience (*upalabhi*). [10] Thus, the (subtle body is) not (destroyed) with the destruction (of the observable body). [11] The warmth (of the living body) is due only to (the subtle body). That (alone) is justified.

[12] *Objection*: (The departure of the life-breath and subtle body of the enlightened from the cycle of rebirths) is denied in scripture.

Response: What is denied is (only the separation of the life-breath) from the embodied individual person (*sharira*). [13] In one recension of scripture, this is clear. [14] And traditional texts also say so.

[15] Scripture declares that those (i.e., the mind and other senses of the enlightened) (merge upon death into) the highest (Brahman) and [16] that (the atman with the life-breath and senses merged in it and the Atman are then) not distinct.

[17] (When the atman of one who knows only the qualified Brahman is about to depart the body), there occurs an illumination at the top of its abode (i.e., in the heart). (The embodied atman goes through) a door that is illuminated by that (light of Brahman). And by the power of knowledge and by the proper effect of constant meditation (*yoga*) on the way that is part of that (knowledge), (the individual departs) through the hundred and first vein (in the heart) under the favor of the one who resides in the heart (i.e., the Lord). [18] (The atman proceeds) by following the rays of the sun.

[19] *Objection*: Thus, it is not (possible for the atman departing) at night.

Response: There is a connection (between the veins and the sun's rays) as long as the body lasts. scripture also declares this. [20] So too, (for the enlightened who die) during the southern course of the sun (i.e., the inauspicious months of the year). [21] This is mentioned concerning yogins and in the texts of both traditions (Samkhya and Yoga).

Chapter 4.3

[1] (The departed who know qualified Brahman travel) along the path beginning with light (of Brahman). This is well-known. [2] (The departed) go from the year (which is between the months and the sun) to the god Vayu (wind), following the absence and presence of specifics (of the path according to different scriptural passages). [3] (The departed then reach the) god Varuna who is beyond lightning because of his connection to water (in the clouds). [4] (Certain gods) are indicated (in scripture) to be guides (for the departed). [5] (They are) established (as guides) because both (the travelers and the path) are nonconscious (and thus need guides). [6] From (the world of Varuna and other gods), (knowers of the qualified Brahman are guided) by the god who belongs to lightning (i.e., Varuna) alone, for so says scripture.

[7] The teacher Badari (asserts that the departed are led to the) goal (*karya*) that can be justified (by that meditation), [8] and that is (the qualified Brahman) since there is the specific mention of this (in scripture). [9] (Qualified Brahman) is designated here because of its nearness to (unqualified Brahman).

[10] On the dissolution of the effect (i.e., the world of Brahman), (the enlightened), along with the Ruler of (the world), attain what is higher: the supreme (unqualified "Brahman without properties") that is beyond (the qualified Brahman). So scripture declares. [11] Traditional texts concur.

[12] *Objection*: Jaimini (asserts that the knower of qualified Brahman attains) the highest (i.e., unqualified Brahman) because that is the plain meaning (of the word "Brahman"). [13] Also because scripture states that. [14] In addition, the firm resolution (concerning knowing Brahman) is not for knowing the effect (i.e., qualified Brahman with properties, but for knowing the highest Brahman without properties itself).

[15] *Response*: Badarayana says that (the gods) lead those who do not focus on the symbols themselves (in meditation) (but focus on Brahman). There is no fault in accepting this twofold division, and (one becomes) what one resolves to become (i.e., either the qualified or unqualified Brahman). [16] Scripture also shows this differentiation (of the fruit of meditating on the symbol itself versus meditating on what is symbolized).

Chapter 4.4: The Nature of Liberation

[1] Once (the light of Brahman) is attained, (the true nature of the individual person [atman]) is manifested. This is so because scripture uses the phrase "its own (nature)." [2] According to the promise (made in scripture), this is liberation (*mukta*, i.e., release from the chain of rebirths).

[3] (The light that the individual's atman enters into is) the highest (i.e., Brahman without properties) as is clear from the context (of the scriptural passage). [4] (In the liberated state, the person's atman abides) in a state unseparated (from Brahman), as is seen from scripture.

[5] Jaimini asserts, based on scriptural references and so forth, that (the liberated atman) attains properties like those of Brahman. [6] The teacher Audulomi asserts that (the liberated atman) attains pure consciousness (*cit*) alone, that being its real nature. [7] Badarayana asserts that there is no conflict (between Audulomi and Jaimini here) since according to scripture the earlier nature of the individual's atman (as consciousness) persists (in the liberated state).

[8] Scripture states that (the liberated person attains all his desires) through will alone. [9] And also for this reason (the liberated person) is without a lord (to rule over him).

[10] The teacher Badari asserts that (those who reach Brahman) have no (body or organs) because scripture says so. [11] But Jaimini asserts that (those who reach Brahman) have (a body and organs) because scripture speaks (of the liberated) being manifold (i.e., able to manifest many bodies). [12] Badarayana holds that (the liberated are of) both kinds (i.e., with or without bodies), just as the Dvadashaha sacrifice (can be of different types according to the will of the sacrificer). [13] In the absence of a body, (the fulfillment of wishes is still possible), as in dreams. This is justified. [14] When (the body and organs) exist, (the fulfillment of wishes occurs) as in the waking state.

[15] The entrance (of a liberated person into many different bodies through divine power is possible), just like (the same flame lighting many different) lamps, since scripture shows this to be so.

[16] (What scripture states about the absence of all dualistic cognition is made) from the point of view of either of two states — dreamless sleep or turning inwardly (*svapyaya*) (to Brahman). That is made clear in scripture.

[17] (The liberated gain all the powers of the Lord) except the power of (creating, sustaining, and dissolving) the universe. (This is known) from the context (of scriptural passages about Brahman with attributes as the Lord

who creates the universe) and from (the individual's atman) not being close (to the creation of the universe, and so forth).

[18] *Objection*: (But the liberated person does have such unlimited powers) according to direct scriptural teachings.

Response: Scripture speaks of the one who appoints the lords of the different spheres and who resides in those spheres (and the individual person cannot do that). [19] And scripture declares that there is (a reality) that does not abide in the effect (i.e., not within the created realm). [20] Both direct experience (*pratyaksha*) and inference show this to be so. [21] And (it is known) from the characteristic mark (in scripture) that (the liberated person and the highest Brahman) share equality only in enjoyment (i.e., the liberated do not gain the cosmic powers of the qualified Brahman).

[22] Scripture states that there is no return (to the manifest world for the liberated). Indeed, there is no return because scripture states that to be so.

* * *

~ Summary of Shankara's Commentary on the Brahma Sutra ~

Book 1: The Nature of Brahman

Introduction. That the subject "I" (*asmat*) and what is other than the "I" (*yushmat*) cannot be equated needs no proof since their spheres (of existence) and properties are as opposed as light and darkness. Thus, it is erroneous to superimpose any object (whose sphere is anything other than "I" and whose properties are objective) and its properties on the subject (whose essence [*atman*] is consciousness and whose realm is subjectivity) or vice versa. However, we have a propensity by our nature caused by false knowledge (*mithyajnana*) to do both. Through the absence of discrimination, what is real is coupled with what is unreal as in "I am that" or "That is mine."

Superimposition (*adhyasa*) is the appearance to consciousness of a form from memory of something previously observed in some other place. Some define this as the superimposition of properties of one thing upon another, or as the error of not apprehending the difference between what is being superimposed and what is superimposed upon, or as erroneously attributing properties contrary to something's actual properties. But all definitions agree that superimposition involves the apparent appearance of the properties of one thing in another. This is exemplified in seeing a mother-of-pearl shell as silver or seeing the single moon appear double (because of an eye disorder).

Objection: But how can an *object* and its properties be superimposed on the subjective inner atman (*pratyag-atman*) which is not *an object*? We can impose the properties of one object on another object, but you claim that the inner atman is totally unrelated to the idea of "that" and is never an object.

Response: (For the unenlightened,) the Atman is not a non-object in the absolute sense since it is the object of the idea of "I."[1] In addition, the existence of the "inner essence" (atman) is well known because it is directly

---

[1] I am differentiating three senses of "atman" in Shankara's work: Atman (identical to Brahman), atman (the ontic essence of an individual person or entity), and an individual person ("oneself") with no ontological implications. Of course, for Shankara they are all one realty in the final analysis and there is no embodiment.

presented (to consciousness). Nor is there a rule that we can superimpose an object only on objects presented to the senses: nondiscerning people (*avikekins*) superimpose the color dark blue upon space although it is not an object of perception. Thus, the position that the non-Atman can be superimposed on the Atman (by the unenlightened) is not unreasonable.

The learned consider this superimposition to be root-ignorance (*avidya*). They consider knowledge (*vidya*) to be ascertained by discriminating the true Atman from what is superimposed upon it. Since there is such knowledge, the Atman is not affected in any way by any good or bad attribute that only results from superimposing the non-Atman on the Atman or vice versa. The mutual superimposition of the Atman and non-Atman — i.e., root-ignorance — is the underlying condition upon which all worldly distinctions are based, both those made in everyday life as well as those laid down in the Vedas that concern the means of correct knowledge (*pramanas*), the objects of knowledge, dharmic injunctions and prohibitions, and even liberation (*moksha*).

Objection: But how can the means of correct knowledge such as perception and inference and scripture have as their locus a knower that is dependent upon root-ignorance?

Response: Because the means cannot operate unless there is a knowing person (*pramatri*), and the existence of that depends upon the erroneous idea that the body, the senses, and so forth are identical to, or belong to, the atman of the knower. Without the body the senses cannot act, and without the senses the means of correct knowledge cannot operate. No one acts without the Atman being superimposed on the body. Nor can the Atman, which by its nature is free of all contact, become a knower without the body. And without a knower, the means of correct knowledge cannot operate. Thus, perception and the other means of correct knowledge and the Vedas have as their object something that is dependent upon root-ignorance.

Human beings are like animals in this regard. When sounds or other sensations affect their senses, animals advance or retreat according to whether the effect is comforting or disturbing. For example, a cow will retreat upon seeing someone approaching with a raised stick, thinking that the person wants to beat her, while she will walk up to a person carrying grass. So too, human beings retreat when they see fierce looking men approaching with shouts and raised swords, but they approach persons of the opposite appearance and behavior. It is well known that animals base their actions on the non-discrimination (of the Atman and non-Atman), and so we conclude that human beings, despite their higher intelligence, proceed in the same way as long as the mutual superimposition of Atman and non-Atman lasts.

So too with regard to the Vedic sacrifices and injunctions and prohibitions. Even the activity of a man who realizes that the Atman has a relation to another world does not depend upon the knowledge derived from Vedanta concerning the true nature of the Atman that is free of all desires, class distinctions, and rebirth — indeed, such knowledge is useless and even contradictory to worldly and religious activity. But before knowledge of the Atman arises, the Vedic texts continue in their operation and have what is dependent upon root-ignorance as their object for injunctions. For example, the injunction "A Brahmin is to sacrifice" presupposes conditions such as class, stage of life, age, and so forth that are superimposed upon the Atman.

Properties of a person's social relations are (non-Atman attributes superimposed on the Atman). Properties that one thinks of the body, senses, and the inner organ are superimposed on the Atman.[2] So too the producer of the sense of "I" (the *aham-kara*) is superimposed on the inner atman that in reality is the actual witness (*sakshin*) of everything. Conversely, the inner atman is the true witness, but it is superimposed on the mind, the senses, and the body. Everyone observes this erroneous superimposition that by its nature is beginningless and endless and is the cause of individual persons (*jivas*) appearing to be the actors in actions and the enjoyers of the karmic fruits of those actions (when only the Atman is real).

In order to free oneself from the erroneous superimposition that is the cause of all suffering and to acquire knowledge of the oneness of the Atman, the study of Vedanta is taken up. We shall show that all the Vedantic texts (i.e., the Upanishads) have this purpose.

Chapter 1.1

[1] *The inquiry into the nature of Brahman then comes after the "ritual portion" of the Vedas in the "knowledge portion" (i.e., the Upanishads).*[3]

---

[2] "Inner organ" (*antahkarana*) is one of several names for the mind (*manas*) — i.e., what produces intention, thought, desire, doubt, and so forth. It is another sense-organ with ideas as its objects. The inner organ is referred to as *manas, buddhi,* or *aham-kara* (the maker of "I," a sense of self). *Buddhi* ("intellect") is sometimes distinguished as a special mental function by which one becomes aware of Brahman (e.g., 1.4.1, 2.3.17, 3.3.12) but not always (2.3.32).

[3] The translation or summary of the *Brahma Sutra's* aphorisms that are given here in italics will reflect Shankara's understanding of them.

"After" means "immediately following," not something new. One who has read the Vedantic parts of the Vedas can enter into the inquiry into Brahman before engaging in the inquiry into social and religious duties (*dharma*) because the two have different results. Knowledge of duties has an impermanent well-being for its fruit and is dependent upon the performance of actions. On the other hand, the inquiry into Brahman has eternal bliss for its fruit and does not depend upon any actions. The object of the inquiry into the ritual portion — acts of duty — depends upon something yet to be accomplished, while the object of the inquiry into Brahman is eternal and does not depend upon human activity. The texts on duty present injunctions for actions, while texts on Brahman merely instruct without enjoining actions since the fruits follow directly (from understanding the texts).

Question: What conditions precede the inquiry into Brahman?

Response: The prerequisites are: (1) the discrimination of what is eternal from what is not; (2) nonattachment to the fruit of one's own actions, both in this life and the next; (3) the attainment of tranquility, self-control, and the other means (of mental preparation); and (4) the desire for liberation from the cycle of rebirths. Only when these conditions exist may one engage in the inquiry into Brahman and come to know Brahman, whether one has inquired into duties or not. The word "after" indicates that the inquiry into Brahman is subsequent to the acquisition of these prerequisite conditions.

The word "then" in the aphorism indicates that there is a reason: the Vedas declare that the fruit of the sacrifice and similar actions as a means for happiness is only temporary since whatever is attained by action here on earth or in a heaven perishes (CU 8.1.6). But the Vedas teach at the same time that the highest aim is realized by the knowledge of Brahman — e.g., "He who knows Brahman attains the highest" (TU 2.1).

The statement of the principal matter also entails all secondary matters connected to it. Thus, if the most important of all objects of knowledge — Brahman — is mentioned, all the objects of inquiry entailed by that knowledge need not be mentioned, just as "The King is going" implies his retinue is also going.

Our interpretation also agrees with scripture that directly represents Brahman as the object of the desire for knowledge — e.g., "Desire to know that from which all these beings are born, and so forth. That is Brahman" (TU 3.1). The object of desire is the complete comprehension of Brahman because this is the highest goal of humanity since it destroys the root-ignorance that is the seed of the cycle of rebirths (*samsara*). Thus, the knowledge that gives complete comprehension is to be desired.

Question: Is Brahman known or unknown? If it is known, we need not enter into the inquiry concerning it. But if it is not known, then we cannot get the inquiry started.

Response: Brahman, who is all-knowing, all-powerful, and eternally pure, conscious, and free, is indeed well-known to us to exist. For the word "Brahman" is derived from the root "*brih*" that means "to be great," and thus we understand immediately that Brahman is all-knowing, and so forth. In addition, the existence of Brahman is known by each person to be his atman. Everyone is aware of the existence of this essence and never says "I do not exist." If there were no such general recognition of the existence of the Atman, everyone would say "I do not exist." And this essence is Brahman.

Objection: So Brahman is generally known, and there is no need to inquire into it.

Response: But there are mistaken opinions concerning the nature of Brahman. Ordinary people and materialists (Lokayatikas) believe that one's "self" is merely a body endowed with awareness. Others believe that the bodily organs endowed with awareness are one's atman. Some believe that the mind is the atman. Others believe that one is but momentary cognitions. Some believe the atman is empty (*shunya*) (of all reality). Some say that there is an actor and also a separate enjoyer (of the fruits of action) or that only the enjoyer transmigrates from body to body. Others teach that in addition to individual persons there is a separate all-knowing and all-powerful Lord. Others think the Lord is the atman of the enjoyer.

Thus, there are conflicting opinions based in part on sound reasoning (*yukti*) and scriptural passages and in part on fallacious reasoning and misunderstood scriptural passages. If one endorses one of these opinions without a prior consideration (of the other positions), one would be barring oneself from the highest good and incur a grievous loss. Thus, one should inquiry into Brahman by means of the Vedantic texts and proper arguments (*tarka*) and aim for the highest good (i.e., freedom from rebirths).

Thus, the next question is what are the (true) characteristics of Brahman. On this, the revered Badarayana states the next aphorism:

*[2] From Brahman proceeds the origin and so forth of the world (*jagat*).*

The phrase "and so forth" indicates the sustaining and destruction of the world. Scripture declares the origin, the order of origin, the sustaining, and the destruction of the world (TU 3.1). All forms of existence are included in the reference to "origin." (The full meaning of the aphorism is this): Brahman is the all-knowing and all-powerful cause from which proceed the origin, sustaining, and destruction of the perceived world that is differentiated into name-and-form (*nama-rupa*) (BU 1.4.7, 1.6.3; CU 8.14.1) that is the support of actors, enjoyers, and fruits of action that are determined in space and time and causal order. This arrangement cannot even be conceived by the mind (and so we must rely on scripture).

The world's origin, sustaining, and destruction cannot in any way proceed from anything but a lord possessing the properties stated above (i.e., all-knowing and so forth). The world cannot arise (as Samkhyas claim) from the nonconscious (*achetana*) matter (*pradhana*), the atoms (*paramanus*) (as postulated by the Vaisheshikas), nonbeing, or a being subject to rebirth (who thus is part of creation). Nor can it proceed from its own nature (i.e., arise spontaneously without a cause) since we observe that that origin needs particular spatial and temporal causes.

Objection: We can infer (without appeal to the Vedas) from this argument the existence of a lord who is the cause of the world but who is other than a transmigrating being. You yourself have brought forth the argument in the discussion of this aphorism.

Response: The aphorisms merely have the purpose of stringing together the Vedantic passages. Those passages are discussed here since comprehension of Brahman is brought about by ascertaining the sense of the Vedantic passages. This is based on discussion, not inference or the other means of correct knowledge. The passages primarily declare the cause of the origin and so forth of the world. Inference does not contradict them and so is not excluded as a means of confirming the sense of the passages ascertained (but is not a means of gaining knowledge). Scripture also allows for argument since some passages declare that understanding assists scripture — e.g., the Atman is to be considered as well as heard (about from teachers) (BU 2.4.5).

Unlike in matters of religious and social duties (*dharma*), in the inquiry into Brahman scripture is not the only means of knowledge: recourse to both scripture and immediate experience (*anubhava*) is to be made appropriately. This is so because experience is the final result of the inquiry into Brahman and because the object of the inquiry is an existing reality. If the object of the knowledge of Brahman were something to be accomplished (by actions, as with religious duties), there would be no reference to experience — the texts and so forth would be the only means of knowledge. So too the origin of something depends upon action, and so injunctions and prohibitions and so forth would be appropriate. But that does not apply to a reality and its properties that exist (eternally) or do not exist (at all). All possibilities depend upon worldly ideas, but the knowledge of the true nature of a reality depends on only the thing known. Upon seeing a wooden post, to think "This is a post or a man or something else" is not true knowledge — the second and third possibilities are false; and the idea "This is a post" depends on the thing itself, and only that idea is true knowledge. And so, true knowledge of all existing things depends on the things themselves. Thus, the true knowledge of Brahman depends entirely on the thing itself, i.e., Brahman.

Objection: But since Brahman is an existing reality, it must be the object of other means of correct knowledge (and not only the Vedas). Thus, this discussion of Vedantic texts is not needed.

Response: Brahman is not an object of the senses, and so it has no connections to other means of correct knowledge (which rely upon external objects). The senses only have external things for their objects, not Brahman. If Brahman were an external object open to the senses, we might perceive the world as connected to Brahman as an effect. But as only the "effect" (the world) is perceived, it is impossible to determine (through perception or inference) whether it is connected to Brahman or to something else. Thus, the aphorism "That from which . . ." does not propound inference (as a means to know Brahman). Rather, it reflects Vedantic passages such as "Strife to know that from which these beings are born, live, and enter upon death. That is Brahman" (TU 3.1). Other passages also declare the cause whose nature is eternally pure, conscious, free (of desires and rebirths), and all-knowing.

That Brahman is all-knowing is to be inferred from it being demonstrated that it is the cause of the world. To confirm this, the text continues:

[3] That Brahman is omniscient is known only from scripture because either [a] Brahman is source of scripture, or [b] scripture is the (only) source of correct knowledge concerning Brahman.

Brahman is the source (*yoni*) of the great body of scripture and the auxiliary sciences (such as logic and grammar) that, being lamp-like, illuminates all things, and thus, so to speak (*iti*), is all-knowing.

Under interpretation [a], the origin of a scripture having the attribute of omniscience can only be found in that omniscient thing itself or its author, and the supreme omniscience and omnipotence of the great being that in sport (*lila*), so to speak (*iti*), produced the sacred texts known as the Rig Veda and so forth without effort, like a person sends forth breath, as stated in "The Rig Veda and so forth have been breathed forth by that great being" (BU 2.4.10).

Under interpretation [b], scripture is the source or cause of the means of correct knowledge by which we comprehend the nature of Brahman, and so scripture is only the means by which we know that Brahman is the cause of the world.

Objection: But the previous aphorism pointed out a text that demonstrated scripture is the source of knowledge of Brahman. So what is the purpose of this aphorism?

Response: The previous aphorism does not clearly identify the scriptural passage, and so one might suspect that the origin and so forth of the world could be determined by inference (independently from scripture). Thus, this aphorism is needed.

Mimansa Objection: Scripture cannot be a means to know Brahman since scripture is about actions, and so those Vedantic passages whose intent is not directed toward action are not needed or only supplement the passages enjoining actions or only serve to enjoin new actions such as meditative adoration (*upasana*). The Vedas do not aim to convey information regarding the nature of existing realities since such realities are the objects of perception and of the other means of correct knowledge. In addition, if the Vedas did give such information, it would not be concerning things to be desired or avoided and thus would be of no use to us. In this way, passages in the Vedas that appear useless have the purpose of praising certain actions. So too, mantras are related to actions. Thus, all Vedic passages are related to actions and so cannot refer instead to existing realities. Thus, we maintain that the Vedantic passages are only supplements to the passages enjoining actions. Or if the Vedantic passages introduce matters that are actually alien to Vedanta, they must refer to meditation and similar actions that are mentioned in those Vedantic texts. Thus, the result is that scripture is not the source of knowledge of Brahman.

[4] Response: Knowing Brahman is the aim of the Upanishads.

In all the Vedantic texts, the sentences indicate Brahman as their meaning. For example, "In the beginning, there was only being, one without a second" (CU 6.2.1), "In the beginning, all this was only Brahman alone" (Aitareya Aranyaka 2.4.1), or "This is Brahman, without cause or effect, without anything inside of out. This Atman is Brahman that perceives everything" (BU 2.5.19). If their meaning is ascertained to be referring to Brahman and their purpose is understood, it would be wrong to give them another sense since that would involve the error of abandoning the direct statements of the text for mere assumptions.

Nor can these passages be auxiliary to actions since certain scriptural passages preclude any reference to action, agents, and results — e.g., "Then by what should he see whom" (BU 2.4.14).

Nor can Brahman be an object of perception and the other means of correct knowledge even though it is a reality (since it is not an object). Thus, that everything has Brahman as its essence (atman) cannot be grasped without the aid of scriptural passages such as "You are that" (CU 6.8.7).

Nor must an instruction be without a purpose if it is not connected to something that is either to be strived for or avoided: Atman, being Brahman (and thus always present), is not something either to strive for or avoid, but from the mere comprehension of this fact all frustration ceases, and thereby we attain our highest goal. Nor can these sentences relate to meditation since once knowledge of absolute oneness has arisen, there no longer exists anything to desire or avoid, and thus the conception of duality by which we distinguish actions, actors, and so forth is destroyed. Once the conception of duality is uprooted by the realization of nonduality, all ideas of duality with its distinction of actions, actors, and so forth cannot arise again. So too, it can no longer cause Brahman to be seen as an object assisting injunctions.

Other parts of the Vedas have authority only insofar as they relate to injunctions. Those parts cannot discredit the authoritativeness of passages conveying knowledge of Atman since these passages have their own result.

Nor can the authoritativeness of the Vedas be proved by inference and reasoning thereby making it depend on things observed elsewhere.

From all this, it follows that the Vedas possess authority as a means of correct knowledge of Brahman.

Objection: The Vedas may be means for gaining the correct knowledge of Brahman, but they indicate Brahman only as the object of certain injunctions, just as the Vedas give information about the implements of the sacrifice, information that is not known in the common life that supplements the injunctions. The purpose of the Vedas is to initiate action or to restrain it, and the purpose of the others passages is to supplement the injunctions and prohibitions. The Vedantic texts must be understood in that way. Knowledge of Brahman is enjoined as the means for those who desire immorality.

Response: There is a difference in the nature of the objects of inquiry: the prior part of the Vedas is something to be accomplished by actions, while the object of the Vedanta is a reality that already exists. Thus, the fruit of knowledge of Brahman must be different in nature from the fruit of the knowledge of duty that depends upon the performance of actions.

Objection: The Vedantic texts give information about Brahman only in connection to the performance of actions — e.g., "The Atman is to be seen" (BU 2.4.5) or "We must seek the Atman that is free of fault and must try to understand it" (CU 8.7.1) or "Let a man venerate him as the Atman" (BU 1.4.7) or "Let a man venerate the Atman only as his true state" (BU 1.4.15) or "He who knows Brahman becomes Brahman" (MunU 3.2.9). These injunctions cause us to desire to know what that Brahman is, and the Vedantic texts teach us that Brahman is eternal, all-knowing, completely self-sufficient, eternally pure, conscious, free, pure knowledge and supreme bliss. From devout meditation on this Brahman, the fruit of liberation from rebirth is attained. On the other hand, if the Vedantic texts were interpreted as having no reference to injunctions concerning actions but only to statements about realities, they would have no purpose.

Response: Statements about existing things can have a use. For example, stating "This is a rope, not a snake" serves to remove the fear caused by the erroneous idea (and thus has a use). Similarly, the Vedantic passages about a non-transmigrating Atman have their own use: to remove the erroneous idea that the Atman transmigrates.

Objection: Merely hearing the true nature of the rope dispels the fear caused by the imagined snake, but merely hearing the true nature of Brahman does not end the hearer's pleasure, suffering, and other properties attached to the condition of being in the realm (*avastha*) of rebirth. For this reason, the scripture enjoins us to action: "The Atman is to be heard about, to be considered, and to be reflected upon" (BU 2.4.5) — consideration and reflection must follow merely hearing about Brahman. Thus, the passages are connected to injunctions concerning actions. And the bodiless state of liberation is the result of meritorious actions.

Response: That argument is invalid because being disembodied is the natural state of the Atman and the fruits of action and of knowledge of Brahman differ in nature. The fruits of performing religious duties and their opposite are non-eternal and refer to the pleasure and pain of the realm of rebirth. However, in the unembodied state of liberation (KaU 2.22, MunU 2.1.2), there is neither pleasure nor pain (CU 8.12.1), and thus liberation is not the fruit of action or the effect of merit gained by acting according to Vedic injunctions. Final release is eternally unchanging, free from all modifications, eternally content, as all-pervading as space (*akasha*),[4] without parts,

---

[4] "*Akasha*" is more like "ether" than empty "space" — it is a substance pervading the universe. It is a fifth element, in addition to air, fire, water, and earth.

completely self-sufficient, and self-luminous. Past, present, and future do not apply to this bodiless liberation. Nor is it subject to merit or demerit and their consequences: "Different from merit and demerit, different from cause and effect, different from past and future" (KaU 2.14). Thus, liberation is the same as Brahman. If Brahman were merely supplementary to religious actions and liberation were the effect of those actions, then liberation would not be eternal but merely preeminent among non-eternal fruits of action. But that liberation is something eternal is acknowledged by all who accept it at all, and thus the teachings concerning Brahman are not merely supplementary to actions enjoined by scripture.

In addition, there are numerous scriptural passages declaring that liberation follows immediately upon knowledge of Brahman — e.g., "He who knows Brahman becomes Brahman" (MunU 3.2.9). This precludes the possibility of anything intervening between the occurrence of knowing Brahman and liberation. No action takes place between seeing Brahman and becoming one with the all-pervading Atman. The removal of any obstacles standing in the way of liberation is the only fruit of the knowledge of Brahman. This position is supported by arguments from others: "liberation results from the successive removal of wrong knowledge, faults, actions, birth, and pain" (Nyaya Sutra 1.1.2). Wrong knowledge is removed by the knowledge that you are one with the essence (atman) of Brahman.

Nor is this knowledge that your atman is one with Brahman merely an imagined association where Brahman is superimposed on the mind or anything else that is not Brahman. Nor is it a purification of action. Such understandings would violate the clear meaning of passages that indicate Brahman and your atman are identical — "You are that" (CU 6.8.7), "I am Brahman" (BU 1.4.10), and "This essence is Brahman" (BU 2.5.19). Passages that declare that the fruit of the knowledge of Brahman is the cessation of root-ignorance would also be contradicted — e.g., "the knot of one's heart is cut, all doubts are dispelled" (MunU 2.2.9). Nor could passages speaking of the individual person becoming Brahman (e.g., MunU 3.2.9) be explained satisfactorily.

Thus, knowledge of Brahman does not depend upon actions. It is analogous to the knowledge of objects of sense-perception, inference, and the other means of correct knowledge in that it depends upon the object of knowledge (alone). It is impossible to establish by reasoning any connection whatsoever between actions and Brahman or the knowledge of Brahman. Nor can we connect Brahman with our acts of representing it as the object of the action of knowing since Brahman is "different from the known and above the unknown" (KeU 1.3) and "By what means can one know that by means of which this entire world is known? How can one know the knower?" (BU 2.4.14). Brahman is also declared not to be an object of knowledge (as with external objects) or the object of acts of meditative adoration (KeU 1.5-6).

Objection: If Brahman is not an object, then scripture cannot possibly tell us about it.

Response: Scripture does not speak of Brahman as an object — its purpose is to turn aside all the false distinctions created by root-ignorance. Scripture does not represent Brahman as an object designatable by "this" but shows that the eternal inner Atman is never an object. Thereby, it removes the false distinctions of knowers, objects of knowledge, acts of knowledge, and so forth that are created by root-ignorance. "Brahman is conceived by one who does not conceive it. One who conceives it does not know it. It is not perceived by those who perceive it. It is perceived by those who do not perceive it" (KeU 2.3). "You cannot see the seer of seeing. You cannot hear the hearer of hearing. You cannot think the thinker of thinking. You cannot know the knower of knowing" (BU 3.4.2). Thereby, the idea of the impermanence of liberation that is due to root-ignorance is discarded.

Liberation has the nature of the eternally free Atman. Thus, the imperfection of being temporary cannot be ascribed to it. The idea that liberation is not eternal is a consequence of thinking that liberation is the effect of the actions of mind, speech, or body, or is a modification (of Brahman) since modifications (such as milk turning into curds) and effects of action (such as making jars) are not eternal. Nor is liberation something to be obtained by action since Brahman constitutes one's atman. Even if Brahman were different than one's essence, it could be obtained since it is all-pervading like space and thus is present in everyone. Nor is liberation the result of ritual purification since purification depends on the actions of adding something excellent or removing some fault — liberation has the nature of Brahman and thus is eternally pure and no excellence can be added to it.

Objection: Liberation is a property of the Atman that is hidden and can be manifested in oneself only by some action, just as the property of clarity becomes observable in a dirty mirror only when the mirror is cleaned by the action of rubbing.

Response: Brahman cannot be the locus of action since an action cannot occur without modifying its locus, and if Brahman were modified by an action it would be non-eternal, and that contradicts scripture. Thus, no action can abide in Brahman. Nor can the Atman be purified by something else since Brahman has no relation to anything else. Nor is the embodied atman purified by ritual actions such as bathing: what is purified is not the Atman in itself but the Atman joined to the body through root-ignorance — we see that bathing and so forth relates only to the body, and so actions here relate only to what is joined to the body. So too, thinking "I am free of disease" relates only to the body joined to the Atman and mistakenly identifies the Atman with conditions of matter.

Thus, it is only the "I," the object of the idea of an ego and the agent (*aham-kara*) in all acts of cognition that (apparently) accomplishes all actions and enjoys their fruit that is purified — not the Atman. Scripture declares: "One eats sweet fruit, while the other watches without eating" (MunU 3.1.1) and when the Atman is embodied "the wise declare that the (embodied) atman associated with the body, senses, and mind to be the one who enjoys" (KaU 3.4). But scripture declares Brahman to be incapable of receiving any additions and to be eternally pure: "He is the one Lord, hidden in all beings, pervading all the world, the inner atman of all beings, the overseer of deeds, dwelling in all beings, the witness, the solitary spectator, devoid of all properties" (SU 6.11) and "He is radiant, bodiless, without wounds, without sinews, pure, all-encompassing, untouched by evil" (IU 8).

And since liberation is nothing but Brahman, it is not something to be purified. It is impossible that it is connected in any way to action but only to knowledge.

Objection: But knowledge is itself an activity of the mind.

Response: Action and knowledge have different natures. An action is independent of anything that already exists and depends on the activity of a person's mind. Meditation and reflection are mental actions, and thus they depend on a person in order to be performed, not performed, or modified. But knowledge is the result of means of correct knowledge that have existing things as their objects. Thus, knowledge depends solely on existing things and not on Vedic statements or the human mind and cannot be made or unmade or modified.

Knowledge differs greatly from meditation. Meditation is only an action resulting from a Vedic injunction and is dependent upon a human being. On the other hand, what is meditated upon (e.g., the fire in meditating on "The fire is man") is a real thing and not dependent upon Vedic statements or human beings. Thus, knowledge is not an action. That holds for all objects of the means of correct knowledge. Thus, the knowledge that has Brahman as its object is not dependent upon a Vedic injunction. If there were injunctions related to Brahman in the Vedas, they would be without a purpose since their have as their object something that can neither be strived for nor avoided.

Sentences in the Vedas that have the appearance of injunctions, such as "The Atman is to be seen" are for diverting human beings from the objects of normal activities and turning the stream of our thoughts to the inner atman. When we act focused on external objects, we are anxious to obtain the objects of desire and to avoid objects of loathing, and we do not reach the highest goal of human beings, even if we desire it. The nature of the true Atman is neither something to be strived for or avoided since "all of this is that Atman" (BU 2.4.6). "When everything has become one's own atman, then whom is there to see and by what means? By what means can one know him by means of whom this entire world is known?" (BU 4.5.15). "This Atman is Brahman" (BU 2.5.19). Thus, knowledge of Brahman refers to something that is not a thing to be done, and so is not concerned with either the pursuit or avoidance of an object. As soon as we comprehend Brahman, all our duties come to an end and our work is over. "Whoever knows the Atman, knowing 'I am he,' then with what desire or with love for what would he cling to his body?" (BU 4.4.12). "Having understood this, one who understands has done all that is to be done" (BG 15.20).

Thus, Brahman is not presented as an object of injunctions.

Objection: No part of the Vedas makes statements that merely depict existing things. All statements are either injunctions, prohibitions, or supplements to them.

Response: The subject of the Upanishads is the transcendent Person (*purusha*), and this is not an aspect of anything else. The Atman is to be comprehended from the Upanishads alone. This Atman is Brahman. It is non-transmigratory and different in nature from what can arise, be obtained, modified, or purified. It is impossible to claim that this Atman does not exist or is not apprehended. That Atman is designated in the passage "That Atman is not so, not so" (BU 3.9.26). It cannot be denied.

Objection: There is no reason to maintain that the Atman is known only from the Upanishads since it is the object of self-awareness.

Response: The Atman discussed in the Upanishads is the witness of that self-awareness. (That is, it is the *subject* in self-awareness, not its *object*, and so cannot be treated as an object.) Neither from the Vedas nor from reasoning does one apprehend the Atman that is the witness and is different from the actor that is the object of self-awareness. It is what is permanent in all beings. It is uniform, one, and eternally unchanging — it is the ontic essence of everything. Thus, it can never be denied for the very person who would do the denying is the Atman. Nor can it be represented as a mere complement to injunctions. And as the Atman of everything, it can neither be strived for nor avoided. All impermanent things perish since they are merely modifications, but the Atman is imperishable since there is no cause why it should perish. So too, it is eternally unchanging since there is no cause for it to undergo any modification. Thus, it is by its nature eternally pure and free.

From such passages as "Nothing whatsoever is higher than the transcendent Person (*purusha*); that is the goal, the highest state" (KaU 3.11) and "The person taught in the Upanishads" (BU 3.9.26), it is justifiable to conclude that this Atman is the chief topic of the Upanishads. If the Vedas dealt only with injunctions, then to be consistent the information about existing things given even within those injunctions must be construed as meaningless. However, if it is accepted that some of the texts are about existing things, then why should they not give information about the eternally existing and unchanging Atman? That does not make the existing thing an action.

Objection: Existing things do not act, but they are instrumental to actions. Thus, the information given about such things merely serves actions.

Response: Even though this information serves actions, this means that the things about which information is given are themselves things that have the power to bring about particular actions. Their ultimate purpose may be to serve in actions, but this does not mean that the information given them does not also serve a purpose. The information about the Atman that exists but is not comprehended by other sources of knowledge has the same purpose: to put an end to all false knowledge. By understanding Brahman all false knowledge that causes transmigration is ended. Thus, a purpose is established that makes passages concerning Brahman the equal to those passages that give information about things useful to actions.

In addition, some Vedic injunctions enjoin avoiding certain acts — e.g., "A Brahmin is not to be killed." If all passages that do not express actions are without purpose, then so are these passages, and that is unacceptable. The word "not" denotes inaction — i.e., refraining from an action — not another action. The idea itself passes away, just as a fire is exhausted after it has consumed its fuel. Thus, the aim of prohibitions is merely a passive state, except in the case of certain vows. The charge of the uselessness of statements about existent things applies only to things in legends.

Objection: The analogy to the rope and snake does not apply. (When you see that the snake is illusory, your actions change, but) when your are told that your atman is Brahman, you remain in the realm of rebirths.

Response: One who realizes that his atman is Brahman does not remain in the realm of rebirths in the same way — that would be contrary to his realizing that he is Brahman. He is not subject to fear and frustration, as is someone who thinks that the person is his body (and so it is like someone realizing that there is no snake to fear but only a rope). A rich householder will grieve when he loses his wealth, but not once he retires from the world. "Pleasure and pain do not touch what is bodiless" (CU 8.12.1).

Objection: But being free of a body only follows death.

Response: The cause of a person being joined to a body is wrong knowledge. The Atman is eternally disembodied. (Thus, once wrong knowledge is destroyed by realizing Brahman, a person loses concern for the body and so is not in the realm of rebirth during this life in the same way as before.)

Objection: Embodiment is caused by the merit and demerit of following ones' duty (*dharma*) or acting contrary to it (*adharma*).

Response: The Atman does not act since it is without a body. You have not established how the Atman comes to be joined with the body or how the action of the embodied atman produces merit and demerit. You cannot argue in circles that embodiment is dependent on merit and demerit and that merit and demerit are dependent on embodiment. So too, an endless chain of rebirth would be a chain of the blind leading the blind. In addition, the Atman cannot possibly become an actor.

Objection: It is like a king acting through other people as his agents.

Response: The king employs servants and pay wages. Nothing analogous can be said of the Atman as the Lord and the body. Only false imagining is the reason of the idea of the connection of the Atman and the body.

Objection: That the Atman is an actor and connected to the body is only meant figuratively, not literally.

Response: A figurative sense of a word can be applied only when an actual difference between things compared is known to exist. Since we know some properties of a lion, we can apply the name figuratively to people. If we did not know the differences between a person and a lion, we could not. And this leads to the fallacious superimposition of the properties of one thing onto another (e.g., silver being erroneously ascribed to a mother-of-pearl shell). Even the learned who know the difference between the Atman and non-Atman confuse the words and ideas just as common shepherds and goatherds do. Thus, applying "I" to the body is not figurative but a superimposition, even when those who affirm the existence of the Atman do it.

Thus, (the idea of) the embodiment of the Atman is caused by an erroneous conception, and one who has attained true knowledge is free of his body even while still alive. The same is affirmed by scriptural passages concerning one who knows Brahman. So too, traditional texts such as *Bhagavad-gita* 2.54 on one whose mind is steady declare that he who knows is no longer connected to any action (i.e., one's actions no longer have any karmic consequences for the actor because the actions are attributed to the Lord). Thus, one who has comprehended Brahman to be the Atman does not belong to the realm of rebirth as he did before.

Objection: Brahman is only a complement to injunctions since hearing about it is to be followed by (the actions of) consideration and meditation.

Response: Reflection and meditation, like hearing about Brahman, are subordinate to the comprehension of Brahman. All injunctions and other means of correct knowledge end with the cognition expressed by "I am Brahman." As soon as the knowledge of the nondual Atman arises, all objects and knowing agents vanish, and there no longer can be any means of proof. When the knowledge arises that "I am Brahman, and this is my essence," the idea of a figurative or false atman comes to an end, and so how can there any longer be any effect arising from that false atman? Prior to attaining this knowledge, the Atman is seen as (an object) — the knowing subject. But just as the body is taken to be the Atman prior to gaining knowledge of Brahman, the ordinary sources of knowledge are valid only until the one Atman is ascertained (and then the Atman is no longer seen as an object).

Samkhya objection: There is an existing nonconscious substance (*pradhana*) that is known by means other than the Vedas, and so we can infer different nonconscious causes. We interpret the Vedantic passages as referring to that matter — e.g., "all-powerfulness" refers to its modification, and "all-knowing" can be ascribed to matter since knowing arises from matter rather than from the transcendent conscious soul (*purusha*) and needs material instruments of knowledge and so cannot exist without matter.

[5] Response: Since the Upanishads state that the cause of the world "sees," the claim of a nonconscious cause cannot be founded on scripture.

Scripture ascribes thinking to the cause. For example, "In the beginning, this world was beingness (*sat*) alone — one without a second. . . . Beingness then thought, 'May I be many! May I multiply myself!' It brought forth fire" (CU 6.2.1, 6.2.3). Other passages indicate that the omniscient Lord is the cause of the world (e.g., MunU 1.1.9). Nor can "all-knowing" be based on nonconscious matter since matter consists of three qualities (*gunas*), not just purity — even if purity (*sattva*) had the potential for knowledge, the other two qualities would obstruct it. And even a modification of the pure quality would require a witness (*saksin*), and matter is without that. Samkhya-Yogins may invoke the transcendent soul (*purusha*) embodied in mater as the witness, but it is more reasonable to assume that the cause of matter — i.e., Brahman — is the all-knowing cause of the world.

Objection: "All-knowing" cannot be ascribed to Brahman: if the activity of cognition is permanent, Brahman could not be a separate knower.

Response: Why can't Brahman be endowed with a permanent cognitive activity? To claim that he possesses eternal knowledge that is capable of throwing light on all objects but is not all-knowing is contradictory. If his knowledge were considered impermanent, he would know sometimes and not others and thus would be not all-knowing, but not so if the knowledge is permanent. So too, a knower can be designated as independent of the act of knowing, just as the sun is designated as independent of its light and heat, even though that light and heat are permanent.

Objection: The sun lights objects that stand independent of it, but Brahman existed before creation, in no relation to any object of knowledge.

Response: But we refer to the sun shining without reference to any object it illuminates. So too, Brahman may be referred to as an agent of knowledge in such passages as "It thought" without reference to any object of knowledge. Nor is there a problem if an object of knowledge is required to refer to Brahman as a knower: it is impossible to tell if name-and-form are either identical to the Lord or different from him, but they existed unemitted prior to creation. Yogins claim to have knowledge of the past and the future through the favor of the Lord, but this means that the ever-pure Lord himself has eternal cognition of the origin, sustaining, and dissolution of the world.

Objection: But prior to the origin of the world, Brahman cannot think since it does not have a body and so forth.

Response: Brahman's nature is eternally knowledge, just as the sun's is eternal luminosity — it does not need any instruments of knowledge. A transmigrating person (*samsarin*) is governed by root-ignorance and requires a body for knowledge to arise in him, but not so the Lord who is free of all impediments to knowledge and so can know free of all obstructions. "No action or organ of action of his can be found. Nor can an equal or a superior to him be seen. His highest power is truly varied. The working of his knowledge and strength are innate to him" (SU 6.8). "He moves swiftly and yet has no feet. He grasps and yet has no hands. He sees and yet has no eye. He hears and yet has no ear. He knows whatever there is to know, but there is no one who knows him. They call him 'the great primordial person'" (SU 6.19).

Objection: But scripture states that there is no transmigrating person who is different from the Lord. "Other than he, there is no seer, hearer, thinker, or knower" (BU 3.7.23). Why then does the transmigrating person need a body in order to know but the Lord does not?

Response: True, there is no transmigrating essence (atman) different from the Lord. Nevertheless, the Lord is connected with limiting adjuncts (*upadhis*) of the body, senses, and so forth. And just as the space within limiting adjuncts such as jars is not different from all-pervading space, so the result of the transmigrating person is not different from the Lord. Just as there is the false idea of different spaces, so there is the false idea that the Lord and the transmigrating person are different due to the nondiscrimination of the Atman from the limiting conditions of the body. The Atman in reality is the only existence, but we ascribe the property of being Atman to bodies that are not the Atman due to a wrong idea. The consequence of the person involved in rebirths is that his thought depends on the body and (other things that are not the Atman).

Samkhya objection: Only something consisting of multiple elements, such as matter (e.g., clay), can be a cause. Thus, Brahman cannot be a cause.

Response: That is not based on scripture. Reason establishes that non-composite Brahman can be a cause, as discussed below (aphorism 2.1.4).

Objection: Nonconscious entities are sometimes figuratively spoken of as conscious — e.g., "the riverbank is inclined to fall." So too, scripture refers to fire and water "thinking" (CU 6.2.3, 6.2.4). Thus, matter can be referred to figuratively as "conscious" since it performs actions. And just as people act according to their objectives and according to their nature, matter evolves by necessity of its own nature. So too, with the phrase "The fire saw" (CU 6.2.3). Thus, thought is to be taken only figuratively where being (*sat*) is the actor.

[6] Response: the word "Atman" is used to refer to the cause of the world, and so the word "sees" is not used in a figurative sense (to refer to matter).

Scripture states that only being existed at the beginning (CU 6.2.1) and proceeds to relate it to conscious individual beings (*jivas*). The word "being (*sat*)" does not refer to matter (*pradhana*). The attribution of consciousness to fire and water is figurative and clearly does not apply here. How could such an individual being be the atman of nonconscious matter? By "atman" we mean something's own nature, and obviously an individual conscious being cannot constitute the nature of what is nonconscious — matter. But if scripture here is referring to conscious Brahman, the use of "atman" in connected to the conscious individual is appropriate. So too in this passage: "That finest essence (*anima*) is the Atman of all of this world. That is reality/truth. It is the Atman. You are that reality" (CU 6.8.7). The "finest essence" is being (*sat*), the subject of that chapter of scripture. "You" refers to Shvetaketu, a conscious being. On the other hand, fire and water are nonconscious objects, and there is no reason to apply "conscious" to them in the literal sense. Any consciousness they would have comes from being (*sat*).

Samkhya objection: But "self" (atman) is often used figuratively — e.g., a king applies "self" to a servant who is carrying out his orders — and so it can be applied figuratively to matter since matter is the "servant" of the conscious transcendent soul (*purusha*). Also, the one Atman can refer to nonconscious things — e.g., the (material) essence of the elements or senses. So consciousness can be taken figuratively with regard to matter.

[7] Response: *Liberation is for one who holds tight to Brahman.*

If nonconscious matter were denoted by "being," then "You are that" would mean the being Shvetaketu was nonconscious — such a contradiction would mean that scripture could not be a means to right knowledge and could not be a means to knowing the true Atman and final liberation. But to assume scripture is not a means to correct knowledge is contrary to reason. In addition, to assert that "Atman" may signify both nonconsciousness and consciousness is unwarranted because it is not legitimate to attribute to words a plurality of meanings. Thus, "Atman" in its literal sense refers only to what is conscious and only figuratively to nonconscious things. Some words have two meanings (e.g., "*jyoti*" designating light and a certain sacrifice), but even if we assume "Atman" designates both groups of things, we cannot know which of the two meanings applies in a case without additional information. In the scriptural passage under discussion, being is distinguished by consciousness, and a conscious being, Shvetaketu, is mentioned.

Alternatively, the preceding aphorism may be understood as completely refuting the idea that "being" has a figurative or double sense at all. If so, then this aphorism supplies an independent reason for not considering matter to be the primary cause.

[8] *Samkhya declares that liberation involves a separation of the person* (purusha*) from matter* (pradhana/prakriti*).*

If matter constitutes being (*sat*), then "You are that" refers to matter. If so, the teacher of Shvetaketu would declare that we should separate ourselves from matter and that our essence (atman) is not the nature of matter. But no such statement is made. Matter is merely the cause of aggregation of the objects of enjoyment and cannot lead to knowledge of the enjoying persons, who are not effects of matter. Thus, "being" does not denote matter.

[9] *Separating consciousness from matter would contradict the merger* (apyaya) *of the individual* (sva) *into the Atman.*

In sleep, the individual person is united with being (*sat*) — he has gone to his own essence (atman, which is the Atman) (CU 6.8.1). A person is called "awake" as long as he is connected to external objects by the modifications of the mind in sense-perception; in dreams, he sees the impressions that these modifications had previously left. In deep sleep, the limiting adjuncts of waking and dreaming are ended, and then the person merges with the Atman, so to speak (*iti*). But the individual's atman does not merge into nonconscious matter. "The inner person when in the embrace of the atman consisting of insight (*prajna*) knows nothing inside or out" (BU 4.3.21). Thus, wise persons merge into a conscious cause of the world denoted by "being," not matter.

[10] *Scripture uniformly teaches that Brahman is cause of the world.*

All Vedantic texts teach that the cause of the world is the conscious Brahman. This uniformity greatly strengthens their claim to be considered a means of correct knowledge, just as the claim of the senses are strengthened by giving us uniform information concerning colors and so forth.

[11] *That is the final, direct teaching of the Upanishads.*

That the all-knowing Lord is the cause of the world is also declared directly: "There is no ruler or lord of him in the world. He has no defining mark. He is the cause. He is the lord of the lords of the sense-faculties. He has no progenitor or lord" (SU 6.9). Thus, it is finally settled that the all-knowing Brahman is the general cause of the world, not nonconscious matter or anything else.

Question: You've shown that the Vedantic texts demonstrate that an all-knowing, all-powerful lord is the cause of the origin, sustaining, and dissolution of the world, and that all Vedantic texts maintain that the cause is consciousness — so why is there any more to this text?

Response: Because Brahman is apprehended in two forms: one qualified by limiting adjuncts (*saguna* Brahman, i.e., the Lord) constituted by the diversity of name-and-form, and one free of any limiting conditions whatsoever (*nirguna* Brahman). For example: "Where there is apparently duality, so to speak, there one can see another. But when everything has become one's own atman, then who is there for one to see? (BU 4.5.15). "Where one does not see, hear, or know another, that is the fulness of reality. Where one sees, hears, and knows something else, that is a smaller reality. Truly, the full reality is the same as the immortal; the smaller is the same as the mortal" (CU 7.24.1). "That Atman is not so, not so" (BU 2.3.6). All the passages declare that Brahman possesses a double nature as either the object of knowledge or the object of root-ignorance. In the state of root-ignorance, Brahman plays two roles: the embodied atman, and the object of devotion. The different types of meditative adoration lead to different results. As one meditates upon the highest Atman as the Lord, so one becomes (CU 3.14.1).

Although the Atman is one, unchanging, and uniform, scripture declares that the Atman reveals itself in different ways in different beings, and so there must be an inquiry into the meaning of the texts to determine the knowledge of the Atman that leads immediately to liberation. Knowledge is conveyed by limiting conditions, thereby raising doubts as to whether knowledge has the higher or lower (form of) Brahman for its object. Vedantic texts teach that both (forms of) Brahman as connected to limiting conditions as an object of meditative adoration and Brahman as free of such connections as the object of knowledge. Different essences (atmans) are to be delineated. (TU 2 lists a hierarchy of different atmans [e.g., the atman of food], i.e., different "essences," with each succeeding one being deeper.)

[12] The essence (atman) consisting of bliss is the highest Atman.

Scripture states that the essence (atman) consisting of understanding (*vijnana*) is different from the atman consisting of bliss (*ananda*) (TU 2.1). But since scripture states that bliss describes the highest Atman, not the embodied transmigrating person (*jiva*). The atman of understanding is embodied. The atman of bliss is the innermost atman. The limiting adjuncts due to root-ignorance lead to misattributing joy to parts of the body. Unlike the transmigrating person, the atman of bliss is not embodied and thus is the supreme Atman.

[13] Objection: *Bliss is a modification and so not the highest Atman.* Response: *The word that you think means "modification" actually means "abundance."*

The text shows that "abundance of bliss" is meant (TU 2.9). (But "abundance of bliss" does not actually qualify the highest Atman [1.1.19].)

[14] Brahman is also indicated to be the source of bliss.

Brahman is the cause of bliss (TU 2.7), but to be the cause of bliss it must abound with bliss, just as a man who enriches others must be rich.

[15] Brahman is referred to in the aphorism on bliss from the Brahmanas.

The blissful one (*anandamaya*) is the highest Brahman, and one who knows Brahman attains the highest (TU 2.1). Brahman possesses true existence, consciousness, and non-finiteness (i.e., transcends the finite realm). Nor is there mention of a deeper inner atman different from the atman consisting of bliss. Thus, the Atman consisting of bliss is the highest.

[16] *Brahman and not (the individual person) is meant because of the claim that the latter is the source of bliss cannot be justified.*

The atman of bliss is the highest atman, not the transmigrating person who is different from the Lord and who is not the blissful one (Brahman).

[17] *The source of bliss is declared to be different from the individual person (and so the latter cannot be the source).*

TU 2 distinguishes the atman of bliss from the transmigrating person.

Objection: If "he who perceives or attains" is different from "he who is perceived or attained," how do you explain scriptural passages that say "The Atman is to be sought"?

Response: (From the point of view of ultimate truth,) that is a legitimate point. But in ordinary life, we see the Atman identified with the non-Atman (the body and so forth) and so we can speak of the difference between the seeker and the sought. But scripture also denies such passages. For example, "Other than he, there is no seer, hearer, thinker, or knower" (BU 3.7.23). The Lord is different from the embodied atman of understanding (*vijnana-atman*) who acts and enjoys — the latter is the product of root-ignorance. They differ just as a real magician differs from an illusory person or how unlimited space differs from the space in a jar that is fixed by that limiting adjunct.

[18] *And because the desire that propels creation is part of bliss, there is no need to infer primal matter as the cause as Samkhyas do.*

The desire to create is mentioned in the chapter on the atman of bliss (TU 2), and feeling cannot be ascribed to nonconscious matter. So nonconscious matter cannot be the Atman of bliss or the cause of the world.

[19] *In addition, scripture teaches the joining (*yoga*) of the individual person with that Brahman.*

Scripture teaches that once one has attained knowledge the individual person is identified with Brahman and attains liberation.

But something must be said about the true meaning of "abundance of bliss." Scripture states Brahman is merely the "tail" or "support" of the atman of bliss (TU 2), but this is merely figurative and not literally true since bliss is not the essence (atman) of Brahman. Brahman is the one essence in all of the various essences. And, as discussed, the highest Atman is not the atman of bliss, and so Brahman cannot be characterized as consisting of bliss. "He reaches that atman consisting of bliss" (TU 2.8) does not refer to Brahman since the passages list lower atmans (the "atman of food" and so forth). "Abundance of bliss" cannot qualify Brahman since there are degrees of bliss but no such qualifications of Brahman. Brahman transcends speech and mind (TU 2.9.1), and so "abundance" is ascribed merely figuratively. Brahman is the cause of all effects, including the atman consisting of bliss, since "He created everything there is" (TU 2.6). Thus, Brahman is the "blissful one," but bliss is not its atman.

[20] *The one that is within an individual person or thing is Brahman since the properties* (dharmas) *of Brahman are declared to be so by scripture.*

The highest Lord (*parama-ishvara*) is the being within the sun and the eye because their properties are the same (CU 1.6.6). Scripture here is not referring merely to the transmigrating person because the passage refers to being free of all evil (*papa*) and that can be attributed only to the Lord. Attribution of bodily properties occurs only when the Lord is treated for devotion as an object formed by illusion (*maya*). But the highest Lord is without form or properties although (from the conventional dualistic point of view) he may be said to possess some of their properties as the cause of effects. He is a locus for meditation, since, like space, he is all-pervading and can be viewed as within the atman of each being. References to his limitations are also for purposes of meditation alone.

[21] *Scripture declares Brahman to be different from the individual person.*

The Lord within persons and things is distinct from the transmigrating person (BU 3.7.9) even though he is the internal ruler of all.

[22] *Space (akasha) is Brahman since Brahman's characteristic marks are mentioned (with regard to it).*

Space is not the cause of the world (despite, e.g., CU 1.9.1) because the word "space" in these passages denotes Brahman because they share some characteristic marks in the passages.

[23] *For the same reason, the vital life-breath (Prana) indicates Brahman.*

For the same reason as "space," the word "life-breath" denotes Brahman since it is connected with marks that are characteristic of Brahman.

[24] *The word "light" also indicates Brahman (and not a phenomenal light) because all quarters of the world are mentioned with regard to it.*

The phenomenal world constitutes one "foot" of Brahma, and the heavens constitute the other three (CU 3.12.6). Whatever illuminates something else can be referred to as "light." Brahman, which is unconnected to any place, can be assigned a place (e.g., the heart or eye or sun) when Brahman is connected to limiting adjuncts (for meditation). Light or fire may be viewed as the outward appearance of Brahman (for meditation), just as the name "Brahman" is a mere outward symbol of it.

Brahman is free of all connections to distinguishing properties, and so whenever a text represents Brahman as the all-pervading Atman it is only as instruction leading to liberation. And whenever a text represents Brahman connected to distinguishing properties, it is for a worldly reward.

[25] Objection: *Because quarters are mentioned, it cannot be referring to Brahman (since Brahman is partless).* Response: *Scripture declares that the mention of the quarters directs the mind toward Brahman.* [26] *This also explains the representation of beings as the feet, and so forth of Brahman.*

Only Brahman can be represented as having beings as parts.

[27] Objection: *This is not so because of the difference from the earlier specification concerning space and light.* Response: *There is no contradiction between the two passages.*

Both passages (CU 3.12.6, 3.13.7) can refer to Brahman: just as a falcon in a tree can be said to be both in the tree and above it, so Brahman can be said to be both in heaven and beyond it.

[28] *Scripture understands life-breath to be Brahman.*

For example: "I am the life-breath, the atman consisting of insight (*prajna-atman*) . . . . meditate on me as life and immortality" (KsU 3.2, 3.3, 3.8). Some characteristics are observed to be different, but the chapter of the text as a whole indicates that the word "life-breath" here refers to Brahman. Life-breath can be identified with the conscious Atman only if the Atman is Brahman since life-breath is obviously nonconscious. Some characteristic marks ascribed to life-breath (e.g., bliss and imperishability) cannot be reconciled with any being but Brahman.

[29] Objection: *Passages about life-breath simply refer to the speakers themselves.* Response: *There is an abundance of references to the innermost atman.*

Life-breath is the atman consisting of insight. The multiple references to the innermost atman (*adhya-atman*) means that Brahman is referred to.

[30] *The instruction proceeds from the sage's vision that agrees with scripture.*

Indra refers to himself as life-breath — the atman of insight (*prajna*) that is Brahman. This comes from an insight gained through scripture.

[31] *If Brahman were not the subject here, that would lead to a threefold*

*meditative adoration (*upasana*) on Brahman, life-breath, and the individual person as different from each other. Elsewhere breath is accepted as Brahman. And the characteristics (of Brahman) are mentioned in these passages.*

There is a single meditation on Brahman spoken of as threefold: the characteristic marks of Brahman itself, life-breath, and insight. Thus, it is settled that Brahman is the subject of this chapter.

Chapter 1.2

Introduction. In Chapter 1, Brahman was shown to be the cause of the origin, sustaining, and reabsorption of the phenomenal world (when views from the dualistic point of view of root-ignorance). But certain scriptural passages only indicate Brahman obscurely. So we must address whether Brahman or something else is being referring to in those passages.

[1] (Brahman is consciousness and is the reality to be meditated upon).

When scripture identify an embodied atman with mind (*manas*) (e.g., CU 3.14), it does not indicate that the individual person's atman should be the object of meditation. Brahman without attributes (*nirguna*) is without mind or the life-breath. These attributes are for Brahmanas an object of meditation.

[2] The properties intended to be expressed are fitting for Brahman.

The properties of life-breath and mind are mentioned as possible subjects for meditation on Brahman (i.e., Brahman as life-breath).

[3] But the properties are not fitting for the embodied individual atman.

The embodied individual atman does not have the attributes of mind and life-breath. Properties such as "all-pervading" cannot apply to an embodied atman. The body is the seat of experience. Brahman is present in the body but not confined to it, unlike the embodied atman. The object to be mediated upon is different than the meditator.

[4] Also because of the reference of the actor separate from the object to be attained. [5] Also because the words denoting them are grammatically different. [6] And because the traditional texts concur.

The object of meditation (i.e., the mind as Brahman) is separate from the meditator and thus does not refer to the embodied atman.

The highest Atman as limited by adjuncts (e.g., the body, mind, and intellect) is referred to by the unwise as embodied. The distinction of actors and objects of activity may be assumed for activity in the world until we learn from "You are that" that the Atman is only one. But once we grasp the truth that there is only one all-pervading essence, the entire practical view of the world of rebirth, liberation, and so forth is ended.

[7] Objection: The highest Atman is not taught in these passages because of the smallness of the abode (e.g., the space within the heart) and because it is designated *as minute.* Response: *Brahman is referred to as such only for the sake of contemplation* (nichayya)*, as with Brahman being said to be space.*

Just as unlimited space can be considered limited when within a confined space, so too the highest Atman can be viewed as limited for purposes of meditation. If Brahman has its abode in different places, it would be subject to all the imperfections of those places — e.g., impermanence, having parts, and lacking unity.

[8] Objection: If Brahman and the individual person are one, then a Brahman would have the results of the person's experiences. Response: *There is a difference in the nature of Brahman and an individual being.*

The embodied atman acts and is affected by pleasure and pain, but the highest Atman is free of all of that. Thus, they are one in being but differ in nature. Brahman is ontic essence of the embodied atman, but the claim "You are that" must be interpreted this way. The enjoyment of the embodied atman is caused by false knowledge and does not affect what is revealed by true knowledge — the highest Atman. Brahman is not affected any more than space becomes dark blue simply because the uninformed believe it so.

[9] The highest Atman is the eater, and, all things in the world are his food. [10] Also because the highest Atman is the subject of the passage (KaU 2.18-23). [11] Both the highest Atman and the individual atman identified with the intellect enter the cavity of the heart, for that is seen in other passages.

Only the highest Atman can be the consumer of things in their totality. When things are reabsorbed (into Brahman at the end of a world-cycle), the highest Atman can be said to be an "eater."

The highest Atman and the embodied atman are both atmans. The embodied atman is the "knower (*jna*) of the world (*kshetra*, 'field')." They are both conscious and of the same nature. One passage (KaU 3.1) states that the highest Atman and the individual atman of understanding (*vijnana-atman*) are like light and shadow — one belonging to the realm of rebirth due to root-ignorance, and one in its real condition. Thus, they are different but of the same nature.

[12] Also because distinct properties of the two are specified in scripture.

The individual atman is the charioteer of the body (KaU 3.3) and the highest Atman is the goal. Or the individual atman is the bird that eats and the highest Atman is the bird that watches (MunU 3.1.1, SU 6.6). The passage figuratively ascribes being the enjoyer to the nonconscious matter (*sattva*) that is responsible for a sense of "I" and is modified by pleasure, pain, and so forth. But this is considered the enjoyer only due to root-ignorance. In reality, neither the mind (*manas*) nor the Atman acts or enjoys — the mind is without consciousness (*achitta*) because it is material in nature and is only a presentation of root-ignorance, and the Atman is not open to modification. Scripture declares the practical assumption of actors and so forth holds only in the realm of root-ignorance, comparable to taking elephants in dreams to exist. What is postulated for everyday existence vanishes for one who has attained discriminating knowledge.

[13] The inner person is Brahman because of the agreement between its properties and Brahman's, [14] its location and so forth attributed to it by scripture, [15] the texts attribute bliss to it, [16] and because of the practices to be followed by those who have heard the secret Upanishadic knowledge.

Brahman is without attributes and name-and-form, but it is taught as having attributes for the purpose of devout meditation. So too, scripture gives it an abode, even though it is all-pervading, for the purpose of realization.

Based on the properties mentioned, the person within the eye (CU 4.15.1) is the Lord and not the individual person.

[17] No other essences (atmans) *but Brahman can be the inner person because all the others are impermanent and because it is not possible to attribute the characteristics of the inner person to any other atman but Brahman.*

Only the highest Atman is permanent, not the reflected knowing atman of an individual person or the atman of a god. But even though Brahman is all-pervading, it may be spoken of as connected to limited places for the purpose of meditation, e.g., in the eye.

[18] The characteristics that are mentioned show that Brahman is the inner ruler (antaryamin) *of the gods and of all others.*

⚫ The inner ruler of the gods, the world, the Vedas, the sacrifice, beings, and the inner atman of a person (BU 3.7.3) must be the highest Atman (Brahman) because of the properties designated in the passage — all-pervading rulership, omnipotence, and unknowability. Organs of actions may be ascribed to the highest Atman due to the organs of action of those it rules. No infinite chain of inner rulers and what is ruled needs to be postulated.

[19] And the inner ruler is not Samkhya's primal matter (pradhana) *since the texts mention qualities not applying to matter but only to consciousness.*

Matter is not conscious, but the inner ruler sees (BU 3.7.23). Nor can being the Atman (which is conscious) belong to matter.

[20] *Nor can the embodied individual atman be the inner ruler since both recensions of the Brihadaranyaka Upanishad speak of it as different from the inner ruler.*

The word "not" has to be supplied from the previous aphorism (to make them consistent). The inner Atman is conscious and unseen — one cannot see the seer of sight (BU 3.4.2). It inwardly rules the organs of action. But the passage refers to the inner ruler as different from the embodied atman and dwelling in the embodied atman. The distinction of inner controller and embodied atman results only from the limiting adjuncts arising from root-ignorance and are not ultimately real. The Atman is only one, but due to limiting adjuncts the one Atman is treated as two — as universal and as indwelling a person (*pratyag-atman*), just as the space within a jar is distinguished from all-pervading space. But scripture can make a distinction between the knower and known objects for worldly purposes of perception (BU 2.4.14) and the other means of correct knowledge, for insight into the apparent world, and for injunctions and prohibitions. Scripture declares that the entire practical world exists only in the realm of root-ignorance and vanishes in the realm of true knowledge (BU 4.5.15).

[21] *The possessor of invisibility and so forth is Brahman, not an individual person, because of the characteristics mentioned concerning it.*

"What is not seen" (MunU 1.1.5-6) is Brahman, not matter or the embodied person, because the properties in the passage are ascribed to the highest Atman (e.g., all-knowing and immutable). So too for the Lord being the source (*yoni*) of all things. Two types of knowledge are enjoined: the lower knowledge of the Vedas, and the higher knowledge by which the immutable is directly grasped (MunU 1.1.2-7). These differ in their fruits: the result of higher knowledge is liberation and bliss — knowledge of nonconscious matter does not give that. The fruit of lower knowledge is prosperity. Turning away from the lower knowledge is preparation for higher knowledge.

[22] *Primal matter and the individual person are not mentioned in these passages because the distinctive characteristics of Brahman are mentioned, as is its difference from these.*

Samkhya objection: Matter may be the source of all beings (*bhuta-yoni*) and can itself be the imperishable (*akshara*).

Response: The highest Atman is the source of all beings, not matter or the embodied individual (*jiva-atman*). Brahman is beyond the unmanifested imperishable. The individual considers himself finite, determined by the name-and-form that are brought about by root-ignorance. The "immutable" has the unmanifested seed of name-and-form as its nature (*rupa*). It depends on the Lord and is the Lord's limiting adjunct, but it is not an effect.

[23] The form of Brahman as the Lord is also mentioned.

The conscious and nonconscious forms cannot be ascribed to matter.

[24] The Cosmic Person (Vaishvanara) of Chandogya Upanishad 5.11 is Brahman since words denoting the same properties specifically characterize both. [25] Also because what is stated in the traditional texts are an indirect indication of the scripture's meaning.

The terms used indicate that the Cosmic Person is the highest Atman.

[26] Objection: *The Cosmic Person is not Brahman because words with different meanings are used and other reasons and because the Cosmic Person abides within the person.* Response: *The instruction is to conceive Brahman as inner and this characteristic is not attributed to any others and because Brahman is referred to as a person. [27] For the same reason, the Cosmic Person is not a divinity nor a great element of the Samkhya theory. [28] According to Jaimini, there is no contradiction here even if Brahman is directly meditated upon as the Cosmic Person.*

All of the gods and elements are limited and the highest Atman is not. The highest Atman may be venerated through the form Vaishvanara.

[29] The teacher Ashmarathya says that this is so from the point of view of Brahman's manifestation as space. [30] The teacher Badari says that this form with a finite size is for the sake of constant remembrance for the purpose of devout meditation. [31] Jaimini says, based on the scripture, that it is because of a false identification (i.e., superimposing the small on the great).

But the imagined identification of the highest Lord with something of a finite size can be employed for meditation.

[32] The wandering ascetics of the Jabala school teach that this one is inside the head.

They teach that the Lord who is the inner Atman of all is in the space between the top of the head and the chin.

Chapter 1.3

[1] The support of heaven, earth, and the rest of the world is Brahman since scripture uses the word "own" denoting the Atman.

("Support" [*ayatana*] is the abode or repository underlying the world in which the world resides.) Brahman is a "bridge" in the sense that it connects two things together, not that it spans a space. By eliminating through knowledge the universe conjured up by root-ignorance, one knows the one homogeneous Atman as the sole repository.

[2] The teaching is that that is the reality attained by the liberated.

By the "support of heaven and so on," Brahman must be understood since that is what the liberated resort to. The idea that the body is our atman, even though the body and other things exist only within the realm of what is not the Atman, is root-ignorance. From this idea, desires and fears arise. On the other hand, no source indicates matter as the support. Texts indicate that the knowledge of the support of heaven and so forth is connected with leaving words behind, and this attaches to knowledge of Brahman. By giving up name-and-form, the enlightened are free of name-and-form and reach the radiant Person (*purusha*) who is higher than the unmanifested (*avyakta*) realm (MunU 3.2.8). It is realized by giving up speech (and other activities).

[3] This support cannot be inferred to be the primal matter of Samkhya theory since there are no terms indicating nonconscious matter.

*[4] So too with any living creature (*prana-bhrit*).*

Omniscience and other such properties do not belong to (finite) individual beings. Nor can the support (of the heavens and earth) be limited by adjuncts and thus not be all-pervading.

[5] The differences of knower and the object to be known are mentioned.

Brahman, not the individual atman, is the object to be known.

[6] And because Brahman is the subject of the passage (MunU 1.1.3), not primal matter or living creatures.

The entire world becomes known if the essence (atman) of everything — the Supreme Atman — is known, not if only an individual atman is known.

[7] And because of the difference between remaining detached and eating (MunU 3.1.1). (Brahman does the former and an individual does the latter.)

The context of the two birds (MunU 3.1.1), one of whom eats the fruit of actions while the other merely observes, clearly refers to the individual being (having the karmic effects of action) and Brahman (which is changeless). But the individual living being is only a product of root-ignorance. But freed from the limiting adjuncts, the living being is not distinct from Brahman any more than the space in a jar is distinct from all space.

[8] The abundance of reality is Brahman since Brahman (and not the individual) is taught to be present in the serenity of deep sleep.

"Abundance" (*bhuman*) here (CU 7.23-24) refers to Brahman and not to an individual or life-breath because the individual consciousness is not present in deep [dreamless] sleep — the bliss of deep sleep belongs to Brahman, not to the individual. The life-breath only figuratively denotes Brahman since it springs from Brahman (CU 7.26.1). "Abundance" is represented as the final truth and so must refer to Brahman, the truth/reality (TU 2.1). One can transcend speech (and the other functions of the organs) only by relying on Brahman, not on knowledge of the life-breath.

[9] Also the characteristics of abundance fit only the highest Atman.

There one sees, hears, and understands nothing else, and so "abundance" must be denoting Brahman (BU 4.5.15). So too for bliss, reality/truth, resting in its own greatness, all-knowing, and being the atman of everything.

[10] The imperishable (akshara) is the highest Atman because it supports all other things up to (and including) space.

Space is woven on the imperishable (BU 3.8.8). It is either "imperishable" or "what pervades" all of the world. It is not referring to the syllable "Om" (CU 2.23.4) which is a means to attain Brahman.

[11] Such support is possible only by Brahman's command.

The command attributed to the imperishable (BU 3.8.9) is from the Lord, not nonconscious matter.

[12] Also because of the exclusion in scripture of all things from Brahman whose nature (bhava) is other than Brahman's.

Brahman is conscious, and all limiting adjuncts are excluded, so the imperishable must be Brahman, and not matter or an embodied atman.

[13] Brahman is mentioned in scripture to be the object of (meditative) perception (ikshana).

Objection: The lower Brahman, not the supreme Brahman, is the object.

Response: The full passage in question makes it clear that the supreme Brahman, the supreme Person (*purusha*) is meant. An object of meditation may not be real, but here the object is identified as an object of seeing, i.e., something real (and open to experience), and so it is the highest Brahman. Brahman is higher than a conscious person (*jiva*) and constitutes the object of perception and the object of meditation. Nothing is higher. It is the supreme all-pervading reality.

[14] The small space within the heart is Brahman for the following reasons: [15] the action of going into Brahman through the space in the heart; because it is described as the phrase "world of Brahman"; it is seen to be so in other Upanishadic passages; "small space within the heart" indirectly indicates Brahman; [16] the property "supports the world" is attributed to the small space; and its greatness is seen in that; [17] and the familiar use of the term "space" indicates that it is Brahman.

The small space within the "city of Brahman" in the shape of a lotus within the heart is all-pervading (CU 8.1.1-3) and contains within it the earth and true desires. Thus, the space is the highest Atman, not the individual atman of understanding (*vijnana-atman*). The "world of Brahman" (*brahma-loka*) in CU 8.3.2 is the world of the real (*satya-loka*) and is applied to the space within the heart, not the world of the god Brahma (Prajapati). So again, the small space within the heart is the highest Lord. "Space" has a settled meaning of "the highest Lord" and is never used for the individual person.

[18] Objection: *The individual person is referred to as in the "space within the heart" in other passages, and so that is meant here.* Response: *It is impossible for the individual to reside in the space within the heart.*

The individual imagines himself limited by the sense of "I" and other limiting adjuncts. That cannot compare to space. So too, properties of the highest Atman like freedom from evil (CU 8.7-11) cannot be transferred and attributed to the individual.

[19] Objection: *But the individual person is referred to as such in subsequent passages.* Response: *It is referred to as such only to reveal its real nature (as nondifferent from Brahman).*

The teaching is about the highest Atman — i.e., Brahman — not the inner embodied atman. "You are that" is about the true nature of the oneself, and what depends upon the unreal limiting adjuncts is not the Atman's true nature. Duality remains as long as the individual person has not freed itself from root-ignorance. This ends only with the rise of knowledge of the Atman whose nature is unchanging eternal knowledge. It is expressed as "I am Brahman." One remains an individual person until one has discarded the aggregate of the body, sense-organs, and mind and has arrived by means of scripture at knowledge that one is not the aggregate and not part of the realm of rebirth but is the real/true — the Atman whose nature is pure consciousness. "He who knows Brahman becomes Brahman" (MunU 3.2.9). It is this real nature of the individual person by which it arises from the body and appears in its own form.

Objection: How can Brahman appear in any other form than its true one? Its true nature is eternal and unchanging.

Response: Before the rise of discriminating knowledge, the nature of the individual (*jiva-atman*), although in reality pure light, is non-discriminated, so to speak, from its limiting adjuncts of the body, sense-organs, mind, sense-objects and feelings. It appears to consist of the powers of seeing, and so forth. It is like a crystal: although its true nature is clear, before the rise of knowledge the crystal is seen, so to speak, as not distinct from the nearby limiting adjuncts having a red or blue color, and so it appears red or blue; when discriminating knowledge arises, one sees its true nature that had been there all along. In the same way, the individual person uses discriminating knowledge and rises from the body to realize its true nature. Thus, non-embodiment and embodiment of the atman are due only to discrimination or lack thereof (KaU 2.22). But the embodiment and non-embodiment are not (ontologically) different (BG 13.31). Thus, the true nature of the individual person is not manifested until true knowledge arises. The manifestation of a different nature is not possible because the true nature of the Atman does not change. The (apparent) difference between the individual person and the highest Lord results only from wrong knowledge, not from any reality since, like space, the highest Atman is not in contact with anything. But the reflected embodied atman is not referred as the "seer" within the eye.

When one awakes from a dream, one discounts the content of the dream but not the reality of the dreamer. So too, there may be no content in dreamless sleep, but the identity of the cognizing atman is not in doubt.

There is no destruction of the knowing by a knower as that is imperishable (BU 4.4.30). The individual person is not different from the highest Atman whose properties are immortality and fearlessness. The unreal aspects of the individual are a presentation by root-ignorance, stained by all the desires and aversions attached to actors and enjoyers and are connected to evils of all kind. Root-ignorance is dissolved by true knowledge. The person is thus led into the opposite state — the true state in which a person's atman is one with the highest Lord and is free of evil and so on. The process is like the imagined snake passing into the rope as soon as the mind of the beholder is freed from its erroneous imagination.

Some, including some of our own school, believe that the individual person (*jiva*) as such is real. The purpose of these aphorisms is to refute these speculations. There is only one highest Lord, who is forever unchanging and whose substance is knowledge. Besides the Lord, there is no other knowledge. By root-ignorance, the highest Lord manifests himself in various ways, just as a magician appears in different forms by means of his magical power (*maya*). The highest Atman is eternally pure, conscious, free, not in contact with anything, and devoid of form. The opposite properties of the individual person are erroneously ascribed to the highest Atman, just as the ignorant ascribe dark blue to the sky.

To prove that there is this error, Vedantic texts insist on a difference between the highest Atman and the individual person, but the Atman and person are not really distinct — the distinction is part of ordinary thought due to the power of root-ignorance. The real purpose of the texts is to show the absolute oneness of the Atman.

[20] The reference to the individual person is for a different purpose.

The reference is to show the nature of the highest Lord, not the person. The person is to attain the Lord and thereby reveal its own true nature. The individual (*jiva-atman*) has authority over this cage of the body and senses during the wakeful state, experiences the dreams created by the impressions, approaches the supreme Light that is Brahman in dreamless sleep, and, getting rid of particular cognitions, attains its true nature.

[21] Objection: *But scripture declares the limitedness of the space within the heart.* Response: *This has already been explained (in aphorism 1.2.7). [22] The space within the heart attains the likeness of Brahman. It is referred to as "his." [23] The traditional texts (e.g., BG 15.6, 15.12) also state this.*

Objection: *The shining substance mentioned in MunU 2.2.10 and KaU 5.15 must be something other than the atman consisting of insight (prajna-atman) — a luminous substance that causes the Atman to shine afterward.*

Response: The highest Atman is referred to: after him, everything that shines shines by "his" light. So too, the light of knowledge illuminates everything. The manifestation of the entire world of name-and-form, actions, actors, and the fruit of actions has the light of Brahman as it cause, just as the light of the sun is the cause of the manifestation of form and color. Whatever is perceived is perceived by the light of Brahman, not only the light of the sun, moon, or stars, while Brahman is self-luminous and not perceived by means of some other light. Brahman manifests everything and is not manifested by another.

[24] Brahman is said to be measured by the size of the thumb. [25] Scripture speaks of this only concerning Brahman within human beings.

The person who is said to be the size of the thumb (KaU 4.12) is the highest Lord/Person, not the atman of insight.

Objection: How can any extension be ascribed to the all-pervading atman?

Response: Only human beings study the Vedas, and so we can speak of the highest Atman being within the heart. The transmigrating person (*jiva-atman*), which is the size of a thumb, is the inner atman. The passage teaches the oneness of the individual person with the highest Atman, not the size of anything (KaU 6.17).

[26] According to Badarayana, gods are also capable of meditating on Brahman since that is possible.

Gods too can hear the Upanishads and may have the desire for liberation and become students to gain knowledge (CU 8.11.3), as can their children who are the seers (*rishis*) (TU 3.1).

[27] Ascribing corporeality to the gods does not contradict this since it is seen in scripture that the gods can assume many different bodies.

The gods can assume forms and be present at many different sacrifices at the same time, although they are invisible. If yogins can animate several bodies at once, so much more so can the gods who possess supernatural powers by their nature.

[28] Nor does the corporeality of the gods contradict the words of scripture since the world arises from the words of scripture, as is known by direct perception and inference.

The world, the gods, and other beings arose from the Vedic words (*shabda*). This is known from the perception (by the seers) of scripture and inference. Traditional texts concur. That word is not the ontic cause — Brahman is. *Types* arise from words, but the *individuals* within each type arise from Brahman. We know from "perception and inference" (here, scripture and traditional texts) that words precede the creation of things. So too from observation: one remembers first the word for anything he wishes to accomplish and then acts.

Objection: What is the nature of a word that creation can proceed from it?

Response: A word, not its letters, is the unit of power, and the intellect (*buddhi*) apprehends the unity in one mental act of apprehension. The word is eternal and recognized each time it is pronounced. Through the denotative power of the word, this world, actions, actors, and the fruits are produced.

Objection: But the letters are no sooner produced then they pass away.

Response: They do not pass away — we recognize exactly the same letters each time they are produced. Letters are not impermanent but permanent properties that are apprehended each time in a single act of hearing. No additional letter or word is needed.

[29] For that reason, the eternity of the Vedas follows.

The eternity of the Vedas has to be assumed because of fixed types of the gods, and so forth, originate from it (in each world-cycle).

[30] Nor is there a contradiction since the same names and forms (appear) in each world-cycle, as is seen from the Vedas and the traditional texts.

Objection: At the end of each world-cycle, all is dissolved, and a totally new production then appears — so how can there be an eternal connection between a word and an object?

Response: It is like an individual going to sleep: when he awakes, there is a new production, but it has the same types of form and words as before.

Objection: In the dissolution of a world-cycle, the dissolution is complete — the world does not merely take up in the next cycle where it left off.

Response: By the favor of the highest Lord, lords such as Hiranyagarbha (the first born) continue in the same form and continue the same kind of existence in each world-cycle. For them, the period between world-cycle is like sleep. So too, the karmic merit and demerit of beings survive. Power (*shakti*) survives, and worlds arise from that power in the same form. The senses and their relation to sense-objects remain the same. With all this, beings with the same names and forms arise again. At the beginning of each world-cycle, the highest Lord arranges the entire world the same way each time, and the same beings appear again.

[31] Objection: *According to Jaimini, the gods are not qualified to attain knowledge of Brahman because they are not qualified for the preparatory (Vedic lower) knowledge, being themselves the objects of meditation.*

Likewise, seers are unqualified for meditations connected to seers.

[32] Also because the gods' meditation is limited only to the realm of light.

Beings in the realm of light are devoid of bodies, consciousness, or the capacity to form wishes (and so are not capable of knowing Brahman).

[33] Response: *But according to Badarayana, the gods are qualified for Brahman knowledge because their competence for this exists.*

The gods do have personal existence, desire, and the capacity to know. If we accept the Vedas as an independent source of knowledge based on the direct perception (by the seers), then immortal beings can see and deal with them due to their perfection of religious duties. According to the Yoga school, one can draw near to one's chosen god. Thus, it is justified to believe that the gods have corporeality and from that it is justified to believe that the gods have the capacity to gain knowledge of Brahman.

[34] Grief arose in King Janashruti upon hearing a swan disparage him as being of the lowest class (a Shudra).

Objection: Then like the gods, Shudras are qualified for knowledge too.

Response: But Shudras cannot study the Vedas, become initiated, or participate in certain rituals, and so cannot attain knowledge of Brahman.

[35] Response: *But that Janshruti was a member of the warrior class is known from scripture and from the indirect indication of his being a descendant of Chitraratha (a known warrior). [36] In addition because of the mention of the purificatory ceremonies that he performed and the impossibility of these for a Shudra. [37] Also because of the inclination (of teachers to impart*

knowledge to him) arising only upon ascertaining that one is not a Shudra. [38] And because the traditional texts prohibit Shudras from hearing, studying, and acquiring the meaning of the Vedas (since they may not perform the rituals).

However, Shudras may be in a position to acquire knowledge of Brahman as the effect of actions in a former life. In addition, knowledge can be acquired by all classes and women through the traditional texts.

[39] Objection continuing aphorisms 24-25: How can Brahman be within the heart and the size of a thumb? Response: Because the entire world trembles in the life-breath that is Brahman.

"Life-breath" in KaU 6.2 refers to Brahman, not normal breath (BU 4.4.18, KaU 5.5). Also, because the fruit in this passage is immortality.

[40] Also because scripture declares Brahman to be light.

The highest light (CU 8.12.3) is the highest Atman, not physical light, because the highest Brahman is the subject of the chapter. In the case of final liberation, there is no course to be followed upon death and no atman to depart from the body.

[41] Space also is Brahman because scripture so declares it to be different from name-and-form.

Space reveals name-and-form (CU 8.14.1). But only Brahman can be different from name-and-form since the world developed by names and forms. Only Brahman can bring about (*nirvahana*) names and forms — the living person (*jiva-atman*) is said to have the creative agency, but that person is (really) Brahman (CU 6.3.2).

[42] Brahman is different from the individual person in deep dreamless sleep and death, and thus they are different. [43] And because Brahman is described as "the Ruler" (i.e., "Lord" of the universe).

The statement in BU 4.3.7 is only about the highest Lord — the atman of insight (*prajna*) — not about the transmigrating embodied atman. It only highlights that Brahman's nature does not involve transmigration (and does not deny the two's identity).

Chapter 1.4

[1] Objection: The Samkhyas can infer from scripture that primal matter (pradhana) is the cause of the world. Response: The Upanishad passage in question shows that the word "unmanifest" (avyakta) is used only in a simile concerning what is contained in the body and refers to the body itself.

Objection: Katha Upanishad 3.11 states that "Higher than the great one (*mahat*, the first Samkhya evolute) is the unmanifest. Higher than the unmanifest is the transcendent person (*purusha*). Nothing whatsoever is higher than the person." (The *purusha* is separate from matter, and) thus, there is scriptural authority for matter as the cause of the world (*jagat*).

Response: There is no place for matter as the cause. "Unmanifest" in the Upanishad can mean anything undeveloped or subtle (i.e., unobservable). Here, the subtle body that develops into the manifested body is being referred to. The point of the passage is the identity of the cognizing individual (*jiva*) and the highest Atman. Scripture here indicates the realization of Brahman by describing the development of the individual who has root-ignorance (*avidyavat*) and is attached to the body and its organs before the release from rebirth. It also indicates that yoga — the withdrawal of speech and the mind into the calm and peaceful highest Atman — is the means of release (KaU 1.3.12). Thus, the wise should give up the activity of the senses and should withdraw the mind from sense-objects and rest on the intellect (*buddhi*), which is capable of discriminating (what is real), and withdraw the intellect into knowledge of the calm and peaceful highest Atman.

[2] The "unmanifest" means the subtle body since it deserves that label.

The transient world that is divided up into various entities by name-and-form can be referred to as "unmanifest" when it is in its primal state as a latent seed before names and forms are unfolded.

[3] The "unmanifest" is not the cause of the world because it is dependent on Brahman, but it serves a purpose as a subtle cause.

Objection: By admitting a subtle body undifferentiated by name-and-form, you admit matter is the cause.

Response: Any undeveloped potential form is dependent on the highest Lord. Without the assumption of a primal state, the power to create of the highest Lord cannot be established. Nor could the unenlightened gain final release since knowledge burns up the seed of potential rebirth. The seed is referred to as "unmanifest" and is by nature root-ignorance.

The "unmanifest" is sometime designated by the words "space," and "imperishable," and illusion (*maya*). *Maya* is designated "unmanifest" because it cannot be defined as that which exists or that which does not exist.

The "great one" of Samkhya theory is either an evolute governed by the Lord or an individual atman dependent upon root-ignorance. Nothing is highest than the supreme Person (*purusha*) (KaU 2.11).

[4] Unmanifest matter is not Brahman also because it is not mentioned

as something that should be known.

[5] Objection: The Upanishads refer to nonconscious primal matter when they say "unmanifest." Response: From the context of the full passage, it is the atman of insight (prajna) that is being referred to. [6] And the question and answer in the passage relate to only three things (fire, the individual person, and the highest Atman), not primal matter.

The text explicitly refers to the highest Atman and also refers to it as the object of knowledge. It is also referred to elsewhere as possessing all the properties ascribed to matter. All this suggests that the individual atman and the atman of insight are not different. As long as root-ignorance remains, the individual atman is (seen as) affected with phenomenal properties, but once root-ignorance ends this atman is (seen to be) one with the highest Atman, as is taught by scriptural passages such as "You are that." But whether root-ignorance is present or not, no difference is made in the Atman — whether a rope is seen as a snake or not makes no difference in the rope. The aphorism is to be understood from the point of view of an imagined different between an individual atman and the atman of insight. But the distinction of the individual embodied atman and the highest Atman results only from root-ignorance.

[7] Just as Samkhya's "mahat" (the great, the first evolute of matter) does not refer to the Atman, neither does "avyakta" (the unmanifest). [8] So too, "aja" ("unborn") cannot refer to matter since no special characteristics are mentioned, just as we cannot identify which bowl is being referred in BU 2.2.3 because no special characteristics are specified there. [9] But some recensions of the Vedas consider the elements beginning with light to be the unborn.

Prior to creation, names and forms lie unemitted in the divine power of creation. That is the primal state of the world in which names and forms evolve.

[10] And there is no contradiction since this is an instruction based on imagery, as with honey denoting the sun.

There is a real difference among embodied individuals and between bondage and release (in the phenomenal realm).

[11] Even the mention in the Vedas for the number of Samkhya categories (i.e., 25) cannot be cited for support for primal matter being the Atman since the categories are different from those in the Upanishad and there is an excess number of Samkhya categories. [12] Life-breath and the others are the five origins (janas), as is seen in a complementary passage. [13] In one recension, food (matter) is omitted, and light is included instead to reach the number five.

Thus, the Samkhya doctrine of matter cannot be based on scripture.

[14] There is a conflict between the recensions as to the items created, such as space and so forth, but Brahman is spoken of in all the Upanishads as the cause.

Objection: It is impossible to prove either that Brahman is the cause of the origin, sustaining, and destruction of the world or that all Vedantic texts refer to Brahman because the texts contradict each other. The order of the creation of space and water and so on conflict in different texts. Some say that creation arose from nonexistence (*asat*) (TU 2.7, CU 3.19.1), and some dispute this (KaU 6.1). One says that the creation of the world occurred spontaneously (BU 1.4.7). Because of such discrepancies, the Vedantic texts cannot be accepted as authoritative for determining the cause of the world.

Response: The texts conflict on the order of creation but not on the creator: the all-knowing, all-powerful, all-pervading Lord of all — the atman of everything, one without a second. The Lord is not dependent upon anything else. The cause is described as the Atman abiding within a series of sheaths beginning with the observable body, and the texts affirm this to be the inner atman within all beings. The texts tell how the Atman became many and declare that it is not different from the created effects. The conflicts do not affect the statements of the cause, and they will be reconciled below (chapter 2.3).

In addition, the conflicts are of no great importance since creation is not what scripture teaches, and our welfare do not depend on those doctrines in any way. Creation is described merely to teach us that the effect is not different from the cause (GK 3.15). The fruit of knowing Brahman is what is important (TU 2.1, CU 8.1.3, SU 3.8) — it is overcoming suffering and death. That fruit is realized by direct experience (*pratyaksha*) as soon as one realizes by the doctrine "You are that" the knowledge that the Atman is not reborn.

[15] Nor does nonbeing (in TU 2.7, CU 3.19.1) mean literal nonexistence because of the connection of the passages to Brahman.

Since the term "being" (*sat*) ordinarily means the differentiated world of name-and-form, the term "non-being" (*asat*) designates only the same substance prior to its differentiation, not literal nonexistence. Thus, Brahman is called in a figurative sense "non-being" prior to the origin of the world. Nor does "undeveloped" mean that the development of the world occurred without a lord. Since scripture declares that after entering the body the Atman has the nature of consciousness, it must have had that nature before it entered.

[16] Because the word "work" (in Kaushitaki Upanishad 4.19) indicates the world, the world is the work of Brahman.

[17] Objection: *Brahman is not meant here because there are indirect indications of the individual person and the primary life-breath.* Response: *This has already been explained above (aphorism 1.1.31).*

The passage is not about life-breath per se. the indicatory marks of an individual are used from the point of view of the oneness (of Brahman).

[18] But Jaimini asserts that the reference to the individual person is for a different purpose, as the question and answer of the passage indicates. In addition, some the Vajasaneyins mention this in their recension.

The general Vedanta doctrine is that the individual becomes one with the highest Brahman in deep sleep, and from the highest Brahman the world proceeds including the life-breath animating an individual. And again, the word "space" may be used to designate the highest Atman, as with the space within the lotus within the heart (CU 8.1.1). In addition, the Upanishads say that all the atmans come forth from the highest Atman. Thus, the highest Atman is the one general cause.

[19] The atman that is to be seen, heard, studied, and meditated upon is the highest Atman because of the correlation of the Upanishadic passages.

Objection: The atman in Brihadaranyaka Upanishad 4.5.6 is the individual (*jiva-atman*) since only that is "dear" to someone. In addition, "the knower of knowing" is the individual.

Response: The full passage makes it clear that this refers to the highest Atman, not the individual. Only knowing the highest Atman achieves immortality, and everything — the universe of names, forms, and deeds — is known only by knowing the highest cause, the highest Atman. That "all this is the Atman" means that the aggregate of existing things is not different from the highest Atman. The Atman is the support of the entire world of objects, the senses, and the mind. It has neither an inside nor outside but is altogether a mass of knowledge. Since the highest Atman is the support of all things, it is the object of direct (meditative) experience (*pratyaksha*).

[20] The teacher Ashmarathya asserts that the individual person is taught to be the object of realization only as an indirect indication, and this proves the declaration that the highest Atman is Brahman.

Ashmarathya is saying that the individual atman is not different from the highest Atman but the individual atman is an effect of the highest Atman.

[21] The teacher Audulomi asserts that the individual person becomes one with Brahman when it departs the body at death after liberation because such

becomes one's state.

Audulomi is teaching that the individual atman becomes one with the highest Atman. As rivers flowing into the sea disappear, having lost their name-and-form, so the wise who are freed from name-and-form (the limiting adjuncts creating individuality) go to the divine person (MunU 3.2.8) and lose their name-and-form and become united to the highest person.

[22] The teacher Kashakritsna thinks that it is because Brahman exists in the individual person (without undergoing any change and so understands "You are that" correctly).

Only this opinion of the three teachers accords with scripture: the individual atman and the highest Atman are not different. The highest Atman only appears as the individual atman. Only this view enables immortality to be the result of knowledge — that would be impossible if the individual atman were in fact a modification of the highest Atman and lost its existence by merging into its causal substance. So too, the simile of the river does not apply since name-and-form abides in the limiting adjuncts, not the atman, and are ascribed to the Atman only figuratively. So too the image of the individual atman being emitted from the highest Atman as a spark from a fire is based only on the limiting adjunct. The unchanging Atman is a mass of knowledge, and by knowledge can one become dissociated from the limiting adjuncts (elements and sense organs) that are the product of root-ignorance. Without the adjuncts (of a body and mind), one does not have the means to gain knowledge. The idea of a knower as actor is part of the realm of root-ignorance. When the Atman is all, one cannot see or know another — thus, all specific acts of cognition are absent. Thus, the difference of the individual atman and highest Atman is not real but due to the limiting adjuncts of the body and so forth that are the products of root-ignorance — they differ in name only. Perfect knowledge has as its object the absolute oneness of the two. So too, liberation is not an event brought about by a cause.

[23] Brahman is also the material cause (prakriti) (of the phenomenal world), so as not to contradict the declarations and illustrations in scripture.

Objection: Brahman may be the controlling efficient cause of the world since matter is not conscious, but it cannot be the material cause. Nor can Brahman be referred as a personal "Lord" (from the ultimate point of view since it does not have the properties of a person). So too, the effect should resemble the cause, and the composite, nonconscious, and impure world cannot reflect Brahman which is the opposite of those.

Response: Scripture states that Brahman is both the efficient (*nimitta*) and material (*prakriti*) cause of the world. Thus, knowledge of everything is possible through cognizing the material cause since effects are not different from their ontic source but are different from their efficient causes, just as everything made of earth is known by knowing one piece of earth (CU 6.1.4-6). Worldly material causes are dependent upon people to shape them, but Brahman is not dependent on any other efficient or ontic cause.

[24] *Scripture teaches of the longing to create (and the creator must be conscious to have a desire).*

The wish "May I be many!" (CU 6.2.3) shows the reflective atman to be the controlling efficient cause and also the material cause out of which the many arise.

[25] *And also because scripture directly teaches that (Brahman) is both (the creator and destroyer of the worlds).*

All things arise from space (and thus from Brahman) and return to it (CU 1.9.1).

[26] *Also because Brahman transforms itself by its own action.*

In the beginning, being (*sat*) made itself the essence (atman) (TU 2.7). This shows that the Atman is both the efficient and material cause. The Atman modifies itself into effects by its own action (*atma-kriti*). It is what is present (*sat*) and what is beyond (*tyat*).

[27] *And because scripture declares Brahman to be the source (*yoni*).*

Being the source denotes a material cause.

Objection: In the ordinary world, only the actions of the efficient cause the actor involves reflection, not the material cause.

Response: Matters of the creation of the world cannot be handled by inferences from worldly events and worldly experiences but only by scripture, and scripture teaches that the conscious Lord is both the efficient and material cause.

[28] *Thereby, all doctrines of the cause of the world are explained.*

Only the Samkhya doctrine of matter has so far been refuted. The same arguments can be extended to lesser arguments on the analogy of defeating the principal wrestler (and so you do not have to wrestle with the others).

Book 2: Refutations and Defenses
Chapter 1

Introduction: The first book showed that the all-knowing Lord is the (efficient and material) cause of the origin of the world, that he is the cause of the sustaining of the world, just as a magician creates a magical illusion, and that he is the cause of this emitted world being reabsorbed into his being (*sat*), just as creatures are reabsorbed into the earth. In addition, the meaning of the Vedantic texts shows that the Lord is the essence (atman) of all beings, and the Samkhya doctrine of matter as the cause of the world is refuted. The purpose of this book is to refute objections that are purportedly based on the traditional texts and reasoning (*tarka*) and to show that those texts do not support the Samkhya doctrine of matter and that the Vedantic texts do not contradict each other on the mode of creation and related issues.

[1] Objection: *If Brahman is the cause of the world, then some doctrines from traditional texts are left without any scope.* Response: *If we reject Brahman as the cause of the world, other traditional texts would have no scope.*

Objection: Some traditional texts declare matter to be the cause of the world. Because these texts were composed by seers they aid in our understanding of scripture, and to reject them leaves them without a purpose.

Response: But other traditional texts teach that the Lord is the efficient and material cause of the world, and to reject them would leave the texts without a purpose. And we have shown that scripture teaches this doctrine, and so the traditional texts that follow scripture must be accepted as authoritative, and the texts that conflict with that must be set aside.

Nor can we assume that some people can perceive matters beyond the world without scripture since there is no cause for such perceptions. Such powers depend upon the performance of religious duty (*dharma*), and that depends on the Vedic injunctions, not traditional doctrines established later. So too, since the various seers contradict each other, only scripture can be the means of a final resolution. Without that authority, we would be left with multiple conflicting opinions, and truth itself would be unstable. The Vedas' authoritativeness in these matters is independent of other means of knowledge and direct, just as the sun is the direct means of our knowledge of the form and color of objects, unlike human doctrines that are not dependent on the Vedas, and is transmitted by a chain of teachers and tradition.

[2] *Also the Samkhya doctrine of matter is not seen in scripture.*

As discussed, the Vedas and common experience do not endorse the Samkhya doctrine, and so any traditional texts that do must be set aside. If texts on Samkhya's evolutes of matter are not authoritative, then they are not authoritative on their source (*pradana*).

[3] *By this reasoning, the doctrines of the Yoga school are also refuted.*

Objection: The Vedas enjoin the practice of yoga as a means of attaining knowledge of Brahman (BU 2.4.5) and give information on the practices (SU 2.8; KaU 6.11, 6.18). Thus, the traditional text that expound the practices — the Yoga Sutra — must be accepted as authoritative. But the Yoga system assumes matter is the cause of the world, and if the same reasoning applied in the last aphorism applies here, then the Yoga system is entirely rejected and is of no purpose.

Response: Some traditional texts are authoritative, and this includes part of the yoga literature on means to full illumination, but some also disagrees with the Vedanta doctrines expounded above. Samkhya and Yoga are singled out because they are widely accepted as means for achieving the highest goal of humanity and are accepted by many competent people. Shvetashvatara Upanishad 6.13 seems to support Samkhya: "That cause is attainable by the application of analysis (i.e., the Samkhya approach). By knowing God, one is released from all fetters." But we reject that the highest goal is achieved by knowledge of the Samkhya system or by yogic practice without reference to the Vedas since scripture declares that there is no other means of attaining the highest aim but the knowledge of the oneness of the Atman conveyed in the Vedas (SU 3.8). The Samkhya and Yoga systems, however, maintain a duality of consciousness and matter, not the oneness of the Atman. We only accept the parts of these systems that comport with the Vedas, such as Samkhya on consciousness being pure and Yoga on the rules for wandering renouncers. We do not object if Samkhya aids by means of arguments in the cognition of truth, but that truth can be known from Vedantic texts alone.

This position applies to all traditional texts based on reasoning (and not the Vedas, e.g., the Nyaya-Vaisheshikas). Reasoning and inferences may be helpful, but knowledge of reality comes from the Vedas alone.

[4] Objection: *Brahman is not the material cause of the world because the world is of a dissimilar nature from Brahman's. That is known from scripture.*

Response: There is no room for objections based on reasoning once the meaning of scripture has been established. Scripture is certainly to be considered authoritative on matters of Brahman as well as on religious duty.

Objection: Unlike religious duty, Brahman is an existing reality, and so there is room for other means of correct knowledge besides the Vedas, as with the case of knowing the earth and elements. If scripture conflicts with what is established by other means of correct knowledge, it must conform with the latter. Reasoning also permits inferring something not actually perceived to the extent that that thing would have the same properties as what is actually seen. This stands nearer to perception than to scripture. And the knowledge of Brahman that ends root-ignorance and achieves final liberation culminates in a direct perception (*sakshatkara*, "established by experience") of Brahman. In addition, the scripture enjoins hearing and reflecting on the doctrine, and so reasoning is to be utilized with regard to Brahman. And reason tells us that the world cannot be caused by a conscious and pure Brahman because the world's differs in character from such a reality.

Response: Cause and effect need not be of the same character: a nonconscious element can be subordinate to a conscious master. The Samkhyas' transcendent soul (*purusha*) is not active and so cannot be the creator, nor is matter (*pradana*) conscious.

Objection: If the effect must resemble its cause, the world would have to be conscious if a conscious Brahman were the cause.

Non-Advaitin Response: There is a difference between the manifested and the unmanifested. Just as the consciousness of a sleeper is not manifested in deep sleep, so too the consciousness of wood and earth is not manifested.

Objection: Nevertheless, one reality is pure and another impure. Nor do perception and inference support the claim of the consciousness of everything. Nor does scripture support you since it teaches that the world is partly nonconscious and partly conscious (e.g., TU 2.6).

Non-Advaitin Response: But scripture attributes consciousness to the elements like fire and water (CU 6.2.3-4) and sense-organs (BU 1.3.2).

[5] Objection: *But the dissimilarity is only between the world and the presiding gods based on the special characteristics of the conscious gods and of them entering nonconscious matter.*

In such passages, consciousness is attributed to the presiding god, not to matter itself.

[6] Vedanta's Response: *Things with contrary natures are observed in the world.*

For example, it is a matter of common experience that persons have conscious and nonconscious parts and that scorpions grow in cow dung. The nonconscious body may arise from nonconscious matter, but it is the support of consciousness. If the cause and effect had all the same properties, the difference between cause and effect would be destroyed. So too, Brahman as the cause and all of the world as the effect share one property: being (*satta*). The opponent cannot point to a nonconscious reality that has Brahman as its cause as the source. And again, we assert that the conscious Brahman is the ontic cause of what is nonconscious. And again, the purpose of scripture is to show that Brahman is the cause and substance of the world.

Nor is Brahman subject to other means of correct knowledge since it is devoid of form and thus not a possible object of perception. It is also free of characteristic marks (*lingas*), and so reasoning cannot infer any conclusions. Like religious duty, it is known only from scripture (e.g., KaU 2.9). Even gods with extraordinary power and wisdom cannot know the origin of the world since they arose only after creation (RV 10.129.6). The traditional texts concur (e.g., BG 10.2). Reasoning is not taken to be independent means of knowledge but as a subordinate aid to experiential knowledge. Also see 2.1.11 below.

Since the states of sleep and awaking, the Atman is not identical to any of them. But since the individual atman disassociates itself from the world in deep sleep and become one with the atman that is reality (*sat*), it must be the same as the transcendent Atman. Since creation arose from Brahman and the principle is that the effect is not (materially) different from its cause, creation is not different from Brahman. In addition, if it is accepted that creation has both conscious and nonconscious parts (TU 2.6), then if a conscious source cannot have nonconscious effects, then so too nonconscious matter of Samkhya cannot have conscious effects.

[7] Objection: *Effects do not exist in their causes* (asat) *before their creation.* Response: *This is a denial only with no object to negate.*

Objection: If the cause (Brahman) is conscious, pure, and devoid of all phenomenal properties such as sound, then the effect (the nonconscious, impure, and phenomenally characterized world) was nonexistent prior to the world's creation. But you claim the effect already exists within the cause.

Response: You negated the effect prior to its origin, and thus there was then no existing object to negate. On the other hand, if the effect does exist within its cause (Brahman), its existence is the same as after its origin as an effect. Even though sound is caused by Brahman (which is silent), the effect with all its properties cannot exist without Brahman as its cause either before or after its origin as an effect, and so it cannot be said that the effect is nonexistent before its origin. Their nondifference is discussed below (2.1.14).

[8] Objection: *In the dissolution of the world at the end of a world-cycle, the cause becomes like the effect. Thus, the doctrine that Brahman is the cause of the world is unacceptable.*

At the end of a world-cycle, the world, along with all its properties and impurities, will infest Brahman when it is reabsorbed. Thus, Brahman at the time of the reabsorption becomes impure and has phenomenal properties. Second, in the reabsorption, all distinctions are ended, and so there would be no specific causes at the re-emergence, and so the new world could not arise with distinct beings, objects of enjoyment, and so forth that we observe. Third, so too those who attained final liberation would in fact be reborn in the next world-cycle. Fourth, if the world were to remain distinct in the reabsorption, then it is not an absorption at all, and there would be an effect existing separate from its alleged cause.

[9] Response: *There are instances (in the world) of such reabsorption without the retention of the properties of the effect in the cause.*

For example, a clay pot can be reabsorbed into a pile of clay without retaining the contaminating properties of a pot — properties of the effects do not affect their cause. You can cite no instances supporting your position — in fact, reabsorption would be impossible if the properties of the effect were retained. Because of the nondifference of cause and effect, the effect has the Atman as its ontic cause and is never separate from its cause.

The same applies within this world, where scripture declares the identity of cause and effect (i.e., Brahman and the world) (e.g., BU 2.4.6; CU 7.25.2, 3.14.1). The cause is not affected by the effects and their properties since the latter are merely the false superimpositions of root-ignorance. Just as a magician is never affected by the magical illusions that he produces because they are unreal, so too the highest Atman is unaffected by the illusion of the world. Just as a dreamer is not affected by his dreams in the waking state or deep sleep, so the permanent witness (the highest Atman) is not affected by the waking, dreaming, and dreamless states of consciousness. That the highest Atman appears in those states is an illusion that is no more substantial than the snake for which the rope is mistaken at twilight. "The individual person is asleep due to the influence of the beginningless illusion of the observable world. When it is awakens, it realizes (in the fourth state) the unborn, sleepless, and dreamless nonduality of the Atman" (GK 1.16).

So too with your second argument about the loss of distinctions in the re-absorption: parallel cases are dreamless sleep and the state of total meditative concentration (*samadhi*). There the Atman enters the state of non-distinction, but the prior state is reestablished because root-ignorance has not yet ended. So too with merging in the real (*sat*) in CU 6.9.2-3: the power of the distinctions based on root-ignorance remains (and so individual persons re-emerge later). Thus, we can infer that in the cosmic reabsorption at the end of a world-cycle, differentiations illusory root-ignorance persists. But third, the enlightened are not reborn because false knowledge has been ended by perfect knowledge. Your fourth argument does not apply since Vedantins reject the claim the world is distinct from (or in) Brahman.

[10] And also because the defects that you assert apply to our doctrines also to your own Samkhya doctrines.

Your doctrine of matter assumes the same: the cause and effect are nondifferent. The cause of the world (matter) at the beginning is devoid of sound and other such properties, but out of it evolves a world with those properties; and at the reabsorption, all specific distinctions are obliterated and pass into a state of non-distinction. If some persons pass into a state of non-distinction and the liberated do not, this could not be the result of (nonconscious) matter. Thus, all the alleged problems you raise apply equally to both your position and ours and so cannot be used against only one.

[11] Objection: *Reasoning is inconclusive, but doctrines can be inferred in a different way that avoids the defects.* Response: *There is no avoiding the defects through reasoning.*

In matters settled by scripture, mere reasoning is not be relied upon. Since thought is uncontrolled, reasoning not based on scripture but resting only on human opinions has no firm foundation. Even arguments made by intelligent people through much effort are shown by even more ingenious people to be fallacious, and the later arguments are in turn refuted by other people. Because of this diversity of opinions, it is impossible to accept reasoning alone as having a firm foundation. Even the reasoning of the most intellectually eminent persons is contradicted by others equally eminent.

Objection: You cannot maintain that no reasoning is ever well-founded since your assertion that reasoning is unfounded is itself based only on reasoning — if reasoning is without foundation, then so is your assertion. In addition, if reasoning is unfounded, then the whole course of everyday affairs would be impossible since people make predictions based on the uniformity of past, present, and future. Moreover, because passages in scripture contradict each other, reasoning is required to ascertain the true meaning of some passages. Also the value of reasoning is actually demonstrated by the later arguments refuting earlier objectionable ones — there is no legitimate reason to maintain that a man must be stupid simply because his elder brother was.

Response: Reasoning is well-founded for worldly matters, but not for matters of liberation. Liberation depends upon knowing the true nature of the cause of the world, and because of its obscurity, that cause cannot be conceived without the aid of scripture. Again, the cause is not an object of perception and is devoid of form and phenomenal properties, and so it is not open to inference or any other means of correct knowledge. Knowledge based on reasoning and whose object is not uniform and permanent and so cannot be the perfect knowledge needed for liberation. Nor are those who accept matter as the cause the best reasoners and accepted by all. Nor can you gather together all past, present, and future logicians to reach a consensus on what is perfect knowledge. On the other hand, the Vedas are eternal and the source of true knowledge and thus the perfection of that knowledge cannot be denied, and there is no perfect knowledge apart from them. Thus, the liberation from rebirth is possible only through the Vedas.

In sum, based on scripture and the reasoning that conforms to it, conscious Brahman is the cause and substance of the world.

[12] By this, the doctrines of the other schools that praiseworthy sages do not accept are also explained.

Doctrines based only on reasoning and not the Vedas — such as the Samkhya's doctrine of matter and the Vaisheshika's atomism — are thereby refuted. Unfettered reasoning is powerless to fathom the depth of the cause of the world that transcends the world.

[13] Objection: *When the objects to be enjoyed merges into the enjoyer (in the experience of Brahman), there is no distinction between the two.* Response: *But the distinction is well seen in common experience.*

Objection: While scripture is authoritative concerning its special subject-matters, it cannot refute what is settled by other means of correct knowledge. The distinction between enjoyers and the objects of their enjoyment is well-established from ordinary experience. But the distinction would not exist if the two were the same, as you claim in the case of Brahman. Thus, you must abandon your doctrine as the material cause of the world.

Response: The nondifference of substance does not mean the lack of distinctions between a cause and an effect. In ordinary experiences, we see waves, foam, bubbles, and other modification of the ocean. Here, the enjoyers and the objects to be enjoyed do not pass over into each other, but they are both not different from the highest Brahman. The enjoyer is not actually a transformation of Brahman, but the creator, although not undergoing any change, is called the "enjoyer" in that he enters into the "effect" (i.e., the body) (TU 2.6). The state of distinction is the result of limiting adjuncts, just as space is divided up by contact with jars and other limiting adjuncts. Thus, the distinction is possible even though both the enjoyer and objects are not different from Brahman, on the analogy of the ocean and its waves and so on.

[14] The nondifference of Brahman and the world as cause and effect is shown by scriptural texts on origin and so forth.

The refutation in the previous aphorism was based on distinctions in ordinary experience, but in reality those distinctions do not exist: the world as "effect" is not different from the highest Brahman that is the "cause." The word "origin" is used to indicate modification and how if one knows the substance one knows all things — e.g., if one knows clay, one knows all pots made of clay (CU 6.1.4). The modifications are names only arising from speech — only the clay is real. Here, "origin" refers only to those modifications, and thus "origin" also arises only from speech — in reality, nothing exists except Brahman (CU 6.8.7, 7.25.2; BU 2.4.6; MunU 2.2.11) and so there is no diversity (BU 4.4.25). Otherwise, it would not be possible that by the knowledge of one thing everything becomes known, as scripture declares. The parts of space limited by a jar are not different from all-pervading space. The water in a mirage is not different from the surface of the desert — the water is seen in one moment and vanishes in the next and does not appear in its own nature. In the same way, this world of multiple objects of enjoyment and enjoyers has no existence apart from Brahman.

Objection: Brahman has within itself elements of diversity, just as a tree is one in itself but has branches, and the ocean is one but has foam and waves, and clay is one but is multiple with regard to pots and plates. Here, the liberation of the enlightened is possible even though Brahman is one: knowledge of the oneness of Brahman leads to liberation, while both ordinary worldly activity and religious duty relate to the diversity within Brahman.

Response: In the passage, only knowledge of clay is declared to be true, while all effects are declared to be unreal and have their origin only in speech. The passage teaches that the fact that the embodied person has its atman in Brahman is self-established (*siddham svato*). This does away with the idea that the individual atman has independent existence, just as the rope does away with the idea of the snake. For one who sees that everything has its atman in Brahman, the entire phenomenal world of actions, actors, and results of actions is nonexistent (BU 2.4.13). The passage "You are that" shows that Brahman being the atman of everything is not limited to any one state. Nor is negation of attributes confined to one state.

Oneness is the one true existence, while multiplicity developed out of wrong knowledge (CU 6.16). If the doctrine of "difference and non-difference" were true, why should a person be condemned as accepting nonreality when they are caught up in the phenomenal existence (BU 4.4.19)? It would also mean that wrong knowledge is not the cause of rebirth. And how could correct knowledge remove the cognition of multiplicity if both types of knowledge were true?

Objection: If so, the ordinary means of correct knowledge (i.e., perception, inference, and so forth) become invalid in the absence of multiplicity because they would have no objects to operate on. So too, scriptural injunctions and prohibitions would be without any purpose. The entire corpus of treatises concerning final liberation (the *moksha-shastras*) would collapse if the distinction between teacher and student is not real (i.e., there is nothing to teach). And if the doctrine of liberation is untrue, how can we maintain the truth of the oneness of the Atman that is part of that doctrine?

Response: The entire complex of the phenomenal world is considered real as along as the knowledge of Brahman being the atman of all has not arisen, just as phantoms in a dream are considered real until the dreamer awakens. Because of root-ignorance, the unenlightened are unaware that Brahman is the atman of everything. They see effects such the body, children, and wealth, as forming part of the Atman or belonging to the Atman. Thus, as long as correct knowledge does not present itself, there is no reason why the ordinary course of worldly and religious affairs should not continue unaffected, just as the activity of a dreaming person does during the dream.

Objection: But scripture too is only part of the unreal "dream." So how can untrue Vedantic texts convey information about the true being of Brahman? We do not see anyone die from being bitten by a rope misconstrued to be a snake or water in a mirage used for drinking or bathing.

Response: Sometimes unreal causes do produce real effects, such as dying (from shock) when someone dreams that they were bitten by a snake.

Objection: But you say those effects are unreal.

Response: The effects are indeed unreal, but not the *consciousness* in which a dreamer has them. The consciousness itself is not obliterated by waking consciousness — upon awaking, we know the content of the dream to be unreal, but we do not consider the consciousness in the dream to be unreal. Scripture confirms this. So too, the body in the phenomenal world is likewise unreal but not the waking consciousness that we have. Injunctions to know Brahman are not defective since the state of consciousness produced by them has for its object the oneness of the all-pervading Atman and there is nothing else to desire. Such consciousness is not useless since its result is the cessation of root-ignorance. Nor is it defective since there is no other type of knowledge that could obliterate it. Before realizing it, the entire real-unreal course of ordinary life continues. Once the phenomenal world based on distinctions is uprooted, there is no longer any occasion for assuming Brahman comprises various elements in itself.

Objection: If Brahman is analogous to clay, then it can undergo modifications (or transformations), just as clay can.

Response: Scripture denies that Brahman undergoes any modifications but is absolutely changeless (*kutasha*) (e.g., BU 4.4.25). And the property of absolute changelessness means that Brahman cannot be both subject to change and not subject to change. And, as discussed, because all properties are denied (BU 3.9.26), Brahman is eternal and changeless. Nor does Brahman undergo a modification when one cognizes its oneness. Nor is any new result created. Thus, when scripture speaks of a new result — e.g., Brahman being modified into the form of this world — is it merely for the purpose of cognition, but nothing independent is created. To maintain that the result of knowing Brahman is that Brahman undergoes a modification would be that the atman of the knower would undergo modification, but the state of liberation is eternal and unchanging.

Objection: If the nature of Brahman is changeless, how can Brahman be described as the Lord and cause of the world, since the doctrine of absolute oneness leaves no room for a distinction of ruler and something ruled? How can you speak of creation while maintaining the absolute oneness and nonduality of the Atman?

Response: The Lord's properties are only name-and-form arising from root-ignorance. Following scripture, we agree that the creation, sustaining, and reabsorption of the world proceed from an all-knowing and all-powerful ruler, not matter or anything else. Name-and-form is nondifferent from the atman of the all-knowing Lord, so to speak — but it is only a figment imagined through root-ignorance. Name-and-form cannot be discerned (*anupakhya*) as either being (*tattva*) nor something distinct from being. Name-and-form is the seeds of rebirth and of the entire expanse of the phenomenal world (*prapancha*) that in scripture and the traditional texts is called the Lord's power (*shakti*) of illusion (*maya*) or nature (*prakriti*). The Lord himself is different from the created name-and-form (CU 8.14.1). Thus, the being (called) the Lord conforms to the limiting adjuncts made from name-and-form, which are products of root-ignorance, just as omnipresent space conforms to the limiting adjuncts of jars and so forth. The Lord stands in the phenomenal realm as the ruler of the so-called individual beings (*jivas*) and atmans of understanding (*vijnana-atmans*) that in fact are one with his own atman. Thus, being a lord and being omniscient and omnipotent all depend on the limiting adjuncts whose essence (atman) is root-ignorance — in reality, none of these properties belong to the Atman. The Atman's true nature is seen by correct knowledge to be free of all adjuncts (CU 8.24.1, BU 2.4.13). Scripture declares that for one who attained truth and reality, the whole phenomenal world does not exist. The *Bhagavad-gita* (5.14-15) also declares that in reality the relation of ruler and ruled does not exist. However, all such distinctions are valid within the phenomenal world (BU 4.4.22, BG 18.61). The nondifference of cause and effect applies only to the true state of reality — when one looks at the phenomenal world from the dualistic point of view, Brahman is like the ocean (with its surface foam and waves). In addition, the view that Brahman undergoes modification is of use in meditations on the qualified Brahman (*saguna-brahman*) (but it does not really occur — it only seems so from the unenlightened dualistic point of view).

[15] *Also because the material cause is seen when the effect is present.*

The effect is not different from the cause since only when a cause exists is an effect seen, as with clay and a jar. Nondifference does not exist between two unrelated things (e.g., a horse and cow, or a clay pot and jar).

Objection: There are differences even when one thing depends upon another — smoke is not identical to fire but is seen only when there is fire.

Response: The reason for accepting the nondifference of a material cause and effect is that the idea of an "effect" is impressed on the intellect (*buddhi*) only when the ideas of a "cause" and "effect" are together, and this does not occur with fire and smoke since smoke may persist after a fire is extinguished. The nondifference of cause and effect is based on both scripture and perception. For example, the nondifference of threads and cloth is perceived in the aggregate of threads — "cloth" is not something in addition to the threads. The infinitesimal parts are identical with the observable parts, and thus we conclude that ultimately the most minute parts are identical with their cause. So too, with air and space being not different from Brahman.

[16] *And because a later effect has its existence due to the existence of an earlier cause.*

Scripture declares that effects have their being (*sat*) in their cause prior to their arising by means of the atman of the cause. Something that does not exist within the cause is not produced from it — oil is not produced from sand. Thus, there is a nondifference prior to the production of the effect, and so the nondifference continues after the production. This applies to the world and its cause (Brahman) — since Brahman, which is neither more or less than all that is, is one, any effect must be nondifferent from this cause. Since Brahman never deviates from existence (*sattva*) in the past, present, and future, so to its effect (the universe) from existence in the three periods. And since reality (*sat*) is singular, so the universe is nondifferent from Brahman.

[17] Objection: *The Upanishads sometimes declare that the effect is nonexistent in the cause since we do not see the effect prior to its production.* Response: *In complementary parts of the passages the word "nonexistent" is used to designate a difference in characteristics.*

Objection: The Upanishads sometimes states that in the beginning the world did not exist (*asat*) prior to its production (CU 3.19.1, TU 2.7).

Response: These passages do not mean literal nonexistence but only that prior to their production the undeveloped effects do not have the properties of name-and-form. Prior to their production, effects were still identical to the cause (Brahman). Later parts of the passages determine the meaning of earlier parts. "Nonexistent" is used figuratively to denote the prior state of what is called "existent" once things are distinguished by name-and-form.

[18] *The pre-existence of an effect in a cause and hence nondifference is established by reasoning and by other scriptural passages.*

That effects exist prior to their origination and are not different than their (material) causes is supported by reason as well as scripture. Butter cannot be produced from clay, and clay pots cannot be produced from milk.

Objection: But the effect does not exist in the material cause since, for example, we do not see butter in milk. Rather, each causal substance has the capacity (*shakti*, "power") to go beyond itself (*atishaya*) for a specific effect — e.g., milk has the capacity only for butter and so forth.

Response: If this power to go beyond itself means the antecedent condition of the effect (before its emergence) is in the cause, you abandon your doctrine. But if the power is causal determination, it can determine the effect only if it is neither other than (the cause) nor nonexistent — if it were either, it would not be different from anything else that is other than the cause and effect or nonexistent. (How then could a cause produce its specific effect, such milk from a cow and not from oil?) Thus, the power is identical to the atman of its cause. In addition, the ideas of "cause" and "effect" are not separate, nor are ideas of "substance" and "property." Thus, the identity of cause and effect and of substance and property must be admitted.

Objection: Cause and effect are different but have an inherent connection (*samavaya*).

Response: Then this inherent connection must itself be connected by something to the cause and effect, which leads to an infinite regress of connections. Or this connection is not connected to the cause and effect it binds together, which leads to the dissolution of the cause/effect relation.

Objection: Inherence is connected to the cause and effect that it joins without the need for any further connections.

Response: Then contact (*samyoga*) also must be connected to that cause and that effect without the aid of the inherent connection since contact is a type of connection. So too, substances, properties, and so on are apprehended as an identity (*tadatmya*), and so the notion of an inherent connection has no purpose. How does inherence abide in the material parts? Does it abide in all the parts collectively or in each separate part? If the former, we could never see the whole since it is impossible for all the parts to be in contact with our organ of perception. Nor can a whole be apprehended by seeing only some of the parts. But if the whole abides in each separate part, a new type of part must be invoked to make the adherence of the whole in each part, leading to an infinite regress. So too, the whole cannot abide in each part since if it is present in one part it cannot be present in the other parts. Or if the whole is present in each part, it must be a different whole in each one. Nor is the whole seen in a part in the way that a universal is seen in instantiation — e.g., cowness seen in each cow. And if the whole were present in each part, each part would produce the effect of the entire whole — e.g., a cow would give milk from its horns.

Every origination requires an agent and a reality in which that action occurs. If the effect does not exist in the cause, the arising of the effect occurs without such a reality and thus is without any being.

Objection: Creation means merely the inherent connection of the effect with its cause and the attainment of the effect of its existence (*satta*) (and of its own atman).

Response: How can something that has not yet come into existence enter into a connection with anything else? Connection with something nonexistent is impossible. A nonexisting effect is like the son of a barren woman — it cannot be referred as existing in any sense.

Objection: If the effect exists in the cause, then activity to produce it would be purposeless. The effect would lie there fully accomplished — no one tries to bring about what already exists.

Response: Work is needed to arrange the cause's substance into the form of the effect (e.g., milk becoming butter). That form already exists in the atman of the material cause. The substance of the cause does not become another substance merely by changing the form. Even when the cause is no longer seen — as with a seed becoming a tree — this only means that the cause becomes seen in another form. The death of a cause and birth of an effect do not involve separate beings any more than a fetus and a new born baby are different beings. An old person is not different from a child, nor a father from the man before becoming a father. This refutes the Buddhist doctrine of momentariness (also see 2.2.20).

So too, if the effect does not already exist in the material cause, the activity of the causal agent would have no object to produce since what does not exist cannot be an object to work upon. A potter can make the pot "arise" only if the pot already existed in the clay.

Milk is simply called "butter" when the milk is in that state. And the fundamental cause of everything appears in the form of this or that effect up to the last effect of all, just as an actor appears in this or that costume. Thereby, the fundamental cause becomes the basis for all current ideas and names concerning the phenomenal world. This establishes by reasoning the scriptural doctrine that the effect already exists before its origin as an "effect" and is not different (in substance) from its (material) cause (e.g., CU 6.2.1). If an effect did not exist before its emergence as an effect and afterwards did not inhere in its cause by the inherent connection discussed above, it would be something different from the cause, and that conflicts with scripture.

[19] Also from the analogy of the piece of cloth and what it is made from.

A folded cloth is the same as the cloth when it is not folded. So too, the effect (a piece of cloth) is not manifested in its parts (the threads) and becomes observable only through the activity of the weaver and loom.

[20] And as with the different breaths.

So too with outgoing breaths even when controlled in yogic exercises: all the breaths exist in the same principal life-breath and are not different from it but appear in different forms as effects.

[21] Objection: If the individual person is not different from Brahman, then faults arise in Brahman from the individual not doing what is beneficial.

Faults (doshas) from an embodied atman's acts would attach to Brahman. And the creative power of Brahman inheres to the embodied atman, and so we would expect the Atman to do only what is beneficial and not undergo birth, disease, old age, death, and the rest of the net of suffering. A pure being would not look upon this thoroughly unclean body as forming part of its atman and would free itself form it. And the embodied atman would remember creating this world. Just as a magician can retract a magical illusion whenever he wants and without any effort, the embodied atman can reabsorb into itself at will whatever it creates. But the embodied atman cannot even abolish its body. Since what is beneficial is not being done, the world could not proceed from a conscious cause (i.e., a lord).

[22] Response: *Because of the declarations in scripture of the difference between the individual person and Brahman, Brahman is greater than the individual person.*

Brahman whose essence (atman) is eternal, pure knowledge, and freedom is different from the embodied atman and is the creative principle of the world. Faults of the embodied atman do not inhere in Brahman — as eternal freedom is its characteristic nature, there is nothing beneficial for it to do or harmful for it to avoid. Nor is there any impediment to his omniscience and omnipotence. But the embodied atman has a different nature, and faults do adhere to it. Nor is that embodied atman the creator because scripture declares that Brahman to be different (in nature) based on the relation of actor and object (e.g., BU 2.4.5, 4.3.45; CU 8.7.1, 6.8.1).

Objection: But there are passages such as "You are that" that declare the embodied atman and Brahman to be not different, and difference and nondifference cannot exist together because they are contradictory.

Response: It is like the co-existence of space existing as the all-pervading space and as the limited space within a jar. And once the consciousness of nondifferences arises within us, the transmigrating state of the individual and the creative property of (qualified) Brahman both vanish, as does the entire phenomenon of plurality arising from wrong knowledge. How could there be any creation or any faults of not doing what is beneficial? The entire apparent world in which good and evil deeds are performed is an error (*bhranti*) based on not discriminating "You are that." The illusion is based on not discriminating limiting adjuncts (the body, the individual psyche, and so forth) from what is real (Brahman). Limiting adjuncts are made from name-and-form that are only the presentations of root-ignorance, and in reality they do not exist in any way. Thus, we confuse the body that is hurt and dies with the true Atman. But until one realizes the nondifference of Brahman and the individual (*jiva-atman*), the scriptural passages that declare the difference between Brahman and the embodied atman are superior for avoiding faults.

[23] So too, your position is unjustified because the difference is the same as with a stone which does not share the same nature with the earth it come from, and so forth.

Minerals are merely modifications of earth, but we observe a great variety of them varying in value. So too for the fruit of different seeds planted in the same ground. Likewise, the one Brahman also contains in itself various individual atmans (*jiva-atmans*) and atmans of understanding (*vijnana-*

atmans), and these produce different effects. But scripture also declares that all effects have their origin only in speech and are like dream phantoms (while the dreamer remains one and unaffected).

[24] Objection: *Brahman cannot be the cause because we notice that we need instruments to make effects and Brahman has none.* Response: *It is like milk turning itself sour while the substance remains the same.*

Objection: Brahman alone cannot be a cause because tools and materials are needed to create. How can Brahman be the cause of the world without these?

Response: Some things have causation as a capacity within them — e.g., milk can turn sour and water can transform into ice without any tools. So too with Brahman.

Objection: Milk requires heat to turn sour.

Response: Milk itself undergoes the change — heat merely accelerates the process. If milk did not already have that capacity for change, heat would not help since heat cannot turn air or space into sour milk. But Brahman does not require any such supplemental aid (SU 6.8). Despite being one reality, it can transform itself into a multiplicity of effects by its own innate powers.

[25] *Also Brahman creates without instruments like the gods and others creating in this world.*

Objection: Conscious agents, unlike nonconscious things, require tools.

Response: Gods, seers, and other conscious beings of great power do not require tools to create. So too, spiders emit webs without instruments.

Objection: Gods create from their bodies and not their consciousness. Spiders must eat small insects to make the material for their webs. But you say Brahman creates from consciousness, not from something material.

Response: We meant merely to show that not all creating is like a potter making a jar. Conscious beings, like Brahman, cannot be assumed to require extraneous means.

[26] Objection: *Brahman as the cause of the world would involve either the possibility of the transformation of the whole of Brahman or the violation of scriptural texts about Brahman being partless.*

Vedanta: It is established that Brahman — conscious, one, and without a second reality — which undergoes transformation without the aid of another is the cause of the world.

Objection: Either Brahman must have parts to enable it to create or else it transforms itself. But scripture clearly states that Brahman is without parts or any distinctions (e.g., SU 6.19, MunU 2.1.2; BU 2.4.12, 3.9.26, 3.9.26, 3.8.8).

Thus, it must transform itself. But if it transforms, this cuts Brahman from its basis (and so the transformed Brahman is no longer the creator and no longer has any of Brahman's powers). It also renders purposeless the injunctions to strive to see Brahman since the effects can be readily seen already and apart from them Brahman does not exist. But if Brahman has parts, it also would be noneternal, and then the scriptural passage that say that Brahman is unborn (and unchangeable) would be contradicted.

[27] Response: *But Brahman as the cause of the world has to be accepted on scriptural authority since Brahman is known from scripture alone.*

Scripture speaks of the creation of the world from Brahman but also of Brahman apart from any changes and that it exists apart from its effects (e.g., CU 3.12.6). Brahman dwells in the heart, but if it passed into its effects the limitations of the individual person would prevent it from uniting to the whole of Brahman, which scripture also declares. Also, scripture denies that Brahman can be an object of perception, while its effects clearly are. Thus, Brahman must be accepted as an unmodified reality. So too, Brahman is without parts since scripture states so. Reasoning cannot find all their powers, conditions, and so forth even for phenomenal objects — how much more impossible is it to conceive the true nature of Brahman with its unfathomable powers by reason alone without the aid of scripture!

Objection: Even scripture cannot make us understand what is contradictory. You claim Brahman undergoes changes but not the entire Brahman — if Brahman is without parts, then it either does not change at all or changes in its entirety. But if it either changed partly or did not change partly, there would be separate natures and thus separate parts.

Response: The (alleged) break in Brahman's nature is only a figment of root-ignorance and not any more real than the moon is really duplicated by appearing double to a person with defective vision. Plurality, with the properties of names and forms, is a fiction of root-ignorance. The distinctions characterized by names and forms are only imagined through root-ignorance. Both the undeveloped and developed distinctions cannot be defined as either the same as Brahman or as different from it. By that plurality, Brahman appears to be the basis of this whole apparent world of changes through modification by reason of these distinctions, but its real nature always remains unmodified and beyond all change. (Brahman does not really transform in whole or in part in any way — "creation" and change are completely illusory.) The fiction of names and forms arises entirely from speech alone, and thus it does not counter Brahman being without parts.

Scriptural passages that speak of Brahman as undergoing change are not meant literally. Their purpose is to teach that Brahman's atman is raised above the apparent world. The fruit of the instruction is attaining the fearless.

[28] And thus it is also in the case of the individual person in dreams and of the gods that various creations occur in one substance.

Scripture teaches that there is the creation of different things in Brahman without this changing its nature. But scripture also teaches that multiple (nonexistent) creations exist in the atman of a dreaming person (e.g., BU 4.3.10) without destroying the person's nature. In the phenomenal world multiple creations seem to exist in the gods without interfering with the unity of their being. So too, with magicians and the illusory creations that they cast.

[29] Also your position is subject to these same faults.

In the Samkhya doctrine of matter, matter is not made up of parts but has different qualities (*gunas*). Either matter in its entirety undergoes change, or you must accept that it has parts.

Objection: Matter does have three parts — the qualities of goodness, passion, and darkness.

Response: Even so, the qualities are themselves without parts, and each quality works with only the other two qualities. And if they consist of parts, then matter is not eternal (or unchanging but created by combining parts). And if you say that matter produces effects through its own power, well, we say the same of Brahman. Thus, your position is open to the same charges you bring against ours.

The same objections apply to the Vaisheshika doctrine that the world arose from (indivisible) atoms (*paramanus*). If atoms do not have parts, then one atom combines with another *in toto* and nothing is added to the bulk, and we never get beyond the first atom. If atoms do have parts, then they are not (unbreakable and partless) "atoms" at all.

Thus, the objection applies to all the positions and cannot be used against merely one.

[30] And because Brahman is endowed with all powers, as is revealed in scripture (e.g., CU 3.14.4, 8.7.1; MunU 1.1.9; BU 3.8.9).

[31] Objection: *Brahman cannot act because it lacks organs.* Response: *This was explained earlier (2.1.25) concerning the alleged need for instruments.*

The highest Brahman can be fathomed only by scripture, not reason. Nor need we assume that Brahman's capacities must be like those of things that we observe. And any requirement of plurality is a figment of root-ignorance. And scripture declares that although Brahman is without bodily organs, it possesses all possible abilities (SU 3.19).

[32] Objection: *Brahman is not the creator because he has no motive to create.*

The highest Brahman is said to be conscious and so acts for some purpose, and thus Brahman is not self-sufficient. Or it is not conscious and so does not act at all. (Instead, only nonconscious events occur).

[33] Response: *But creation is a mere pastime for Brahman, like our recreation in this world.*

Creation is mere sport (*lila*) for Brahman, proceeding from its very nature without any purpose at all. No further purpose based on reasoning or scripture can be found. Creation seems profound and difficult to us, but to the Lord, with his unlimited power, it is merely play (accomplishing no further end). He is conscious because scripture states that he is all-knowing.

And it must be remembered that the scriptural doctrine of creation does not refer to the highest reality but only to the apparent world of name-and-form that is imagined through root-ignorance.

[34] *Partiality and cruelty cannot be attributed to the Lord because the Lord takes other factors (i.e., beings' past karmic acts) into consideration (in creating beings). That scripture shows.*

Objection: The Lord cannot be the cause of the world because then he would be open to the charge of prejudice in dispensing happiness and pain. He would be like an ordinary person in that regard. He would have to be considered cruel in his dispensation, not essentially good, as scripture claims.

Response: Scripture declares that the Lord is bound by the law of karmic rewards, including in the creation of the world in each world-cycle. The inequality of the circumstances of beings is due to their own merit and demerit — the Lord is not to blame. The Lord's action is analogous to those of the rain-giver: different plants grow from the common rain but depend on different seeds.

[35] Objection: *Brahman cannot take karmic merit and demerit into consideration before the first creation because the fruits of actions then had no distinctions (to distribute among different actors).* Response: *The world and the cycle of rebirths have no beginning.*

Objection: The Lord is responsible for the first creation and thus is responsible for the first distribute of merit and demerit. Work cannot depend on diversity of conditions and then diversity of conditions depend on work — things initially were free of inequalities.

Response: There was no initial set of conditions: the world of rebirth is without beginning — a beginningless series of seeds and sprouts.

[36] This is also justified by reason and comports with scripture.

If the world had a beginning, it would have sprung into existence without a cause. Liberated persons would also reenter the cycle of rebirths, and rewards and punishments would be allocated without reference to previous good or bad acts. That the Lord is the cause has already been rejected. Root-ignorance could not be the cause since it works uniformly — it could be the cause of inequalities only after actions begin due to differences in one's anger, hatred, and other passions. Without merit and demerit, no one could come to exist, but without a body merit and demerit could not form. Thus, the doctrine of a beginning of the world is unreasonable. But a doctrine of beginninglessness explains all of this like the seed and sprout. Scripture and traditional texts also support this (RV 10.190.3, BG 15.3). How could there be a living person embodied by Atman (*jiva-atman*) (CU 6.3.2) before creation?

[37] Brahman is the cause of the world also because all the properties necessary to create the world are present in Brahman.

The Upanishads show that Brahman is all-knowing, all-powerful, and possessing the great power of illusion (*maya*).

Chapter 2.2

Introduction. This chapter refutes Samkhya and other systems that are obstacles to true knowledge based solely upon reasoning and not scripture. The Samkhyas and others cite the Upanishads and the dull-witted may conclude that those doctrines are means to right knowledge. Thus, it is necessary to show their doctrines to be fallacious.

[1] The primal matter postulated by Samkhyas cannot be the creator of the world because nonconscious matter cannot explain the orderly arrangement of the world, and for other reasons.

Objection: Just as clay jars have as their cause something with that property (i.e., clay), so the world of pleasure, pain, and dullness have a cause consisting of pleasure, pain, and dullness — and those properties constitute the threefold nature of matter (*pradhana*). Nonconscious matter evolves itself spontaneously into multiform modifications according to the purposes of a conscious soul (*purusha*). Its existence can also be inferred from the limitations of all effects (because they are the conjunction of several things).

Response: If it is to be explained only on the strength of analogies, then we say that we never see nonconscious things spontaneously modifying them to serve the purposes of a particular person. Instead, we see that conscious workers are needed. Nor does the orderly arrangement of the world look like it has been shaped by nonconscious matter alone. Nor can we say that all effects are endowed by their very nature with pleasure, pain, and dullness since this does not explain why some effects are internal and some external when only pleasure, pain, and dullness are internal. As to the limitation of effects: if they are products of the three *gunas* (purity, passion, and darkness), then the *gunas* must depend on the conjunctions of prior conditions because they too are limited.

[2] *Also nonconscious matter cannot have a tendency to act.*

No activity is seen in nonconscious matter alone. A conscious cause of the world is needed — without it, the world could not be produced.

Objection: We do not see activity of a purely conscious being alone.

Response: True, but we see activity in nonconscious things only in conjunction with conscious beings.

Objection: We never see the activity of the conscious being even then, and so we must attribute the activity to what is actually seen and its support.

Response: The activity does belong to the nonconscious things, but it only occurs when consciousness is present.

Objection: Consciousness cannot move and so cannot produce an effect.

Response: Something without motion can produce motion, as with a loadstone and iron. So, the all-knowing, all-powerful, and all-pervading Lord who is the atman of all things can move the world, but he himself is unmoving: he can impart a tendency to move even though he is without one himself.

Objection: There is no room for a power to move in the oneness of Brahman, and so it cannot induce in something else a tendency to move.

Response: Again, the Lord is only erroneously connected with motion since the realm of name-and-form (i.e., *maya*) is brought about only by root-ignorance. (In reality, Brahman does not move or change at all.)

[3] *Objection*: *Primal matter can undergo transformations, as milk and water do, without conscious agents.* Response: *But even there conscious agents are involved in the transformations.*

Objection: Milk and water flow by their own nature for our benefit.

Response: Since other nonconscious things do not act without a conscious agent, we can infer a conscious agent here (e.g., BU 3.7.4, 3.8.9).

Objection: Aphorism 2.1.24 above contradicts this aphorism.

Response: That aphorism merely shows that in ordinary experience an effect may occur independently of any external instrumentality — that does not contradict the doctrine that all effects depend upon the Lord.

[4] Also because there is (in Samkhya theory) nothing extraneous to primal matter, there is nothing for it to rely upon to cause it to act.

The three material qualities are in a state of equilibrium in matter — if there is no external cause, how are these qualities impelled to activity? The transcendent soul (*purusha*) is indifferent and does not move anything to action or restrain anything from action. Thus, it is impossible to see why matter should sometimes modify itself and sometimes not, unlike the activity or nonactivity of the all-knowing and all-powerful Lord with his power of illusion.

[5] Nor can it be like grass transforming into milk in a cow since such a transformation does not occur elsewhere (i.e., transformations occur only in specific order, and nonconscious matter could not decide which transformations should occur where).

Objection: The transformation of grass into milk is due to its nature. Matter transforms itself without a cause — if there were a cause we would see it and apply it directly to grass. So, we can infer the same for other things.

Response: But grass only becomes milk when eaten by a cow, not when it is left uneaten or eaten by a bull — if becoming milk had no cause, that would not be so.

[6] Even if we admit that it is possible that primal matter could transform itself without outside aid, it still could not do so because of the absence of any purpose (artha) to change since it is nonconscious.

Even if transformation could occur spontaneously, it must be for a purpose. But what purpose (can nonconscious matter have)? Pleasure or liberation? Not pleasure: you claim that the transcendent soul (*purusha*) cannot feel pleasure or pain. Nor liberation: you claim the soul is already liberated, and so the activity of matter would be without a purpose. If both: liberation would impossible because there is an infinite number of things to enjoy. Nor to satisfy a desire: neither a transcendent soul nor nonconscious matter feels any desire.

Objection: If matter is not active, the person's power of sight and the creative power of matter would have no purpose.

Response: But then the creative power of matter would never cease, any more than the person's power of sight, and so no liberation could take place.

Thus, matter cannot be active for the purpose of a transcendent soul.

[7] Objection: The soul can move primal matter like a lodestone can move iron or a lame man with sight can guide the blind. Response: Even if that were

so, the same defect still exists since matter cannot create by itself.

Objection: The transcendent soul is like a lame but sighted man sitting on the shoulders of a blind person guiding him along.

Response: Then you abandon your old doctrine that matter can move itself or have a tendency to act. And how can an indifferent soul move the material body? A lame man can speak to the blind man, but the soul is without actions and properties. Nor is it like a loadstone since the soul is permanently near the body, and so movement would never cease. So too, the loadstone must be moved by a conscious agent to affect iron.

With matter being nonconscious and the soul being indifferent and no third principle connecting them, the two cannot be connected. If the connection is by some capacity that matter has, then the connection is permanent and liberation is impossible. But the highest Atman is characterized by both indifference (and thus nonaction) that is inherent to its nature (*svarupa*) and at the same time uses its active power of illusion (*maya*). This is the uniqueness (*atishaya*, "preeminence") in the case of the highest Atman.

[8] And because of the relation of a principal to subordinates, the three qualities in Samkhya theory — goodness, passion, and dullness — cannot act upon their own to make primal matter act.

The three qualities of matter are in equilibrium and so cannot themselves make matter move. What could disturb the equilibrium? None of the qualities are subordinate to the others, and there is no additional principle.

[9] Even if the existence of primal matter could be established by inference in another way, it still could not act due to the absence of the power of consciousness.

Objection: The three qualities are inherently unstable and can enter into mutually unequal relationships even while remaining in equilibrium.

Response: If so, the orderly arrangement of the world cannot be explained since the three qualities are not conscious. If you try arguing that matter is conscious, you have given up your doctrine — the claim that there is one and only one conscious cause of the world would be our claim about Brahman. And if the qualities could enter into mutually unequal relationships while remaining in equilibrium, then some other cause would keep them from being unequal or their initial condition could not change.

[10] And because of the contradictions involved, the Samkhya doctrine is untenable.

Samkhya doctrines are inconsistent. For example, sometimes they claim seven senses and sometimes eleven, or sometimes there are three inner organs and sometimes only one. And they contradict scripture on the Lord being the cause of the world.

Objection: But the followers of the Upanishads' claim that Brahman is the atman of all things and the cause of the world is also objectionable: it makes Brahman both the cause of suffering and also what suffers — two aspects of the same Atman. Liberation from suffering is impossible — the waves and the water (Brahman) are permanently one, and the water is never without waves. And thus scripture has no purpose. So too, suffering and its cause belong to different categories, as with the person who desires and what is desired: if the object of desire and the desirer were one, we could not describe the person as "having desire" since it would be satisfied.

Response: Because of the oneness of Brahman, there is no duality of the cause of suffering and the sufferer. The one unchangeable Brahman does not enter into a relationship of the cause of suffering and the sufferer. (Both the appearance of suffering and the sufferer lie in the realm of root-ignorance.)

Objection: Burning is a pain, and this affects the conscious being, not the nonconscious material body. Otherwise, with the end of the body, suffering would end, and there would be no need to seek liberation.

Response: The living being is the sufferer burned by the sun. But a conscious being is not seen to be burned or suffer without a body. Nor can you explain what suffers since the transcendent soul and the material body are not connected. And how do you explain the connection of the sufferer and the cause of suffering? Even if one quality (*sattva*) were the cause and another quality (*rajas*) were the effect in the realm of suffering, still the soul is not connected to the qualities. If you say the soul only appears to suffer "as it were" (*iti*), well, we too apply "as it were" to the Atman since suffering is not real — suffering and the relation of the cause to the sufferer are not real but only the effect of root-ignorance.

If you claim that an individual being (which is eternal) suffers and that matter (which is also eternal) causes that suffering, then that suffering is eternal and liberation is impossible.

Objection: Only the potentiality and the cause of suffering are eternal. Suffering itself requires the two to be connected through the nondiscrimination of matter being separate from the transcendent soul (*purusha*).

Response: But you accept that this nondiscrimination through the *guna* of "dullness" is itself eternal. And if there is no fixed rule for the order of the arising and ceasing of the influence of each material quality, then there is also no fixed rule for the termination of the cause that effects the connection of matter and the transcendent soul (i.e., nondiscrimination), and so the lack of liberation is inevitable.

For us, there is only one reality and that cannot enter a relation of subject and object. And scripture declares that the plurality of effects originates from speech alone. We admit the relation of suffering and sufferer only for the (unreal) phenomenal world.

We now turn to the Vaisheshikas' atomism and its doctrine that properties inhering in the substance of the cause produce properties of the same kind in the substance constituting the effect — e.g., white threads producing a white cloth and not one of another color. Thus, they argue that if a conscious Brahman is the cause of the world, we should expect to find consciousness inherent in the effect (i.e., all things in the world should be conscious), but we do not see that. But following the Vaisheshikas' own reasoning it can be shown that their system is not necessarily truth:

[11] So too, the nonconscious could arise from conscious Brahman just as you claim that the big and the long are produced from the short and spherical (i.e., infinitesimal dimensionless atoms).

The Vaisheshika claim that atoms are the cause of effects through combinations. White atoms in combination produce white dyads, but you also claim that combining dimensionless atoms produces something that does not replicate the atoms — objects with dimensions. Spherical atoms combine to form nonspherical objects, and tiny atoms combine to form large objects. If so, nonconscious objects can arise from a conscious Brahman.

Objection: Unlike the combination of material atoms into different material shapes, the world is the negation of an alleged conscious cause — not an effect similar to the alleged cause.

Response: Just as the property of being spherical can produce nonspherical effects (through combinations), so it is with consciousness — effects unlike their causes appear. (Also see above 2.1.6 against the Samkhya.)

[12] From either the Samkhya or Vaisheshika point of view, no action is possible. Thus, there would be an absence of creation.

Objection: Things arise from atoms connected by an inherent relation. They are broken down into atoms at the end of the world-cycle, and the creation of the next cycle begins with action (*karma*) springing from atoms of air. This action results from an unseen principle (*adrishta*) that joins the atoms in which it resides together. Thus, the entire world originates from atoms. From properties of atoms the properties of compounds arise.

Response: Such action requires a cause since without a cause no initial action can take place within the atoms. But prior to the creation of the world, no action is possible because no bodies existed at that time (to be acted upon), and so no individual atmans can be attached to bodies. The same with all other things. Observed causes can only occur after there are things to act upon, and so things cannot be the cause of the action by which the world is created. But neither can an unseen cause: if it inhered in either the transcendent soul or matter, it cannot be the cause of action in atoms since it is nonconscious. Such a soul cannot be the cause because at the time of the beginning of the world, its consciousness had yet not arisen, and later it has no connection to matter. If consciousness and matter were connected, then action would never cease since there is no principle restricting action. Thus, there is no definite cause, and no initial action in the atoms could take place, and thus no subsequent actions are possible.

In addition, how is the contact of atoms imagined? It cannot be total penetration, for then there would be no increase in size, but we see an increase when things combine. Nor can it be only partial contact since that would mean that atoms have parts, contrary to your position. And if atoms consisted of parts, then the conjunction of whole atoms is unreal and could not be the cause of real things. Dyad compounds and so forth could not originate, and there could be no cause of actions since there would be no definite cause. Nor do you claim that the unseen principle is the cause of the creation of the world. Since there is no possibility of an action to bring about the connection of atoms or their separation, neither connection nor separation could occur, and thus there can be no creation of the world or its destruction at the end of a world-cycle.

[13] The inherence of properties in a substance leads by the same reasoning to an infinite regress of substances, and thus creation could not have occurred.

You Vaisheshikas accept that the dyad of two atoms is absolutely different from those two atoms and is related to them by an inherent connection. But this leads to an infinite regress since that connection is itself absolutely different from the two atoms and so requires another connection to relate itself to each atom, and so on and so on.

Objection: We experience the inherence as always connected with the things between which it exists, not as unconnected to them or as dependent upon another connection. So there is no infinite regress.

Response: But then since conjunction is experienced in the same way, conjunction would not require an additional principle of inherence. If you claim that conjunction requires something more because it is different from what is connected, then inherence also requires something more because it also is different, and so on and so on. And the impossibility of one part of an infinite chain means the entire chain is impossible.

[14] Also because either activity or inactivity would persist eternally since inherence would lead to no changes.

Atoms must be either active by nature, inactive by nature, both, or neither — there is no fifth option. But none of these four options are possible. If atoms are active by nature, their activity would be permanent and no destruction of the world at the end of a world-cycle would be possible. If they are inactive by nature, no activity could ever arise, and so no creation at the beginning of a world-cycle could occur. Being both active and inactive by nature is impossible because that is self-contradictory. And being neither is impossible since either a cause would create activity or the absence of a cause would result in inactivity (— one or the other must occur).

[15] And because we see that things have color, the doctrine of invisible atoms is refuted.

Objection: All things composed of parts can be divided into their parts and so on until we reach the indivisible and eternal atoms that are the origin of the entire material world.

Response: (Invisible atoms could not produce color.) If atoms have color and other properties, they are not infinitesimal and permanent but observable and impermanent, and thus some more subtle cause must be at work.

Objection: Something must be permanent — we would not have formed the word "impermanent" unless there was something to contrast with it.

Response: But what is permanent may be Brahman, not atoms. Nor can the existence of anything be established merely by common use of a word. Common use is established only if the word and what is designated are established by the means of correct of knowledge. And if atoms are established as permanent because we cannot see them, then the permanence of dyads is also established (and so on up to all observable objects being permanent).

Objection: Atoms must be permanent because there is no cause to break them but only causes to break or destroy compounds.

Response: Something may be destroyed by other causes, like a solid piece of gold being melted by fire.

[16] Whether atoms are invisible and so we cannot account for color, or they have color, this doctrine is defective and thus untenable.

Do earth atoms possess more properties than atoms of water, fire, and air? If so, they would be larger, but you claim all atoms are the same size. If all atoms are the same size, then there can be no difference in properties and all atoms could have no more properties than atoms of air — thus, we could not touch the earth. And if all atoms have the same properties, we would experience them all in everything. Both are contrary to experience.

[17] It is also not accepted by those who are praiseworthy.

In addition, there are other objections. The six Vaisheshika categories (substance, property, action, generality, particularity, and inherence) are said both to be absolutely different and have different characteristics and also to be dependent on substance. But if something is absolutely different from substance, it cannot depend on it, just as different things in the phenomenal world do not depend on each other. But if they depend on each other, then when one thing is present so are the others, but that would make everything just different modifications of matter. Smoke and fire are seen to be different, but not substance and different properties — we see substance only by its properties. The same reasoning applies to the five other categories.

Objection: Although substance and property are different, each cannot exist without the other. So too for substance and the other four categories.

Response: If so, then substance and property must be non-separate in place or in time or in nature. Not in place: you assert that the cloth made of threads occupies the same place as the threads, not any separate space, but the properties of the cloth are new and not those of the threads. Nor in time: if so, then the two horns of a cow are permanently inseparable (since they were created at the same time). Nor in nature: property and substance would then be inseparable and cannot be distinguished.

Objection: Conjunction is the connection between things that can exist separately, while inherence is the connection between things that cannot exist separately.

Response: In either case, the cause exists separately before the effect, and a connection requires two items. Nor can an effect enter into a connection after it begins to exist and still be an inherent connection or causation. Nor can prior activity cause a conjunction of cause and effect.

Nor is there any evidence for the existence of a conjunction or inherence apart from the things that are connected. Nor simply because we have the names and ideas of them: the same thing may be the subject of several names and ideas when considered in relation to other things — the same person may be described as a man, a Brahmin, a father, a son, a brother, and so on.

In addition, we only observe contact between things that have parts. Thus, neither atoms, a transcendent soul, nor the mind could have contact.

Objection: We then can imagine that these have parts.

Response: Assuming things that do not exist permits us prove anything since there is no rule only certain nonexisting things can be assumed.

Objection: At least we must assume that an inherent relation between a thing and what it abides in — the abode and what abides in it.

Response: That has the fault of circular reasoning: only when the separateness of cause and effect is established can the relation of "abiding" and "abode" be established, and vice versa. We reject both distinctions of "cause" and "effect" and "abiding" and "abode" (as applying to what is real).

In addition, atoms are limited, like regions of space are, and must consist of parts and thus are not permanent (but created from the combination of the parts). We claim that all things form a series of ever increasing minuteness and are capable of dissolution until the highest cause — Brahman — is reached.

Objection: Compound things can be created only by combining parts and can be destroyed only by decoupling parts.

Response: Again, the hardness of gold is destroyed and rendered liquid by fire, not by the separation of parts. So too, the solid shape of atoms may be decomposed by passing back into an undifferentiated condition of the highest cause. So too, effects do not arise only from combination — e.g., water becoming ice, or milk turning sour.

All in all, the atomism doctrine is very weak and opposes the scriptural claim of the Lord as the general cause.

[18] Creation of aggregates would not occur even from a combination of the action of Samkhya primal matter and Vaishshiska atoms.

So much for the Samkhya and Vaisheshika doctrines. Now let's turn to Buddhism. Three principal positions can be distinguished: (1) everything is real (Sarvastivada); (2) only consciousness is real (Vijnanavada/Yogachara); (3) everything is empty (and thus unreal) (Shunyavada/Madhyamaka).

Sarvativadins hold that everything internal and external is real. What is external is an element (*bhuta*) or something elemental in nature. What is internal is mind (*chitta*) or something mental in nature. External objects and internal states of consciousness are products of the aggregation of parts. But Buddhists cannot explain how aggregation is brought about — the parts of the material aggregates are without consciousness, and the seed of the mind in their theory requires a prior aggregate (the body), and Buddhists do not accept an eternal, conscious being or ruling Lord that could bring about such aggregations. Nor could physical or mental parts aggregate on their own. Nor can there be a mental abode: such an abode is either permanent or momentary — but Buddhists reject permanence, and what is momentary cannot exert any influence to bring about the action of atoms. But without aggregates, there could be no worldly existence.

[19] Against the Buddhist doctrine of "dependent co-arising": causes cannot be the cause of one another. Rather, each cause can only cause the next item in a series.[5]

Objection: Aggregates form through mutual causation beginning with root-ignorance and thus do not need any other principle of combination.

Response: Even if there is a causal relationship between each member of the dependent co-arising formula, the members cannot exist without aggregates: what caused the existence of the (prior) aggregates that are needed for root-ignorance and so forth to function? As discussed concerning Vaisheshika atomism, the formation of aggregates cannot be explained by permanent atoms and individual souls — how much less can aggregates be explained by momentary atoms unconnected to souls and without an abode.

Objection: Root-ignorance and the other members of dependent co-arising cause the aggregates.

Response: But how can those cause the (prior) abode without which they were not capable of existing in the first place?

Objection: The cycle of rebirths (*samsara*) is eternal. The aggregates succeed one another in an unbroken chain (with no first member), and root-ignorance and so forth abide in those aggregates.

Response: Do the aggregates necessarily produce another aggregate of the same kind or something not predicated on the principle of similarity in kind? If the former, than someone with a human body could never be reborn as an animal, god, or demon. If the latter, a person might be turned instantaneously into an elephant or a god and then into a man again. But you reject either consequence.

In addition, for you there is no permanent being to desire or to enjoy liberation, and so liberation from rebirth cannot occur or be sought.

---

[5] Dependent co-arising (*pratitya-samutpada*) has the general formula "y arises dependent upon x; without x, y could not arise." There is also a standard twelve-step formula showing how rebirths of people arise dependent upon root-ignorance.

[20] *Nor can a momentary earlier element cause a later one because of the cessation of the prior element when the later one arises.*[6]

Your doctrine of momentariness makes a causal chain between the members of dependent co-arising impossible. What exists in one moment ceases to exist in the next, and thus there can be no cause/effect relation between two items since what has ceased to exist cannot cause a later event.

Objection: The former fully developed momentary existent still becomes the cause of the later existent.

Response: That is impossible: for a momentary existent to exert influence on a later event, the former must be connected in a second moment to something after its moment of existence has expired, and that contradicts your doctrine.

Objection: The mere existence of the antecedent entity constitutes its causal power.

Response: But we cannot conceive the origination of an effect that is not imbued with the nature of its cause: if something cannot be deemed a "cause" only after the "effect" is in existence, for then the "effect" exists before contact with the "cause" and so is not an "effect." And the nature of the cause cannot continue in the effect since that would violate your doctrine of impermanence. Nor can there be a relation of cause and effect even without the cause coloring the effect since the cause then would be available at all times to affect all things.

In addition, the origination and destruction of something must constitute that thing's form or another state of it or be something altogether different. But all three possibilities contravene Buddhist principles. If the origination and destruction of something constitute that thing's form, the words "thing," "origination," and "destruction" could be used interchangeably, which they are not. If origination and destruction designate different states of the thing, then the thing exists more than one moment, which violates the doctrine of momentariness. If origination and destruction are altogether different from the thing, then that thing must be everlasting since it is never connected to origination or destruction.

[21] *(If something arises) when there is no cause, there can be no claim of causation (i.e., that thing is not an effect). But if the cause does not cease, then the cause and effect exist simultaneously.*

---

[6] As noted above, "causation" in this discussion is a matter of *emergence* (like butter from milk), not efficient *causation* (like one billiard ball causing another one to move). Impermanence raises an issue for both material and efficient causation.

We have shown that under the doctrine of impermanence once a momentary entity becomes nonexistent, it cannot be the cause of a later entity.

Objection: An effect may arise without a cause.

Response: But you hold that the mind and mental properties arise from conditions (*pratyayas*). In addition, if things could arise without causes, then anything might arise at any time.

Objection: A momentary cause lasts until the effect is produced.

Response: Then the cause and effect exist simultaneously, and this contradicts your doctrine of momentariness.

[22] In the latter case, neither an observable nor unobservable destruction of the cause is possible since there is no interruption of the cause.

Objection: Absolute destruction (*nirodha*) of entities occurs constantly and is of three types: destruction preceded by a thought, destruction not preceded by a thought, and the absence of anything occupying space.

Response: The first two types of destruction are impossible. (Space is discussed below in aphorism 24.) These types would involve either the end of a continuous stream of entities to which the thing belongs or the nonorigination of a thing in that stream. The former is impossible: each entity in the stream causes the next in an unbroken chain, and so the series cannot be interrupted. The latter is impossible: when an entity is destroyed, its substance does not disappear but continues to exist in another form (e.g., the clay of a broken clay jar still remains) and thus has a connected existence.

[23] The Buddhist position is untenable either way due to these defects.

The cessation of root-ignorance and so forth is covered by aphorism 22. Root-ignorance is uprooted either by perfect knowledge or by its own accord. But the former means the abandonment of the Buddhist doctrine that the cessation occurs without a cause, and the latter would mean that the Buddhist path to liberation is useless.

[24] The case of space does not differ.

Scripture states that space is real and not merely the absence of something. It is also inferred as the entity underlying sound. In addition, if space were the mere absence of entities — the third type of destruction — then when one bird is flying in it there is no room for another bird to fly. If another bird could fly in the space, then the space is an entity and not the mere absence of things. A space that is distinguished by the absence of any thing must be real and not merely the nonexistence of that thing. In addition, Buddhist scripture accept space as the entity supporting wind. But Buddhists contradict themselves on maintaining that space, along with the other two types of destruction, is both indescribable and yet eternal. Eternality or non-eternality cannot be ascribed to what is not real but only to what is real. Anything to which that distinction applies is not an undefinable negation. (Thus, destruction is not the mere absence of a thing.)

[25] *A permanent entity has to be admitted because of our ability to remember.*

Memory and recognition would not be possible if everything arose and vanished each moment. Memory is possible only if it belongs to the same person who had the perception upon which it is based — what one person experiences is not remembered by another person. But if one agent is connected to both moments, the doctrine of momentariness must be abandoned.

Objection: Cognition occurs because the similarity of the two momentary cognitions.

Response: But one who remembers does not merely grasp a similarity. There is a connection that momentariness cannot capture. With a memory, the conscious subject never has any doubt that he also had the previous experience, not anything about a "similarity." Even when there is some doubt about what is seen, the subject has no doubt that he is the same subject who yesterday had a sensation and remembers it today. (This also refutes the Shunyavada claim of the emptiness [*shunyata*] of reality.)

Whenever something obvious from ordinary experience is not admitted by philosophers, they try to establish their opinion and refute contrary opinions by means of words, but they convince neither others nor themselves.

[26] *Nor does something ever arise from nothing, since that is never seen.*

Objection: Entities can arise only after the destruction of their causes. Thus, entities arise from nothing — plants sprout only after their seed is destroyed, for otherwise all effects would arise from all causes at once.

Response: Existence does not arise from nonexistence. Destroyed entities are all the same — nonentities. Thus, nonentities all have the same characteristics, and so anything could arise from anything — sprouts could arise from the horns of a rabbit.

Objection: There are different kinds of nonentities.

Response: Then those "nonentities" are really entities and no less real than the entities that were destroyed. In no case does a truly nonexistent entity have any causal power — like the horns of a rabbit, it is nonexistent. And if something existent did spring from what is nonexistent, all effects would be affected by that cause, but we observe that effects are all positive entities distinguished by particular characteristics. And all causes are also positive entities. Even when a seed is destroyed in making a sprout, there are particles of the seed that are not destroyed.

[27] If something did come from nothing, people could attain a goal without effort.

If something did come from nothing, lazy, inactive people could attain their goals without labor since "nonexistence" can be obtained without much trouble. Farmers could grow rice without cultivating their fields. And no one would have to exert themselves to attain a heaven or liberation.

*[28] The doctrine of the nonexistence of external objects (*abhava*) is not true because such objects are perceived.*

Let's move on to the Buddhist Vijnanavada according to which acts of knowing, the objects known, and the resulting knowledge are all internal to the intellect (*buddhi*), and so there are no external objects. External objects would be either unobservable atoms or aggregates that cannot be defined as different or not different from the atoms. (If external objects are different from atoms, they cannot be said to be composed of atoms; if they are not different, they are invisible too.) So too with universal properties.

Objection: Cognitive states of consciousness are modified according to different ideas; the form of these ideas is determined by ideas, not by any external objects. Thus, the object of knowledge and the act of knowing are the same — we are never conscious of one without the other. Perception is like a dream: ideas that appear to the mind in a dream, a magical illusion, a mirage, and so forth appear in the form of a subject and objects, but there are no external objects. So too, ideas that occur in our waking state are equally without any external objects. The variety of alleged external objects results from trace impressions (*vasanas*) left by previous ideas. In the beginningless cycle of rebirths, ideas and impressions succeed each other as causes and effects (with no first idea), like seeds and plants. Thus, external objects do not exist (but are merely constructs [*kalpanas*] projected from the mind).

Response: The nonexistence of external objects cannot be maintained because external things in the world are perceived — what is perceived cannot be said to not exist (i.e., be unreal [*asat*]). Simply to claim that we are not conscious of external objects and that there are no objects apart from the act of consciousness is an arbitrary statement that proves nothing.

Objection: We do not say that objects are not perceived but only that there are no *external* objects existing separate from our subjective perceptions of them. (The idea of "objects" is strictly internal and perceived.)

Response: That objects exist apart from consciousness must be accepted because of the nature of consciousness itself — no one who is conscious of a post is conscious of his perception alone but of an object. Even those who deny external objects claim their internal object of cognition is "like something external." The objects in our consciousness appear to us as something external. (We cannot deny the sense of externality is part of the phenomenology of our perceptions — we may claim that discrete "objects" are only mental constructs but not this without denying perceptions are veridical.)

Objection: But external objects are impossible.

Response: The possibility or impossibility of something depends on whether the means of correct knowledge are applicable, not on preconceived ideas of what is possible or impossible — what is possible is whatever is apprehended by perception or another means of correct knowledge, and what is impossible is whatever cannot be so apprehended. And external objects are apprehended by all the means of correct knowledge. So too, if there were no objects, the ideas of objects could not have the form of the objects. And the invariable congruence of an idea and an entity has to be considered proof that the entity constitutes the means to the idea, not that the idea and entity are identical.

In addition, when we are conscious first of a pot and then of a piece of cloth, our consciousness remains the same — what varies in the two acts are the properties in the state of consciousness. The difference between the changing content from the unchanging state of consciousness proves that the idea and the object are distinct. The same holds for perception of an object and the later memory of it. And so too for taste and smell.

Two ideas that occupy different moments and pass away as soon as they become objects of consciousness also cannot apprehend each other or be apprehended by each other — i.e., ideas of a knower and a cognition cannot be related. This presents problems for the doctrines of momentariness, emptiness, the distinction of ideas, the distinction of the act of knowing and what is known, the possibility of former ideas leaving trace impressions to arise later, sense-impressions and subsequent cognitions, existing and nonexisting things and things that are both existing and nonexisting (*sat-asat dharmas*) caused by root-ignorance, and bondage and liberation.

If we are conscious of an idea, we are also conscious of its external object. An idea cannot illuminate itself any more than fire can burn itself. You refuse to accept the common and completely reasonable view that we are conscious of an external object by means of a mental state that is different from the object. It cannot be asserted in any way that the mental idea of an object is the object of our consciousness since it is absurd to think that something can be the object of its own activity.

Objection: If an idea must be apprehended by something other than itself, then that something must also be apprehended by something different and so on ad infinitum. Or if each cognition is self-luminous, then the assumption that a further cognition is needed is uncalled for.

Response: The idea alone is apprehended by the conscious witness, and thus there is no need to assume that there must be something else to apprehend that witness ad infinitum. The witnessing person and the idea are different in nature and stand in the relation of knower and thing known. The existence of the witnessing self (atman) is self-proven and thus cannot be denied. If an idea were self-luminous, then ideas exist that are not apprehended by any means of knowledge and without a knowing witness. But for a lamp to become luminous, there must be a conscious agent to light it and some instrumentality, and the same applies to an idea. And ideas have the properties of arising and passing away, being multiple, and so forth (but the witnessing atman is one and permanent). In sum, an idea, like the light of a lamp, requires a distinct conscious agent to become observable.

[29] Also because the waking state is different in nature from a dream.

Experiences in the waking state differ from those in a dream, as do their objects. Things that we are conscious of in dreams are later negated (*badha*) by our waking consciousness, like magical illusions are negated by ordinary consciousness. But objects of ordinary consciousness are never negated under any circumstances. So too, the objects in dreams are the result of the impression of memories while objects perceived in ordinary consciousness are immediately presented. Such perceptions also differ from memories.

These Buddhists absurdly deny what is right before them — it is not proper to deny the reality of one's own experience. And since they are unable to demonstrate the groundlessness of perceptions in the waking state, they attempt to demonstrate it from certain commonalities with ideas in the dreaming state. But fire cannot be demonstrated to be cold simply because it has some properties in common with water, and we have already established the difference in nature between the waking and the dreaming states.

[30] In addition, there would be no existence of sense-impressions since sense-objects would not be perceived. (There are no prior experiences to create impressions.)

Objection: The variety of mental ideas can be explained by the variety of trace impressions without recourse to external objects.

Response: But mental impressions are impossible without prior perceptions of external objects. So too, positive and negative judgments make no sense unless there are external objects and not only mental impressions. In addition, there must be some reality to be modified for impressions, but you deny that any such permanent abode of consciousness can exist.

*[31] And there cannot be a permanent "storehouse consciousness" (*alaya-vijnana*) due to momentariness of everything.*

Objection: The storehouse consciousness provides such a reality. It is the abode of the mental impressions.

Response: Cognition is momentary and impermanent and so cannot be the abode for trace impressions. Unless something is equally connected to the past, present, and future or is unchanging and all-knowing (like Brahman), remembrance and recognition and anything else subject to mental impressions tied to place, time, and cause cannot be explained. But if you claim that the storehouse consciousness is permanent, you abandon the Buddhist doctrine of momentariness.

This refutes the doctrine that the external world does not exist and the doctrine that only ideas exist. Now for the third Buddhist school — the Shunyavada. It asserts that everything is empty (*shunya*) (and so not real). But this doctrine is contradicted by all means of correct knowledge and thus needs no further refutation. The existence of the apparent world is guaranteed by all the means of correct knowledge. A general principle is proven by the lack of contrary instances, and thus this world cannot be denied unless someone finds a new reality (that shows this world not to be real [*sat*]).

[32] Buddhism is unjustifiable from every point of view.

From whatever angle, Buddhism is examined, its probability gives way like the walls of a well dug in sandy soil. It has no foundation to rest upon, and thus to try to use it as a guide for practical concerns is sheer folly.

In addition, that three conflicting schools arose from the Buddha's teachings shows that either the Buddha was a person given either to making incoherent (*asambaddha*) claims or his hatred of all beings induced him to propound absurd doctrines that leads them into utter confusion. Thus, Buddhism has to be completely disregarded by all who are concerned about their own happiness.

[33] The Jaina doctrine is not tenable because of the impossibility of contrary properties existing in the same thing (at the same time).

Jainas advance seven points of view for approaching any object including the contradictory properties of being and not being. But contradictory properties such as existence and nonexistence cannot be ascribed to the same thing at the same time, just as observation shows us that something cannot be both hot and cold at the same time. Under the Jainas' seven categories approach, things are "either such or not such." (Nothing is categorically affirmed or denied.) This results in no definite cognitions, and that can be no more a source of true knowledge than doubt can. The claim that something may have more than one nature that falls under the alternative approaches — "somehow it is" and "somehow it is not" — is not a definite cognition. So too with the person making the assertion and the result — partly they are and partly they are not. In sum, the means of correct knowledge, the object of knowledge, the knowing subject, and the act of knowing are all indefinite. One who proclaims a doctrine of altogether indefinite contents does not deserve to be listened to any more than a does drunk or a madman. How then can the Jaina's Tirthankara claim any authority? It is unjustified to declare that the categories are indescribable: if they are so, they cannot be expressed in words, but they are described — to call them "indescribable" involves a contradiction. And how can his followers act on a doctrine that is indeterminate? If the heavens and liberation "exist or not exist" or are "eternal or not eternal," then anyone seeking a heavenly world or liberation will lack the necessary determinate knowledge. And if the categories are ascertained to be such and such and at the same time are not ascertained to be such and such, and the result of their being ascertained is perfect knowledge or is not perfect knowledge, and imperfect knowledge is the opposite of perfect knowledge or is not its opposite, you clearly are talking more like someone intoxicated or insane than like a sober and trustworthy person. So too, their doctrine of the transcendent soul (*jiva*) is indeterminate, and their doctrine of an enlightened soul must be rejected since the contradictory properties of being and non-being cannot belong to any of the categories.

The above arguments also mean that one entity cannot have contradictory properties and that it is impossible to describe something as one and many, permanent and impermanent, separate and not separate, and so forth.

[34] Also because the transcendent soul would not be all-pervasive.

Jainas claim that the soul is not omnipresent but limited to the size of whatever body it occupies and thus is impermanent (and thus not eternal), like a jar. But being the size of a human being means that in a rebirth it would not fill an elephant and would be too big for an ant (and so we cannot be reborn as an animal). So too, stages of life are a problem — a person changes size from being a baby to an being a youth to being old.

Objection: Perhaps the soul consists of infinite number of parts that can compress or expand.

Response: Are those infinite number of parts capable of occupying the same space or not? If the infinite number cannot, then they cannot fit in any finite body. If they can, then they may all occupy only the space of a particle and thus be minuscule and not the size of a body.

[35] Nor can the contradictions be removed by assuming a succession of parts since this involves the defect of the changeability of the soul and so forth.

Objection: Perhaps the soul changes size by some particles being added in large bodies and some being subtracted in small ones.

Response: That the soul can change and thus is impermanent conflicts with the Jaina doctrine of the soul's permanence. In addition, the particles that can come and go cannot have the nature of the soul any more than can the body. The Jaina doctrine of liberation also then fails: the pure soul cannot rise from the mud of works if it is impermanent and no particular particles are essential to it. If some particles are permanently part of the soul and some only temporarily, we cannot determine which are which. We can also ask where the particles come from and where they reside when they are detached from the soul. They cannot spring from matter and return to it since the soul is immaterial. Nor is there evidence of some reservoir of immaterial soul-particles. And again, the soul would be of an indefinite size.

Objection: The soul may have no fixed size, but it is permanent like a stream of water is (even though the content of the stream is constantly changes) or a permanent stream of changing cognitions.

Response: If the stream is not real, we once again have the doctrine of the emptiness. If it is real, then the soul changes and so is not permanent.

[36] And since the size of the soul is permanent in the state of liberation, the size of the soul prior to liberation also must be permanent — there is no difference between them at any time.

The soul must be the same in size in any body or in liberation. The same problems hold for the Buddhist doctrine of an enlightened Arhat.

[37] As for a creator god: (The universe is eternal, and so) the Lord (arose after creation and thus cannot be the creator) for that would be impossible.

Since the Lord arose after creation, he cannot be the creator or material cause of the universe. (The Lord could not be either the efficient or material cause of the universe.) If he were the creator, then as the subsequent ruler he assigned positions to beings as he liked and thus he must have animated by hatred, passion, and so forth. Nor could he make beings' dispositions with a view to their merit and demerit — that assumption leads to the fault of circular reasoning: the Lord as well as the deeds of living beings would have to be considered in turns both as acting and as acted upon. This is so even with a chain of such deeds that has no beginning, for in past time as well as in the present such mutual dependence of the two would take place. Or the Lord is another kind of soul that is without action. Rather, beings fix their own position in the world by the endless chain of their karmic deeds.

[38] If the Lord and matter are distinct, they could never be connected.

If the Lord were distinct from the universe and persons, there could be no possible connection between them — it cannot be contact since the Lord, the world, and atmans are each all-pervading and without parts. Nor is there inherence since we cannot define what is the abode and what is abiding in it. Nor can there be any other relation since the relation of cause and effect is in dispute. But we say that the Lord and the world are completely identical (*tadatmya*). This is based on scripture, not observation. But your appeal to scripture as composed by omniscient authors for establishing the Lord involves circular reasoning: omniscience being established on the authority of scripture, and scripture being established on the omniscience of the authors. (But scripture is authorless and eternal.)

[39] And thus the universe could not be directed by the Lord.

Objection: The Lord produces actions in matter, just as a potter produces action in clay.

Response: Matter under your theory is not an object of perception and so cannot be the object of the Lord's actions. Bodies only exist subsequent to creation, so the creator does not have one.

[40] Objection: *God directs the universe like a person directs his or her organs.* Response: *Then God would have experiences and so forth associated with organs, and these lead to rebirth.*

We experience pleasure and pain and so infer that the inner atman rules the sense-organs, but the Lord does not experience pleasure and pain resulting from matter, and so the analogy does not apply. And we observe that actions require some substantive reality, but the Lord has none, and so the Lord cannot act. And if the Lord did have a body, he would be subject to rebirth and no longer be the Lord.

[41] God would then last only a finite time and not be omniscient.

Objection: The Lord, matter, and beings are all of infinite duration.

Response: Either the omniscient Lord knows the size of himself, matter, and beings, or he does not. If the latter, he is not omniscient. If the former, then they all (including himself) have definite dimensions and number; consequently, they must have a finite duration since ordinary experiences tells us that anything of definite dimensions ceases to exist at some point. Thus, if when all transmigrating persons (*jivas*) attain liberation, the realm of transmigration would come to an end and then the Lord will have nothing to rule. That would mean that his omniscience and ruling power will have no objects to know or act upon. So too, if matter and atmans have an end, then they also must have had a beginning (i.e., they cannot be eternal), and if things have a beginning and an end, we must accept the Buddhist nihilist Shunyavada doctrine of emptiness (and hence they have no reality). Thus, either way, we must reject the argument that the Lord is only the controlling efficient cause of the world rather than also its material cause.

[42] Against the Bhagavatas: *Because of the impossibility of their being created, individual persons are eternal and so cannot emerge from the Lord.*

Bhagavatas believe in one god — Vasudeva — who is pure knowledge and the one reality. He appears in four forms: the highest Atman (Vasudeva), from which individual persons (*atmans*) spring; from a person, the mind (*manas*) springs; and from the mind, the sense of "I" (*aham-kara*) springs. Thus, the highest Atman is the material and efficient cause of the other three.

Response: We accept the highest Atman as the material and efficient cause of the world, and we do not reject the Bhagavatas constant concentration on Vasudeva, for scripture proclaims that we are to contemplate the Lord. So too, we accept that the highest Atman divides himself into different forms since scripture says that (e.g., CU 7.26.2). But we deny that the other entities emerge from Vasudeva. If persons and so forth emerged from him, they would be impermanent and not eternal, and so they could not merge back with the highest Atman without being destroyed. Liberation in reaching the highest Atman would thus be impossible. That the individual atman has no origin is dealt with below (2.3.17).

[43] *And because an instrument cannot be produced from the agent who wields it.*

We never see an instrument, such as an axe, spring from a person, and so we reject that mind emerges from a person and the sense of "I" from the mind. Nor is there any scriptural support for their claim.

[44] *Even if Vasudeva possesses knowledge, the defect is not remedied.*

Objection: We understand the emergent entities, not as human persons and so forth, but as gods.

Response: Are these gods the same in properties as Vasudeva? If so, they are unnecessary. And there would no longer be one reality. Or are Vasudeva and the emergents each equal in excellence? If so, the objections in the last aphorism apply since they cannot produce each other and none are supreme. Experience shows that a cause must be superior to the effect in some respects, but then the Bhagavatas must reject that here: there is no difference in knowledge, power, and so forth between Vasudeva and the emergents. Nor can the forms of Vasudeva be limited to four since everything is a form of Brahman.

[45] In addition, their doctrines have many contradictions.

Internally the system is inconsistent: eminence of knowledge, ruling power, and so forth are ascribed to Vasudeva in some places and treated as separate gods in other. In addition, the system contradicts the Vedas.

Chapter 2.3

Introduction. We have concluded that other philosophical systems are worthless because of contradictions within them. Now we will address the charge that the Vedas are also self-contradictory concerning creation, starting with whether space has an origin or not.

[1] Space is not created since that is not stated in scripture.

Scripture states fire, water, and earth are produced (CU 6.2.3), but not space. No scriptural text shows that space has an origin, and scripture is our (only) authority for the origin of transcendent things. So we must conclude that space has no origin.

[2] Objection: *But scripture does state that space sprang from the Atman (TU 2.1).*

A conflict of scriptural passages remains: some passages say that creation started with fire and some say with space.

[3] Response: *The second text is to be taken in an indirect sense, not the final truth, since it is impossible for space to be created.*

The passage on the origin of space must be taken as figurative since it is impossible for space to be created. The Vaisheshika analysis of creation shows that space cannot be an effect of causation since there is no apparatus for such causation because space is unique: inherent causation requires more than one member of the same category, and non-inherent causation requires the connection of primary substances. Things that do arise (e.g., fire) are in a different condition (within their cause) before they arise, but space would be the same before and after it arose since it is all-pervading and distinct from earth and the other elements. Space is one, and phrases such as "The space in a jar" are only figurative. So too for texts about the creation of space.

[4] *Other Vedic passages also state that space is eternal.*

The space (*antariksha*) between heaven and earth is said to be immortal (BU 2.3.3), what is immortal has no origin. Scripture states that space is the body of Brahman, and thus it could have no beginning. (But see his commentary on aphorism 7 below.)

[5] *And it is possible for the same word (here, "sprang") to have both direct and indirect meanings, as with the word "Brahman."*

The word "Brahman" is used in a secondary sense as food and so forth (TU 3.2-6). So too for "sprang" in regard to space: it means that Brahman is space's eternal ground.

Objection: How can space not have an origin if Brahman is "one without a second" (CU 6.2.1)? For if space co-exists for eternity, Brahman has second. How then can everything be known just by knowing Brahman (CU 6.1.3)?

[6] Response: *The declaration that space is not created stands unaffected because of the nondifference of all effects from Brahman (and so all things are known by knowing only Brahman). This is confirmed in scripture.*

Everything is nondifferent from Brahman. This is possible only if everything originates from the one Brahman. The Vedas hold that this is established only through the doctrine of the nondifference of the material cause of its effects. We come to know what was not known by knowing the cause of an effect. The aggregate of effects is identical with Brahman. Thus, space is known by knowing Brahman. All is the Atman (BU 2.4.6). Brahman alone is immortal (MunU 2.2.11). Hence, space is an effect of the Atman.

The conflicting order of creation of fire and space in the Taittiriya and Chandogya Upanishads can be reconciled by interpreting the latter to say that Brahman, after having created space and air, created fire as the first of all the other created things. One scriptural passage cannot be self-contradictory, but a conflicting passage can be interpreted to fit the meaning of another passage. Scripture does not ascertain something to have a certain nature by deception (*maya*), fraud (*vanchana*), or untruth (*alika*).

Brahman and space are nondifferent. "Knowledge of everything" through knowing one thing (i.e., the one substance of everything, Brahman) relates to everything being the creation of Brahman, the one without a second.

[7] But division persists wherever there is a transformation (i.e., change of nature or form), as is observed in the world.

Wherever we observe effects (i.e., transformations of a substance), such as jars from clay, we also observe division, and whatever is not an effect is not seen as divided. And we see space divided since we see it separated from earth. So space is an effect, as are direction, time, mind, and atoms.

Objection: By that reasoning, the Atman must be an effect (i.e., a modification of something else) since it is divided from space.

Response: Scripture states that space sprang from the Atman (TU 2.1). If the Atman were a modification, all effects would be without the Atman since scripture mentions nothing beyond the Atman, and the Atman would be an effect (of some other reality and thus not be real or the atman of anything else). Thus, we would be driven to the nihilistic Buddhist Shunyavada doctrine of emptiness. But the Atman is self-established (and so requires no means of correct knowledge). Its existence is not established by a means of correct knowledge (*pramanas*): it is the atman that utilizes the means of correct knowledge to establish the existence of space and other entities, and thus it is established prior to the employment of those means. It is impossible to refute what is a self-established entity for it is the very nature of the one who would attempt to refute its existence — the heat of a fire (i.e., the fire's essential nature) cannot be refuted by the fire itself. The knowing agent (the Atman) does not change in different time periods — by its nature, it is eternally present, and as such the Atman cannot be destroyed even when the body is. Indeed, we cannot even conceive of the Atman becoming something different. Thus, the Atman, unlike space, is not an effect.

Effects need not arise from the same class of things as the cause — e.g., threads do not belong to the class of "conjunction" through which cloth is formed. A rope can be made from different substances — e.g., cloth or cow hair. Thus, Vaisheshika inherent causes need not be of the same class as the effects. An atom or the mind may give rise to an action. The same substance can be modified into different effects. In sum, it is not a law of the Lord that only certain causes in conjunction produce an effect.

Thus, we must rely on scripture that the entire world sprang from one Brahman, and that space was produced first followed by the other elements in succession. (See aphorism 2.1.24 above). Brahman does not participate in the nature of the elements since it is not observable, and it does not participate in the nature of space (BU 3.8.8). Thus, Brahman existed without space before creation.

Space is not eternal because it is a substratum for noneternal properties, just as jars are the substratum of noneternal properties and so are noneternal. But the Atman is not the substratum of noneternal properties. The "immortality" of space mentioned in scripture (BU 2.3.3) is analogous to the immortality of gods since the origin and destruction of space has been shown to be possible. Because space arose, it is not truly all-pervading. Brahman is compared to space in its omnipresent and eternity only to indicate its supreme greatness, not to maintain that they are equal, like when we say that the sun moves with the speed of an arrow. Other passages state that Brahman is greater than space. Nothing compares to Brahman (SU 4.19, BU 3.4.2).

Thus, both scripture and reason show that space is a created effect of Brahman.

[8] In the same way, air is explained as an effect of Brahman.

Conflicting passages on the relation of space and air are to be explained the same way.

[9] But there is no origin to being (sat) since that is impossible.

Brahman, whose essence (atman) is being, has not sprung from anything else because that is impossible — a cause has to be greater than its effect and nothing is greater than Brahman. Nor could it spring from something limited since we observe that nothing more general springs from something limited. Nor can Brahman spring from nonbeing (asat) since nonbeing has no atman and since scripture rejects that view (CU 6.2.2). Scripture also states that Brahman has no progenitor (SU 6.9). Nor does the fact that Brahman has effects mean that it is itself an effect — without some primary material cause (mula-prakriti), there would be an infinite regress of causes. And whatever is that cause will be our Brahman.

[10] Fire is produced from air, for scripture states so. [11] And water is produced from fire. [12] Earth is produced from water. The word "food" means earth because of the topic and color, and other scriptural passages say so.

Contradictory passages on the origin of air can be reconciled: air springs from fire and not directly from Brahman, but Brahman is the ultimate cause. Similarly for water arising from fire and for earth ("food") from water. Brahman exists in its effects as their essence (atman).

[13] But through deep meditation (abhidhyana) as the Lord, Brahman alone is the creator. This is confirmed by his indicatory marks (lingas).[7]

The highest Lord abiding in atmans sends forth specific effects (for each

---

[7] "*Abhidhyana*" also means "desire" or "longing" and the aphorism can be translated along that line.

atman), as indicated by their specific marks. He creates various effects after profound deliberation. Scripture states that the Lord dwells in the earth and presides over the elements' activity. Texts indicate that he is the creator (TU 2.6, CU 6.2.3) and the atman of everything (TU 2.7).

[14] The order of dissolution at the end of a world-cycle proceeds in reverse of the order of creation. That is proved (by reason).

Traditional texts and reason both affirm that the order of the reabsorption into Brahman must be the exact reverse of the order of creation.

[15] Objection: The intellect (vijnana, "insight") and mind (manas) are in between Brahman and the elements in the sequence of creation and dissolution because there are indirect indications of their existence. Response: There is no difference between their place and their organs' place in the order of creation and dissolution.

The bodily organs are not different from the elements, and so their origination and reabsorption are in the same order as the elements'. The separate mention of the elements and senses in some places is to understood as the maxim about Brahmins and mendicants (i.e., all mendicants are Brahmins but not vice versa).

[16] The mention of "creation and dissolution" is meant literally in relation to what moves and what does not move (i.e., all of creation). When applied to the Atman, it is meant in an indirect sense since it is applicable only when a body is present.

The atman of an individual person has no beginning and no end, only the body does (CU 6.11.3). If the atman perished along with the body, the religious injunctions and prohibitions referring to the enjoyment of pleasure and the avoidance of the unpleasant in the next rebirth would make no sense. "Birth" and "death" when applied to the individual person have to be taken in a secondary sense of referring to the body that the atman dwells in.

[17] The individual's atman is not created because scripture does not state that, and because the atman is known to be eternal from scripture.

The essence (atman) of a living person (jiva) is not subject to creation or dissolution. Scriptural passages on creation do not mention it, and other passages say it is eternal. That atman is not subject to being born and is not an effect or modification of Brahman. It arises from Brahman but is not a distinct product from Brahman since scripture does not include it as such. The atman appears separate only because of its contact with limiting adjuncts such as the intellect. The person's atman is eternal, has no origin, and is unchanging; the unmodified Brahman constitutes the person; the person's atman is Brahman (CU 6.3.2, 6.11.3, 6.8.7; KaU 2.28; TU 2.6; BU 1.4.7, 1.4.10, 2.5.19, 4.4.25). The limiting adjuncts dissolve but not the atman (BU 4.5.14). Its essence is knowledge (*vidya*), but it has no cognitions after leaving the body (because it has no limiting adjuncts for instruments). Thus, it is the unmodified Brahman that exists as the living person. The difference in their characteristics results only from the limiting adjuncts.

Objection: The person's atman must be a modification of Brahman since it is divided, and as a modification, it must have an origin.

Response: The Atman is not divided (SU 6.11) and only appears divided because of limiting adjuncts, just as space appears divided by its connection to jars. The one undivided Brahman only appears divided up the intellect (*buddhi*), mind, and so forth due to limiting adjuncts (BU 4.4.5). The adjuncts color the nature (of the embodied atman), not that anything is separate from it. In the rare instances where scripture speaks of the atman arising or being destroyed, it is about the connection or disconnection of the atman with limiting adjunct, not the atman itself. "Reabsorption" (of the individual's atman) is a matter of losing its connection to limiting adjuncts, not the dissolution of the atman into Brahman (BU 4.5.13). That the living person in fact is Brahman removes apparent contradictions. The differences in properties is only a matter of the atman being associated with limiting adjuncts. In sum, the living person does not originate or become reabsorbed.

[18] Based on scripture, the Atman is known to be conscious (jnah, a "knower"). (This consciousness is eternal because it is not created.)

Objection: Consciousness is only contingent — it is produced by the connection of the Atman to the mind (*manas*). If the living person were essentially conscious, there would be no unconsciousness — one would remain conscious always, even in deep sleep, coma, and possession.

Response: The Atman has eternal consciousness as its nature, just as fire has heat. Consciousness is eternal because it is not produced but is the unmodified highest Brahman. We know this from scripture (TU 2.1; BU 3.9.28, 4.5.15, 4.3.11, 4.3.14, 4.3.30; CU 8.12.4). The senses only serve for determining special objects of consciousness (CU 8.12.4). When in deep sleep, the person is conscious, but it is not manifested because it has no objects of consciousness (BU 4.3.23), just as there is unmanifested light pervading space when there is no object to illuminate.

[19] Because scripture mentions the atman as departing the body at death, going to a new realm, and returning in a new rebirth, the atman must be infinitesimal in size. [20] The relation of one's own atman to the latter two

events of going at death and rebirth confirms this size.

Scripture speaks of the individual atman going out of the body and returning (BU 4.4.1-2, BU 4.3.11). Thus, this atman must be finite in size, and scripture states that it is infinitesimal, not the size of the body (as discussed).

[21] Objection: The individual person is not infinitesimal because it is heard from scripture to be otherwise (i.e., that is all-pervading). Response: *Those passages relate to the other (the highest Atman, i.e., Brahman).*

Statements about the atman's size being other than infinitesimal (BU 4.4.22, TU 2.1) refer to the highest Atman or indirectly only indicate the connection of the individual atman to the greatness of the Atman.

[22] Scripture states that directly and also infers the minuteness of the individual atman. [23] There is no contradiction between an individual person being infinitesimal in size and the sense that it pervades the entire body: it is like sandalwood paste where one drop contacting any part of the body gives pleasure to the entire body.

The connection of the atman to life-breath (MunU 3.1.9) must indicate the individual atman. It can also be inferred from passages (SU 5.9). Its size and place within one part in the body does not prevent sensations from extending over the body, just as sticking a foot in a cold pond produces a sensation of cold over the whole body. So too with sandal wood paste.

[24] Objection: That is true for sandalwood paste because of its particular property, but it does not apply to individual atmans. Response: *Scripture states that the Atman lies in the heart (but pervades the whole body). [25] Or another analogy: the individual atman pervades the body like sense-experience pervades the world in the case of ordinary experience.*

Inference cannot remove the doubt of whether the atman extends over the whole body like the skin and has the sense of touch inhering in it, or is all-pervading like space, or is infinitesimal like a drop of ointment that is minute and abides in only one spot.

Objection: How can a property extend past the substance it inheres in? *Response:* It is like light from a lamp.

[26] Consciousness extends beyond the body like the sense of smell extends beyond the object giving rise to the smell.

Smell separates itself from the object in which it inheres, and thus it is reasonable to infer that consciousness can extend beyond the mind.

[27] Scripture declares that.

Scripture declares that the individual atman pervades the entire body (e.g., KsU 4.20, BU 1.4.7) through consciousness as a property.

[28] Objection: *The atman and consciousness are distinguishable because they are taught separately in scripture.*

The embodied atman is the actor and consciousness is the instrument of action.

[29] Response: *But the individual atman is said to be consciousness because of the dominance of that mode (i.e., the intellect), just as in the case of Brahman.*

The atomic size is actually a property of the intellect (*buddhi*), not the atman. The atman is nothing but the highest Brahman and has the same all-pervading extent as Brahman (BU 4.4.22). Pleasures and pains are limited by the mind (e.g., stepping on a thorn only hurts the foot). The individual in the cycle of rebirths is the essence of the mind's properties (e.g., desire, hatred, pleasure, and pain). Apart from these properties, the individual does not exist in the cycle of rebirths. Only due to the limiting adjuncts such as the mind does the Atman appear to be an actor and the enjoyer of the fruits of actions.

Some scriptural passages treat the Atman as both finite and infinite (SU 5.9), but the latter cannot be meant figuratively since Brahman constitutes the atman of the individual; thus, treating the individual atman as finite must be meant only figuratively. The Atman is not an actor or experiencer and does not transmigrate but is ever free. However, it comes to have such states by the superimposition of the intellect as a limiting adjunct in different states. The "lower" atman is meant figuratively by its connection to the mind (SU 5.8) or to indicate knowing the Atman (MunU 3.1.9). So too with passages that distinguish the individual atman and knowledge (KsU 3.6) — it means that the invisible Atman takes possession of the entire body through the mind as the limiting adjunct, or otherwise it is merely a way of speaking. For the distinction between a property and its entity does not exist in the case of the individual atman. So too, it is the mind that lies within the heart, not the atman. In addition, what has left the body cannot return to that body. In sum, as long as the individual atman is in cycle of rebirths, it has as its essence the properties of its limiting adjuncts and can be referred to as infinitesimal. So too with the atman of insight (*prajna-atman*). Just as passages about meditating on the qualified Brahman refer to the highest Atman as possessing minuteness because of the properties of its limiting adjuncts for its essence, so too with the individual atman.

Objection: If the individual atman and the mind are different entities, their connection will come to an end. Then the atman will be thoroughly undefinable and thus nonexistent at least with regard to rebirth.

[30] Response: *The individual atman persists within the individual as long the individual person continues to be reborn. There is no fault in this claim since that is observed in scripture.*

The intellect and other limiting adjuncts remain connected to an embodied atman as long as the individual person exists in the cycle of rebirths. The connection is severed only by perfect knowledge of Brahman.

But in reality there is no individual embodied atman — it is only imagined by its association with the limiting adjunct of the intellect. There is no other conscious substance but the all-knowing Lord whose nature is eternal freedom (e.g., BU 3.7.23, 3.8.11, 1.4.10; CU 6.8.7). Scripture declares the connection with the mind (BU 4.3.7, 4.4.5). "Consisting of knowledge" in these passages means merely "consisting of mind." This can be inferred from where knowledge is listed as merely one property (BU 4.4.5). Ways of speaking such as "as if thinking" and "as if moving" lead to the same conclusion: the Atman does not think or move, but the mind joined to it does. The connection of the Atman to the limiting adjuncts depends on wrong knowledge that can be removed only by correct knowledge of Brahman.

Objection: There is no connection of the atman to the mind manifested in the individual (e.g., in deep sleep) since we are not conscious then, and so the connection does not last as long as rebirths continue.

[31] Response: *But the manifestation of consciousness in the waking and dream states is possible only because it already exists within a person, just as in the case of virility which is not constantly observable in all states either.*

Just as the potentiality for virility exists when it is not manifested, so too for the intellect (*buddhi*).

[32] To maintain otherwise, one must argue that there is either perpetual perception or perpetual nonperception — one or the other is therefore limited.

The internal sense-organ (*antahkarana*) that is a limiting adjunct of the individual (*jiva-atman*) is called in different places "the mind (*manas*)," "the intellect (*buddhi*)," "insight (*prajna*)," or "consciousness (*chitta*)," depending on the state the person is in.[8] It is the limiting adjunct that explains why the embodied atman is not omniscient like Brahman: everything is not perceived all at once due to its restrictive effect. (The mind is a limiting adjunct that

---

[8] Shankara does not analyze the mind, and all these terms are interchangeable for the inner organ (2.4.6, 2.3.32). The mind (*manas*) is a life-organ (*prana*) (2.4.6) that has all objects in the past, present, and future as its "sense-objects" (2.3.32), but *pranas* are not sense-organs (*indriya*) (2.4.17). Sometimes Shankara distinguishes *buddhi* from *manas* and treats it as higher and closer to Atman (e.g., 3.3.14, 4.1.2; see KaU 3.10).

enables cognition but also limits the transcendent consciousness.) Without the limiting adjunct, there would either perpetual perception or perpetual nonperception. Either the Atman or the senses must be limited, but the former is not possible since the Atman is not capable of modifications, and the power of the senses cannot be limited without obstructions. Thus, we must accept the inner organ as regulating the presence of perceiving or not perceiving (BU 1.5.3). The explanation in aphorism 29 is thus correct.

[33] The individual person (atman) must be an active agent (karti). Otherwise, scriptural injunctions about an agent would have no purpose. [34] Also scripture teaches about the individual person roaming. [35] Also because the individual person takes up its sense-organs. [36] And because the mention of the atman as an agent concerning work. If it were not so (e.g., the intellect as the agent), there would be an indication to the contrary.

This must be the individual atman limited by the mind since the highest Atman does not move and so forth. Nor does the intellect do anything.

Objection: But if the atman is the doer, it is distinct from the mind, and there could be no restriction on the atman's actions. (The individual *jiva* would be as free as the highest Atman.)

[37] Response: Just as there is no restriction in the case of individuals' perception, so there is no restriction in the case of their actions.

Perception in the individual is unrestricted: conscious perception does not depend on anything else — the sense-organs merely present the objects of perception. In addition, the individual is not totally free in the case of actions since actions depend on differences in place, time, and causes, but the individual is still an agent.

[38] The individual atman with adjuncts must be the agent — if the intellect (vijnana) were the agent, there would be a reversal of power.

That is, the intellect would control the atman and not vice versa. The instrumental role of the intellect would be replaced with the power of agency.

[39] And because if the intellect were the agent, meditative concentration (samadhi) would be impossible.

Deep concentration as taught in the Vedantic texts has the aim of the realization of the Atman (BU 2.4.5, CU 8.7.1, MunU 2.2.6). This is possible only if the atman is the agent (since only the individual gains liberation).

[40] And because it is like a carpenter. He exists under both conditions.

(*Objection*: if the individual is the agent and the organs of action are by their nature in the individual, then there would be perpetual action.)

Response: The atman's agency is not its nature but contingent upon limiting adjuncts. If agency belonged to an atman's nature, we could not be free of rebirth because we could not be free of action (and action only brings more karmic effects, not liberation), any more than fire could be free of heat.

Objection: Liberation could be attained (without enlightening knowledge) by avoiding the occasions for actions, just as fire is endowed with the capacity of burning but does not burn if no fuel is present.

Response: Anything acquired through action is impermanent. If the atman had an innate capacity (*shakti*) of action, it could not avoid all action, and liberation would be impossible since it cannot be brought about by action because (by its nature) action is not eternal. The individual atman is an agent due to contact with limiting adjuncts and not by its nature (BU 4.3.7, KaU 3.4). When in union with the adjuncts of the body, the senses, and the mind, the Atman is called the enjoyer of the fruits of action (KaU 3.4). The condition of being an agent and enjoyer is presented by root-ignorance alone. To those who discriminate, there is no individual (*jiva-atman*) apart from the highest Atman that is a seer or enjoyer (BU 4.3.23).

The embodied atman is like carpenter who has a mind and who has working tools, but he is not perpetually at work. So as long as the atman is joined with duality presented through root-ignorance, it is the agent in the waking and dreaming states who undergoes pain. But as soon as the embodied atman enters itself (i.e., its true essence — the highest Atman), it frees itself from the complex of effects and instruments and enjoys full peace in the state of deep sleep and also in the state of liberation. Even in dream sleep, the intellect is not totally at rest. The atman is an agent in its functions with regard to its instruments (e.g., in contact with the mind), but it is not an agent by its own nature and has no parts. Vedic injunctions refer to the atman being an agent only with regard to the realm of root-ignorance.

Deep meditation (*samadhi*) is an action enjoined by conventional agentship. Thus, it does not require that the Atman be the agent here.

[41] But the agency of the individual atman comes from the highest (i.e., Brahman qualified as the Lord) as stated in scripture.

Opponent: The individual atman (*jiva-atman*) is not dependent upon the Lord for its agentship but is impelled by its own likes, dislikes, and so forth.

Response: The individual person in a state of root-ignorance is blinded by darkness and cannot distinguish itself from the complex of effects and instruments of action. The realm of rebirth in which the individual atman appears as an agent and enjoyer is brought about through the permission of the Lord who is the highest Atman and who presides over all actions — he is the witness residing in all beings and the cause of all consciousness. Thus, scripture teaches that the knowledge of Brahman arising through the favor (*prasada*) of the Lord leads to liberation. The Lord is the guiding cause behind all actions, including everyday experiences such as agriculture.

Objection: If the ultimate power in causal agency belongs to the Lord, it follows that he must be unjust and cruel (because we suffer), and the individual atman must undergo consequences for things it did not do.

[42] Response: *But the highest Lord makes the individual person act according to the efforts made by that person. Thus, the injunctions and prohibitions of the ritual part of the Vedas are not meaningless, and so forth.*

The Lord makes a person (*atman*) act according to the merit and demerit earned by his former actions. (Liberation is not a matter of "grace" — Brahman is the nonpersonal power behind all events.) Like rain falling on different plants that then grow according to their different seeds, the Lord causes the seeds of prior actions to sprout, whether good or bad (aphorism 2.1.34). The Lord arranges favorable or unfavorable circumstances for the persons according to their past actions. The Lord causes the person (*jiva-atman*) to make their specific acts depending on what he or she did earlier. But scripture states that it is the person who acts. Otherwise, Vedic injunctions be purposeless and our efforts useless since the individual would be (a robot) entirely dependent on the Lord's actions. The beginningless of the cycle of rebirths means there was no first act by the person.

[43] *An individual person is a part* (amsha) *of Brahman because the person is mentioned in scripture as different. Also some passages tell otherwise of Brahman's identity with fishermen, gamblers, slaves, and others.*

Scripture declares that the individual atman is part of the Lord, as spark is part of fire. But "part" really means "part, so to speak" since a being such as the Lord who is not composed of parts cannot have parts in a literal sense. But the individual and the Lord not identical because scripture also states that there is a difference between the highest Atman and the individual atman in their properties (CU 8.7; BU 4.4.22, 3.7.23).

Objection: But a view of "difference and nondifference" (*bheda-abheda*) is more supported by scripture — e.g., the Lord and the individual have the relation of master and slave (but both share the Lord's being). This accounts better for passages stating that the individual atman is a part of the Lord.

[44] *This is follows from the words of the mantras (e.g., CU 3.12.6).*

Some aphorisms suggest that the Lord has parts including individuals.

[45] *And it is also stated in the traditional texts.*

For example, "An eternal part of myself became a living individual person" (BG 15.7) suggests parts.

Response: The part/whole relation is known to hold in ordinary life, but from scripture we learn that the relation of part and whole and that of ruler and ruled may go together (in one reality). So too, there is nothing contradictory in assuming that the Lord, who is provided with the most excellent limiting adjuncts, rules individuals who have only their inferior limiting adjuncts.

Objection: If individual persons are parts of the Lord, then the Lord experiences pains. And thus, one who attains Brahman will feel greater pain (i.e., all the pain that the different parts bring).

[46] Response: The highest Atman is not touched by the sufferings of individuals, just as light is not affected by what it illuminates.

The highest Lord does not feel the pain of the state of rebirth in the same way that the individual atman does. The individual person (*jiva-atman*) is, as it were, under the influence of root-ignorance identifies with the body and suffers the pain occurring to the body. But he Atman itself is imagined to be affected by the pain that is not in fact real. This is caused by the nondiscrimination of the Atman from the limiting adjuncts of name-and-form produced by root-ignorance. The highest Lord, however, never identifies himself with a body nor imagines himself to be afflicted with pain. The Lord is as unmoving as the light of the sun that only seems to move because of limiting adjuncts (e.g., the reflected light moving in a shaking cup). Thus, the Lord is unaffected by pain although pain is felt by the part of him called the individual person as presented by limited by the adjuncts.

[47] That the Lord is unaffected by pain is stated in traditional texts and scripture.

The highest Atman is eternal, without properties, and is no more stained by the fruits of action than a lotus is by muddy water. The individual person (*jiva-atman*), on the other hand, whose essence is action is connected to rebirth and liberation (MunU 3.1.1, KaU 5.11).

Objection: You reject the doctrine of "difference and nondifference" and maintain that scripture teaches nondifference and that Brahman has no parts. You say the one highest Atman is the inner essence (atman) of all beings. Why then are there worldly and Vedic injunctions and prohibitions?

[48] Response: Scriptural injunctions and prohibitions are possible because of the association of the Atman with the body, just in the case of light being associated with the fires that burn good and bad things and so forth.

Injunctions and prohibitions are possible because of the erroneous connection of the Atman with limiting adjuncts. No obligations apply to one who has attained the highest goal of perfect knowledge of Brahman, and so the precepts do not apply to them (but they are obligatory for the those who are not liberated). This does not mean that the liberated person can do what he likes: only wrong knowledge of imagining the Atman to be connected to the body impels actions, and that imagination is absent in one with correct knowledge (and so the enlightened have no compunction to act at all).

[49] *Since the individual person does not extend beyond the body, there is no confusion of the results of one person's actions with those of another.*

Objection: Since the Atman is only one, there must be a confusion of the fruits of action from different individual persons (*atmans*).

Response: There is no connection of the highest Atman with bodies, and limiting adjuncts do not extend beyond the individual, and so there is no confusion of actions or their karmic fruit.

[50] *The individual person is only a mere reflection of the highest Atman.*

Individual atmans are merely reflections (*abhasas*) of the highest Atman, and one reflection does not connect to the actions and fruits of another reflection, just as one trembling reflection of the sun in the waves of water does not cause any other reflections to tremble. Thus, there is no confusion of actions and karmic results. And since the reflections are only the imagined result of root-ignorance, rebirth (which is based on the reflections) is also only the imagined effect of root-ignorance — with the removal of that ignorance, the cognition results that the individual atman is in reality nothing but Brahman.

Only those such as the Samkhyas and Vaisheshikas who believe in multiple transcendent souls, all of which are all-pervading, have the problem of a confusion of actions and fruits. If one soul is connected to pain by being embodied in matter, all souls should suffer.

Objection from the Samkhyas: The differences of the fruit of different embodied souls result from differences in the circumstances in each case of the activity of matter aiming for liberation. Otherwise, the activity of matter would serve no purpose.

Response: You have no evidence of such differences.

Objection from the Vaisheshikas: Differences of the fruits for different souls result from each transcendent soul (*purusha*) having its own mind.

Response: Since each such soul is all-pervading, each mind must be connected to all the souls. Thus, there is no difference in causes and thus no difference in effects.

Objection: Then the difference is due to the unseen principle (*adrishta*).

[51] Response: The unseen principle does not allocate karmic results of works to individuals.

According to the Samkhyas, the unseen principle abides in matter and is the same for all souls, and so it cannot be a cause that limits fruits to particular individual souls. For the Vaisheshikas, the principle connects a soul with a mind, but there is no reason to believe that different principles limit their action to different individuals (since each soul is all-pervading).

[52] And the same problem occurs with mental acts such as resolutions to act since the conscious soul for Samkhyas and Vaisheshikas is all-pervading and thus is not limited to the one who resolves.

For Vaisheshikas, resolutions are still made through the non-particular connection of a mind and the soul in proximity to all souls.

[53a] Objection from the Vaisheshikas: *Even though souls are each all-pervasive, there is a distinction of results from the difference of the limited place within each soul where contact is made with a body.*

Although souls are all-pervading, the connection with the mind takes place for different embodied souls in the part of the soul that is limited to the body, and thus results of action remain distinct.

[53b] Response: *Since all individual souls (according to the Vaisheshikas) are each infinite, each would be in all bodies.*

Souls would not be limited to one body. And since souls are without parts, one "part" cannot limit the soul's effect. In general, there are no instances of a plurality of entities occupying the same place.

Opponent: Different properties occupy the same entity, e.g., the color and so forth (of an object).

Response: Properties are nondifferent in that they are all identical to the object in which they belong. In themselves, they have different characteristics, but there is no difference in properties of the different souls.

Chapter 2.4
The Vital Organs

[1] The same arguments concerning space arising from Brahman apply to

the arising of the vital bodily organs (pranas) in a person.[9]

Objection: Scripture conflicts concerning whether the bodily organs were created or not, and so no position can be formed, or the passages suggesting their creation should be taken as figurative since scripture expressly states that the organs existed before the creation of the worlds.

Response: (As was said about space,) the organs arise from the highest Brahman, along with the worlds, gods, and beings (BU 2.1.20, MunU 2.1.3).

[2] The creation of the organs must be accepted because of the impossibility of the scriptural passages about origin having an indirect meaning rather than of a direct, literal meaning.

Passages about the organs' origin must be taken literally. Otherwise they would conflict with the basic assertion that by knowing the highest Atman one knows everything (MunU 1.1.3) — the organs are not separate realities that would not be known by knowing Brahman, but entities arising from the highest Atman (MunU 2.1.3). The statements about the organs existing before the creation of the worlds mean that they existed prior to the effects of the subsequent cause of later things (i.e., the god/lord Hiranyagarbha) and so appear to be uncaused from the later effects' point of view. The passages are not about the organs existing prior to Brahman but about existing in Brahman where there are no distinctions based on name-and-form.

[3] Also because the word "created" is used in its literal sense earlier in scripture. [4] And because the creation of speech along with life-breath and mind is preceded by the creation of the elements from Brahman.

[5] The organs must be seven in number because they go with the person in rebirth and are specified in scripture (MunU 2.1.8).

Passages with other another number of organs refer to modifications.

[6] The hands and so forth are also called "organs," since they assist an individual while the Atman abides in a body, and so the number of organs varies in scripture.

Different functions are referred to in scripture as "organs." Thus, there are eleven organs: five senses, five organs of action (speaking, taking, moving, evacuation, and begetting), and the inner organ that is responsible for desire and so forth. (The chief breath is not an organ.) Other numbers for organs (e.g., seven as two ears, two eyes, two nostrils, and the mouth) are explained.

---

[9] "*Prana*" as the "life-breath" of a person is usually distinguished from the bodily organs (*pranas*), but sometimes is included as the chief *prana*. *Prana* is also sometimes a substitute for Brahman. So too, the material organs are not always clearly distinguished from their function — e.g., the eye and perception.

[7] The organs' functions are infinitesimal in size.

Thus, they are invisible. Nor are they all-pervading, going outside the body.

[8] And Prana (the chief life-breath) is the foremost.

Prana is a product of Brahman, like the other breaths. It is the oldest and most important function in the body (CU 5.1.1) since we could not live without it (BU 6.1.13).

[9] Prana is neither air nor a power of an organ since it is mentioned separately from those.

It is an independent reality within the body, like the atman, and the other organs are subordinate to it. It is not overpowered by death (BU 1.5.21).

[10] But Prana is subordinate to the atman. The organs are like the senses, since they are taught together, and for other reasons. [11] But scripture shows that they are not senses, and so no fault arises here in not calling them "instruments." [12] Scripture teaches that the organs are of five types (BU 1.5.3) like the mind. [13] Prana is infinitesimal in size.

In the body, Prana is invisible and limited in size. Passages in scripture about Prana being all-pervading are about the one universal atman of all the life-breaths (i.e., the organs and their functions).

[14] But scripture also teaches that Agni and other gods guide the organs.

The organs within the body get their power from gods (e.g., Agni [fire] and Vayu [wind]) and are under their guidance.

[15] That organs are connected to the possessor of senses (i.e., a body). [16] This is so also because of the Atman's constant relation to a body.

Although gods guide the organs, scripture teaches that the embodied atman is the lord of the instruments of the body and enjoyer (of their action).

[17] As distinguished from Prana, the organs (indriyas) are designations for the senses and organs of action. [18] This distinction is mentioned in scripture. [19] And the organs are dissimilar in characteristics (from Prana).

The word "breath" literally designates only the chief life-breath but is used secondarily to designate the senses and organs of action. The bodily organs are independent of Prana and different in nature, but they all like the mind arose from Brahman (MunU2.1.3). Prana is not recognized as an organ but belongs to another category. It remains awake when the organs sleep. The staying or departing of Prana, unlike the senses and organs, is the cause of the maintenance or destruction of the body and is not overcome by death. It remains active in deep sleep when the other "breaths" are asleep. Speech depends on Prana. On the other hand, the senses, not Prana, are the cause of the perception of sense-objects.

[20] *But scripture teaches that the creation of conceptions and shapes (i.e., names and forms) is by the maker who made the three types of elements (i.e., water, fire, and earth). [21] According to scripture, the body is created from the earth and from the other two elements (i.e., fire and water) as well.*

The maker is the highest Lord, not the individual atman. The multiple things of this world are names and forms that evolve by the highest Lord (CU 8.14.1) who is also responsible for the tripartite arrangement of things. The living person (*jiva-atman*) is not absolutely different from the highest Lord but is qualified as "living" only because of the limiting adjuncts. It is a matter of the Atman entering the body, not a manifestation of the Atman.

[22] *Because of their distinctive nature, the organs have a distinctive designation.*

Each is a distinctive conglomerate of the three elements.

Book 3
Chapter 1: The Path of Rebirth

[1] *The individual at death passes out of the body still enveloped by the subtle elements to attain another body. This is known from the question and answer in scripture. [2] The individual is not enveloped solely by water since the envelop has three components (i.e., fire, water, and earth), but water alone is mentioned because of its predominance. [3] Because the vital functions go forth with the individual to the next rebirth, as do the other "breaths" (the senses and organs of action) and elements.*

The transmigrating individual atman is accompanied by limiting adjuncts: the chief life-breath, the senses, and the mind. It takes with it root-ignorance, the karmic effects of good and bad actions, and the impressions left by previous lives. The atman is enveloped by the subtle parts of these elements. It leaves one body and obtains another (BU 4.4.1-4).

[4] *Objection: The functions do not go forth because scripture states that they enter such deities as Agni (BU 3.2.13). Response: Such statements are only meant in a figurative sense.*

It is figurative because we never observe such things entering the body — it means only that Agni and the other gods stop their guidance of the functions at death. And the atman could not go at all if we denied the limiting adjuncts to it that are formed by the organs. And without the adjuncts, the atman could not enjoy the fruits of past lives in a new body.

[5] Objection: *Water is not mentioned in the first instance (concerning a ritual and water taking the shape of a man).* Response: *The word "water" must be meant because it is the only word that makes sense.* [6] Objection: *The atman does not depart enveloped in water since that is not stated in scripture.* Response: *It is understood to be so by those who perform the ritual.* [7] *Or alternatively, the statement is figurative because the speakers have not yet come to know the Atman. Scripture declares that.*

[8] *After the karmic effects of good actions that lead to a rebirth in a heaven are exhausted, a person follows the path dictated by other karmic effects to rebirth on earth or elsewhere. This is known through scripture and the traditional texts.* [9] Objection: *The individual gets his rebirth due to ritual conduct, not due to any karmic effect of the past actions.* Response: *According to the teacher Karshnajini, the scriptural passages suggest that the word "action" is used indirectly to indicate all karmic effects.*

Objection: All karmic effects from one's past actions are used up in a heavenly rebirth, and so there is nothing left over to determine a new rebirth after that.

Response: Some residue remains from previous lives. The good effects of performing the ritual sacrifices and so forth led to heaven, and the remaining bad effects survive and lead to being embodied in this world.

[10] Objection: *Unless conduct alone is the cause rebirths rather than their effects, then conduct is valueless.* Response: *Karmic effects are dependent upon that conduct,* [11] *even though the teacher Badari states that nothing but good and bad acts themselves are meant.*

That ritual work and conduct (*karana*) are sometimes spoken of as different is analogous to the distinction sometimes made between Brahmins and a subclass of them.

[12] Objection: *Scripture declares that the path of rebirth is through the moon to heaven even for those who do not perform the sacrifices, and so forth.*

Thus, there is no difference for those who performs the Vedic rituals and for evil-doers.

[13] Response: *But the course declared by scripture is that those who have suffered in the abode of Yama (the god of Death) still have an ascent and descent (from the moon).* [14] *The traditional texts also declare this.*

Those who do not perform the rituals first ascend to the moon, but they do not enjoy a heaven but descend into a hell ruled by Yama.

[15] *In addition, there are seven hells for the evil-doers mentioned in the Puranas.* [16] *Since Yama's control extends over all of them, there is no*

contradiction in texts mentioning different overseers of the hells.

[17] *What is meant in these passages by the "two paths" are the path of knowledge and the path of action, since that was the topic under discussion.*

The path of knowledge (which includes meditative cognition [*vidya*]) is the way of the gods, and the path of action (sacrifices and giving alms) is the way of the fathers. Those who do not follow either path do not reach the moon but are reborn as small animals.

[18] *Going to the moon is seen not to be applicable to a person in a third state other than this ascent and descent from moon. [19] In addition, this is observed in the world as well in the traditional texts. [20] So too, it is seen that some creatures are born without mating, [21] including the third class of animals born from heat.*

There are four classes of living beings: animals that bring forth their young from their bodies, those born from eggs, animals born from heat, and plants sprouting from seeds. The last two are not produced by sexual inter-course and so do not require rituals. Sometimes the last two are spoken of as one class and elsewhere as separate classes, so there is no contradiction in referring to them together as "the third."

[22] *The person descending from the moon attains similarity of nature with space and air. That is justified. [23] Based on the authority of scripture, this descent occurs soon after death.*

The subtle body, which is similar in nature to space and air, descends from the moon to this world, but it does not remain in that form for long. These bodies fall to earth in raindrops and enter rice and so forth.

[24] *Scripture also declares that the descending person before being born enters into what is already ruled by another (i.e., plants), as in earlier stages.*

Persons that do not ascend past the moon descend to earth and become attached to plants that are already animated by atmans. These persons do not become embodied in the plants and do not experience the enjoyments of plant life but are only outwardly connected to the plants — references to them in scripture as "becoming plants" only means that they become "enclosed" in plants. These persons then enter animals through the process of digestion. But some persons become plants as a result of their unholy acts.

[25] *Sacrificing animals is not unclean, as it is stated in scripture.*

Plants do not embody the atmans of those who had sacrificed animals. The Vedas give authority for the sacrifice. The knowledge of which actions are good and which are bad is based entirely on scripture. The sacrifice is an exception to the general precept against harming animals.

[26] Next the person is connected with the one who inseminates, and then [27] from the womb a new body is born.

The *jiva-atman* with its residual karma enters the womb and gains a body in which it can experience the fruits of that residue.

Chapter 3.2: The States of the Atman and Brahman

[1] According to scripture, creation (by the person dreaming) occurs in the dream state between waking and dreamless sleep.

The first question is whether the entities created in dreams are real (*paramarthika*) like the entities of the waking state or merely illusory (*maya*). Dreams are an intermediate state in between the waking world and the world of bliss (i.e., dreamless sleep) (BU 4.3.9).

[2] According to some interpretations of scripture, the Atman is the creator while sons and other desired things are the created.

Opponent: The creations in dreams must be real for scripture declares it (BU 4.3.10). The atman in dreams shapes things of desire (KaU 5.8). It is admitted that the world of our waking state is made by the atman of insight (*prajna*) and so is real. Thus, our dream world is equally real (BU 4.3.14).

[3] Response: *But this creation in the dream state is mere illusion (*maya*) since the true nature of (real) entities is not fully manifested in dreams.*

What is manifested in dreams is a mere illusion without a speck of reality about it. It does not have all the properties of real things of place, time, and materials, and it cannot be refuted in the way things in the waking world can be. For example, there is no room within a dreamer for a chariot. Nor can a dreamer go to a distant place and return in a moment. So too, a dreamer's body remains visible to others while he or she is dreaming of being far away. And in a dream we do not see entities in far off places as they really are. Dreams also conflict with time — at night one may dream it is daytime. Causation does not work for thoughts or actions in a dream. The existence of a dream chariot and horses is refuted in the waking state. Dreams contradict themselves — e.g., men later become trees. Scripture states that dreams are within the body (BU 2.1.18) and that dream entities have no real existence. Any passages suggesting dreams are real must be taken figuratively. Thus, experiences in dreams are mere illusory appearances.

[4] Objection: Scripture and experts in reading dreams state that a dream is also an omen of future events.

Dreams can foretell future good or bad fortune.

Response: What is indicated may be real, but the dream remains unreal. If the creation of chariots literally occurred in dreams, it would be even more difficult to ascertain that the Atman is self-luminous than it is in waking states. Any statements about the creation of chariots must be accepted as figurative to make them agree with the statements about them being unreal. Nor is the highest Atman the shaper of dreams — the individual atman is (BU 4.3.9). But the atman of insight is active in dreams: as the Lord of all, it presides in all states.

We only maintain that the world of dreams is not real in the sense that the waking world is. But then again, the waking world is not absolutely real either. For the entire expanse of things (*prapancha*) is an illusion (as shown in 2.1.14). The waking world remains fixed and distinct up to the moment that the individual cognizes that Brahman is the essence (atman) of all things. The world of dreams, on the other hand, is obliterated daily by the waking state. Thus, the waking world, although itself merely an illusion, is valid until enlightenment and thus is relatively real compared to dreams.

[5] From deep meditation on the highest (Lord), what is covered becomes uncovered, since a person's bondage and liberation are from him.

Objection: The individual atman is like a spark to the fire of the highest Lord (i.e., Brahman with attributes) and thus sharing the highest Lord's knowledge and rulership. Thus, what the person creates in a dream is real.

Response: Even if the Lord and individual atman stand in the relation of whole and part, it appears obvious to perception that their properties are different in nature. Their equality of properties is hidden by the veil of root-ignorance. (And so the individual cannot create realities as the Lord does.) Some persons who meditate with diligence on the Lord and at last dispel their root-ignorance attain through the favor of the Lord extraordinary powers and the insight that makes the hidden equality of properties observable, just as through strong medicine a blind man gains sight. Thus, the properties of the Lord do not become manifest by their own accord in every person. A person falls into rebirth and attains release through the Lord as the cause. Bondage is due to the ignorance of the Lord's true nature, and liberation is due to the knowledge of it. "By knowing God, all fetters fall off. By the destruction of all defilements, birth and death cease. By meditating on him, there is a third state on the dissolution of the body: sovereignty over all, and a state of absolute isolation in which all desires are fulfilled" (SU 1.11).

[6] Or the covering occurs because of the Atman's connection with a body.

Objection: But if the individual atman is part of the highest Atman, why should its knowledge and lordship be hidden? The spark has light and heat.

Response: The state of concealment of the individual atman's knowledge and lordship is due to the Atman being connected to a body, senses, mind, intellect (*buddhi*), sense-objects, sensations, and so forth, like fire still hidden in wood. These limiting adjuncts are made from name-and-form as presented by root-ignorance — its knowledge and lordship remain hidden (*tirobhava*) as long as the individual is possessed by the erroneous notion of not being distinct from those adjuncts.

Objection: So isn't the individual separate from the Lord in this state of the concealment of his knowledge and power?

Response: It is impossible that they are separate (CU 6.3.2). The individual atman is nondifferent from the Lord, but its knowledge and power are obscured by its connection with the body. Thus, the dreaming person is not able to create real chariots and so forth from its wishes. If the person possessed that power, no one would ever have an unpleasant dream. Dreams are equal to the waking state in appearance only because they arise from mental impressions (*vasanas*) received from the waking state.

[7] The atman in the state of dreamless sleep resides in the nerves (nadis) *and in the Atman, as known from scripture.*

The individual atman resides in the nerves, the heart, and in Brahman. "Abiding in Brahman" does not mean that the abode and the one who abides are different — the two are absolutely identical. The two are not sometimes united and sometimes not. But the individual atman in dreamless sleep has entered its true nature. Brahman is the lasting abode of the individual atman in the state of deep sleep. In deep sleep, the limiting adjuncts have ceased, but the individual atman does not cognize that it has become one with Brahman because there is no distinction of a knower and known object. Without any limiting adjuncts, the embodied atman is without cognitions and thus does not recognize that it is one with reality (*sat*, i.e., Brahman). But the ascertainments from deep sleep are that the individual atman is unconnected to the worlds that appear in the waking state and that Brahman is the atman of the individual.

[8] Thus, awakening from dreamless sleep is waking from the highest Atman (BU 2.1.20, CU 6.10.2). [9] But it is the same person who returns from dreamless sleep. This is based on action, memory, scriptural authority, and Vedic injunctions.

Objection: How do we know that the person awakening from oneness with reality (*sat*) is the same one who entered that state? When a drop of water is poured into a large quantity of water, it would be hard to get out the very same drop — how do we know awaking is not like that?

Response: Four reasons. First, the person who awakens completes the ritual of the person from the day before. (If these are different persons, we would not know who earned the fruit, and this goes against the Vedas.) Second, the one who awakens remembers his experiences, not others'. Third, scripture tells us that the same person arises (BU 4.3.16; CU 8.3.2, 6.10.2). Fourth, if someone could become liberated simply by falling asleep, the Vedic injunctions for actions and knowledge would be pointless. If the person who arose after deep sleep was other than the prior person, then that new person either existed earlier in another body — and what is the point of that person awakening in another body? — or he would be someone who attained liberation but somehow found himself back in the realm of root-ignorance again.

Nor does the "drop of water" analogy apply: the water merges completely into the pool of water, but here the individual still has its karmic residues of past action and ignorance (in deep sleep). (Thus, the person still has individuality while the water drop loses all distinctions.) In addition, the individual atman is not different from the highest Atman like the drop of water — Brahman is only figuratively called an "individual atman" because of its connection with limiting adjuncts. The phenomenal existence of the individual atman only lasts as it continues to be bound by such adjuncts. Each set of adjuncts continues through the states of deep sleep and waking; in the former, it is like a seed, and in the latter, it is like a fully developed plant. As long as individual (*jiva-atman*) continues to be connected to a set of adjuncts, we deal with it as if it is different from the Atman. Thus, the proper inference is that the same person awakens from sleep.

[10] *A person who is senseless in a swoon attains only a partial state of sleep, since that is only alternative to the waking and sleeping states.*

This partial state of oneness with reality (*sat*) in partial deep sleep is not considered a fifth state of consciousness.[10]

[11] *Brahman is without a twofold characteristic (*linga*) even in different places because scripture teaches that it is without characteristics everywhere.*

Some passages in scripture suggest that Brahman is affected by differences — "with attributes" such as form and "without attributes" — and thus is dualistic in nature. But the highest Brahman cannot in itself possess double characteristics — it is impossible that the same thing can both possess

---

[10] No altered states of consciousness (e.g., visions) are considered.

characteristics (e.g., color) and not possess them because of the contradiction. So too with Brahman and the limiting adjuncts presented by root-ignorance: an entity having one nature does not have a different characteristic merely by being qualified in connection with limiting adjuncts. A crystal that by its nature is clear does not become red when it is near a red object, even though it will appear that way — that the crystal itself is pervaded by red is entirely erroneous. (It is an illusion to see the crystal itself as red.) This is especially so since the limiting adjuncts are only imagined by root-ignorance. Scripture teaches that Brahman is free of attributes and is changeless — e.g., "The Atman is without sound, touch, form, taste, or smell. It is without beginning or end. It is unchanging and greater than the great one" (KaU 3.15). Thus, when we have to choose between two characteristics, Brahman should be understood as devoid of any attributes and not admitting the alternative.

[12] Objection: *Brahman cannot have only one characteristic since scripture teaches that it has differences.* Response: *Scripture negates each of differences individually.* [13] *Also some schools teach this.*

Objection: Scripture teaches different forms of Brahman — e.g., it has four feet or sixteen parts or is dwarfish or has the three worlds as it body (CU 3.18.1, 1.3.22; Prashna Up. 6.1; KaU 3.1; BU 1.3.22).

Response: These differences result from limiting adjuncts, not Brahman (e.g., BU 2.5.1). There is no diversity in Brahman (BU 4.4.19). Differences are spoken of for the sake of meditation (*upasana*), but showing Brahman's nondifference is the real purpose of scripture.

[14] *Brahman is indeed formless since that is the dominant theme in the Upanishads (e.g., CU 3.8.8, CU 8.14.1, MunU 2.1.2, BU 2.5.19).*

Brahman is unconnected with any world and thus is without form (*arupa*). Those passages indicating that Brahman has form do not aim at setting its nature but aim instead at enjoining the adoration of Brahman (as an object of meditation). Verses can be accepted as long as they do not lead to contradictions, but where there is conflict the aphorisms whose main subject is Brahman being formless must be viewed as having greater force.

[15] *Like light that appears to assume the form of things it contacts, Brahman appears to have different forms. Otherwise, scriptural passages about Brahman having form would be without meaning.*

Just as the light from the sun or moon becomes bent or straight, so to speak, depending on the object it contacts, so Brahman assumes, so to speak, the form of earth or another limiting adjunct that it entered into contact with. Thus, there is no reason that scripture should not teach that Brahman has this or that form for the purpose of meditative adoration. Such passages do not contradict the basic claim that Brahman is formless since the forms are merely due to the limiting adjuncts, not Brahman. The limiting adjuncts are presented by the primordial root-ignorance that leaves room for all practical activities of life, whether religious or nonreligious. But any feature brought out by the adjuncts is not a real attribute of that thing.

[16] *Scripture declares Brahman to be (consciousness) and no more.*

Scripture declares the Brahman consists of consciousness (*chaitanya*) alone and to have no form or other features. The Atman's nature consists of simple nondifferentiated consciousness, just as a lump of salt has the same salty taste inside as well as outside and no other taste.

[17] *Scripture also reveals this, as do the traditional texts.*

For example, "not so, not so" (BU 2.3.6). Brahman is different from the known and is also above the unknown (KeU 1.4). "All speech, along with mind, turns away from it, unable to reach it" (TU 2.9). A now-unknown Upanishad tells of Bahva teaching Brahman to a Brahmin by silence: "He said to him, 'Learn Brahman' and became silent. And after a second and third request (from the student), he replied 'I am teaching you, but you do not understand. Silent is that Atman.'" "The highest Brahman without beginning or end . . . cannot be said either to be or not to be" (BG 13.12). And the god Narayana taught Narada: "Illusion (*maya*) is the cause for you seeing me endowed with the qualities of all beings — but do not know me as being so."

[18] *Illustrations such as the sun's reflection in water are appropriate.*

The Atman is consciousness only (*chaitanya-matra*). It is without any differences and transcends speech and mind. It can be described only by denying that all other characteristics apply. The one luminous sun appears multiple when reflected off multiple waves of water. So too with Brahman: it is one and unchanging and appears multiple only due to limiting adjuncts. The one Atman of all beings abides in all individual beings — it appears as one and as many at the same time, just as the one sun is multiplied by its reflection in different pools of water.

[19] *Objection: There is no similarity and thus no basis for the illustration since there is nothing comparable to the water since Brahman alone is real.*

The sun and the water are two different material objects. Brahman is not a material thing but is present everywhere and everything is nondifferent from it. (Thus, there is no second reality to reflect Brahman.) The limiting adjuncts are not separate from it and occupying a different place. Thus, the cases are not parallel.

[20] Response: *Brahman participates in the increase and decrease of the things it has entered since it abides within those things. Thus, since both the illustration and the point being illustrated have the same features, the illustration is applicable.*

Any analogy is limited. Brahman and the sun/water analogy have one common feature: the unchanging sun's reflected image changes with changes in the water; thus, its image participates in all the features and conditions of the water even though it is unchanging. So too, Brahman's "image" changes with the limiting adjuncts but Brahman itself never changes — it only seems to conform to the limiting adjuncts. Brahman participates, so to speak, in the properties and states of a limiting adjunct within which it abides, but only "so to speak" (*iti*) since Brahman is never modified.

[21] Scripture also declares this.

Scripture declares that the highest Brahman enters the body and other limiting adjuncts (BU 2.5.18, CU 6.3.2).

Question: Is Brahman absolutely one in which the entire apparent plurality of the world vanishes, or is it itself a being that is as multiform as the world? Doesn't Brahman have two characteristics — being (*sat*) and knowledge (*bodha*, or perception, apprehension, thought, sentiency)?

Response: Aphorisms 11-14 refute the claim that Brahman has a plurality of properties. Nor are they meant to show that Brahman is being rather than knowledge (BU 2.4.12). In addition, how could Brahman be the atman of conscious individuals if it were not conscious? So too, it is being (e.g., KaU 6.13). But there is no plurality of characteristics: being, knowledge, and sentiency are all the same. Scripture does not permit us to maintain the Brahman can be characterized as knowledge different from being or as being different from knowledge — otherwise there would be a plurality Brahman's nature, and no being can possess more than one nature. If being is knowledge and knowledge is existence, the two do not exclude each other. (It is like "*satya*" meaning both "reality" and "truth.")

Question: How can the texts represent Brahman as both having form and being without form?

Response: When a text teaches the highest knowledge (i.e., Brahman is without form), passages suggesting form still entail that Brahman is formless; and when a text teaches a form of Brahman, it is only for purposes of devout meditation (not the highest knowledge). Thus, there are two classes of texts — one about Brahman without form and one about Brahman with form.

Objection: The Vedas enjoin the annihilation (*badha*, "subration") of the appearance of the world of duality (*dvaita-prapancha-vilaya*) because it stands in the way of true knowledge of Brahman.

Response: The Upanishads do not enjoin any action toward Brahman but only have knowledge of Brahman as their purpose. And what is the nature of this "annihilation"? It is not literal annihilation of the world, for no person could do that. Or the world would disappear when the first person is enlightened. But if you believe that the phenomenal world is superimposed upon Brahman through root-ignorance, then all we need is knowledge of Brahman (CU 6.2.1, 6.8.7) — the knowledge arising on its own throws aside root-ignorance, and the variety of worldly manifestations arising from names and forms (as realities independent of Brahman) vanishes like images in a dream (but Ishvara's creation remains as it is). Since Brahman is without plurality, cognizing Brahman dissolves the illusory world of plurality at the same time, just as pointing out the true nature of a rope gives rise to the cognition of the true nature of the rope and the dissolution of the appearance of a snake at the same time. And what is done once need not be done again.

Question: Does the individual (*jiva-atman*) upon whom the injunction to know Brahman is laid belong to the phenomenal world or to the real element (Brahman) that underlies the phenomenal world? If the former, the individual is dissolved when Brahman knowledge arises. If the latter, the individual is unreal and so there is no reality toward which the injunctions are directed. So who, acting upon injunctions, attains final liberation?

Response: The same result occurs either way. Once it is realized that Brahman is the true being of the individual and that the individual is an illusion due only to root-ignorance, there remains no being upon whom injunctions could be laid and so no room for injunctions.

Question: Why then are there injunctions to know Brahman?

Response: The injunctions are not to enjoin knowledge but only to direct attention toward the reality (*tattva*), like "Listen to this!" in ordinary life only directs attention. Even when one is face to face with an object of knowledge, knowledge may not arise, and all another person can do is point it out. True knowledge (unlike actions) cannot be brought about by injunctions since it does not depend upon the will of a person but only on what really and unalterably exists and the valid means of knowledge. The Vedic texts concerning Brahman aim at knowledge, not injunctions (which concern actions). Dissolving the entire phenomenal world and valuing part of the world (as injunctions require) cannot go together, and so the two classes of texts must be distinguished. So too, the injunctions are not uniform but differ concerning Brahman with attributes and Brahman without them.

[22] Scripture indeed denies the limitation of the forms of Brahman and then speaks of something more.

"There are two forms of Brahman: one embodied and one unembodied; one mortal and one immortal; one stationary and one moving; one is what is real here and one is what is real other than that" (BU 2.3.1). The text then goes on to state "not so, not so" (BU 2.3.6) (to deny all phenomenal forms and properties to Brahman), and there is nothing higher to say than this.

Objection: The context of this passage means that both forms of Brahman and also Brahman itself — the possessor of the forms — are all three negated. Or Brahman has two aspects and both are denied as beyond speech and the mind and so cannot be conceived but must be denied while the phenomenal forms are perceptible and so not to be denied.

Response: All three are not negated for that would leave only the nihilistic emptiness of the Buddhist Shunyavadins. Whenever the reality of something is denied, it is always with respect to something real — e.g., the unreal snake is negated with reference to the real rope. A denial is possible only if something real is left. If everything is denied and no reality is left, the denial of the entity intended to be negated is rendered impossible and that entity becomes the reality that cannot be denied. In addition, scripture affirms the existence of Brahman (BU 2.1.1, TU 2.6, KaU 6.13) and cannot be overridden. Its denial would stultify all the Vedas. That Brahman transcends all speech and thought clearly does not mean it does not exist. It cannot be supposed that after the Vedas establish Brahman's existence that they teach his nonexistence. Thus, texts on Brahman's transcendence of speech and thought (TU 2.4.1) must be viewed as implying its existence.

Thus, "Not so! Not so!" means this: Brahman's nature is eternal, pure, conscious, and free. It transcends speech and thought and so does not fall within the category of an "object." It constitutes the inner atman of all things. Scripture denies all plurality of forms to Brahman but leaves Brahman itself untouched. All material and immaterial forms are denied. The second form of Brahman as the Lord and the first form as propertyless are both phenomenal and denied. (Thus, *nirguna* Brahman is also treated as a form arising from root-ignorance.) The second form is characterized by mental impressions and forms the quintessence of what is immaterial; it is denoted by the term "person" (*purusha*) and rests on the subtle Atman (*linga-atman*). Brahman is qualified by forms (by the unenlightened), and so we speak of the "forms of

Brahman." However, "Not so! Not so!" negates the entire aggregate of effects superimposed upon Brahman by root-ignorance, but it does not negate the root (*mula*) of these imagined constructs (*kalpanas*) — Brahman-in-itself. Thus, whatever is thought cannot be Brahman. Effects have no real existence and so can be negated. But Brahman cannot be negated since it is the basis for all erroneous superimposition. In sum, scripture denies the reality of all phenomenal entities superimposed on Brahman-in-itself and leaves Brahman-in-itself untouched. And there is no reality beyond Brahman (BU 2.3.6).

Objection: How can scripture negate the two forms after affirming them? After all, it is better not to touch dirt in the first place than to wash it off after touching it.

Response: Scripture does not set forth the two forms as something real. It only mentions them since they are things mentioned in the sphere of ordinary thought that are falsely attributed to Brahman in order to negate them and thereby establish the true nature of formless Brahman.

The text negates only the plurality that is falsely superimposed on Brahman but leaves Brahman-in-itself untouched. The first "Not so!" may be negating the material and the second the mental, or it may be the totality of elements and impressions. Thus, all things phenomenal are negated but not Brahman itself. If the negations were meant to negate everything whatsoever and to end in complete nonexistence, the text would not next say that there is nothing beyond or separate from Brahman. In sum, "Not so! Not so!" does not mean that Brahman does not exist. The text instead means that there is no teaching concerning Brahman higher than the negations of plurality to "the Real of the real" (BU 2.1.20). That again does not negate everything but leaves Brahman.

[23] Scripture also states that Brahman is not observable.

Because Brahman is not observable in the world, it cannot be apprehended by the senses (MunU 1.1.6, 3.1.8; BU 3.9.26; TU 2.7). It is in fact the witness (the subject) in any apprehension. Traditional texts also state that Brahman is unobservable, unchanging, and not fathomable by thought. (But it can be experienced in meditation [above v. 1.3.13].)

[24] In addition, Brahman is realized by the complete meditative concentration of the mind, as is known by both scripture and traditional texts.

Yogins in a complete meditative concentration of mind (*samadhi*) see the unmanifested Brahman free from all plurality. This is a presentation before the mind (of Brahman) that is brought about through meditative adoration. This is supported by scripture: "The self-born pierced the openings of the body outward. Thus, one looks outward and not inward into oneself. But a certain wise man, seeking the eternal life, turned his sight inward and saw the atman within" (KaU 4.1); "The partless one is not grasped by sight, speech, or any other sense faculty. Nor by austerities or rituals. But by the light of knowledge when one's being is clear, it is seen by one meditating" (MunU 3.1.8) Traditional texts also support this: "He is seen as light by yogins meditating upon him sleeplessly with controlled senses."

Objection: This involves a duality of an individual (the *jiva-atman*) knowing a higher Atman.

[25] Response: *The shining one (i.e., the Atman) during activity appears dual, like light appears diffuse from the objects illuminated, yet according to repeated declarations in scripture it is not differentiated (avaisheya).*

Light appears diffuse through the objects it illuminates, but it is really nondifferentiated and the apparent plurality is due only to limiting adjuncts supplied by root-ignorance. So too with the distinction of atmans due to limiting adjuncts while all atmans and the Atman are not different.

[26] *Thus, the individual person enters into oneness with the nonfinite (ananta), as scripture indicates.*

The nondifference of all atmans (from each other and from Brahman) is natural — their (apparent) difference is due only to root-ignorance. After dispelling such ignorance, the individual atman passes over into oneness with the highest Atman (MunU 3.2.9, BU 4.4.6).

[27] Objection: *Both difference and nondifference (between Brahman and the individual person or the world as taught in the* Bheda-abheda *school) are mentioned.* Response: *It is like the relation between a snake and its coils.*

Scripture does refer to the highest Atman and the individual atman as distinct entities (e.g., MunU 3.1.8, 3.2.8; BU 3.7.15), but it also refers to them as not different (e.g., CU 6.8.7; BU 1.4.10, 3.4.1, 3.7.15). To accept the latter would render the former useless. But it is analogous to a snake and its coils: viewed as a whole, the snake is one and nondifferentiated, but an element of difference appears when we look at its parts.

[28] *Or it is like the relation of light to its source — both are luminous.*

The sun and its light are not different and yet we speak of them so.

[29] *Or else, the relation between Brahman and the individual person has already be given earlier in aphorism 25.*

Only if bondage is due to root-ignorance is liberation possible. If the individual atman were really independent of the highest Atman, on the

analogies of the snake and its coils or the sun and its light, then (its separation from that reality could not be overcome, and thus) its bondage in the
cycle of rebirths would be real and could not be overcome.

Nor does scripture teach "difference and nondifference" as equally valid.
Scripture aims at establishing nondifference and merely presents "difference"
when presenting something else as something known from other sources of
knowledge such as perception (within the dream). "Difference" is only a
matter of what is conventionally recognized, and so there actually is no
difference as in the cases of the snake and the sun.

[30] *And because of the denial of difference given in scripture.*

For example, "there is no other seer but he" (BU 3.7.23). And this follows
from the denial of the existence of the world apart from Brahman.

[31] Objection: *There must be some reality superior to Brahman since
scripture mentions a bridge, limitation, connection, and difference (e.g., CU
8.4.1-2, 6.8.1; BU 4.3.21). [32]* Response: *The Atman is referred as a bridge and
so forth because of the similarity between speaking of ordinary crossings and
attaining Brahman.*

Nothing deserves to be accepted as existing separately from Brahman
because no means of proof for such a reality is specified (in the Vedas). Nor
does the Vedic claim that Brahman is a "bridge" warrant positing such a
reality. All that is connected is the ordinary individual and world with
Brahman. Attaining Brahman is like "passing a test," not going beyond it —
no further reality is involved. We have already established that all things that
have a beginning spring from, subsist through, and return into Brahman, and
that effects are not different from their cause. Nor can anything not have a
beginning and exist apart from Brahman since scripture affirms that only
being existed in the beginning, one without a second and that through
knowing Brahman all things are known.

[33] *So too, Brahman is described as having four quarters for the sake of
making it easier to grasp by the intellect (*buddhi*) in meditation. [34] So too
statements about connection and difference are made concerning particular
places (from the point of view of limiting adjuncts), as in the case of light
illuminating an object and so forth. [35] Also because this position is justified.*

Sunlight is said to be differentiated because of limiting adjuncts (i.e., the
objects it illuminates), and when the adjuncts are removed it is said to be
united with its source. The connection of the individual atman to the highest
Atman is the only connection possible since it is the Atman's own nature and
thus is imperishable. It is like no other connection and can only be explained

by the Atman's true nature being obscured due to root-ignorance. So too for any differences spoken of in scripture since it declares there is only one Lord — the highest Atman.

[36] So too from the denial of the reality of everything else.

Scripture denies that anything exits besides Brahman (e.g., CU 7.25.1-2). No other essence (atman) is inside the highest Atman.

[37] Thereby, the all-pervasiveness of the Brahman is established in accordance with scriptural statements about its extent and so forth.

It is established that the highest Atman pervades all the world. Passages about "connections" are not to be taken literally to suggest plurality of realities or limitations of Brahman. Traditional texts concur.

[38] From the Lord of the universe comes the karmic fruit of action since this position is justified and [39] also because that is declared by scripture (BU 4.4.24).

The distinction between ruler and the ruled is discerned during conventional existence, but Brahman is both. The fruit of action springs from the Lord, not from the actions themselves. He alone is capable of effecting the proper results since the actions themselves pass away as soon as they are done and thus have no power to bring about results at a future time since nothing can spring from nothing. Nor can a principle that is supposedly the result of the action bring about the fruit in the future since any such principle is nonconscious and can act only if moved by a conscious being.

[40] Objection: *For those reasons from scripture, Jaimini asserts that ritual conduct itself is what produces the positive fruits of actions.*

The sacrifice itself must bring about the result through a principle that connects action with a result, or otherwise the scriptural injunctions have no object. So too, one uniform cause cannot account for the great variety of effects. And if the Lord were the cause, then he would be responsible for partiality and cruelty. In addition, if the act itself did not bring about the result, it would useless to perform it at all.

[41] Response: *But Badarayana asserts that the earlier one* (purvam, *i.e., the Lord) bestows the fruits of actions since he is mentioned as the cause of the fruits.*

The Lord brings about the fruit, acting with a view to the deed done by the person, or, if you prefer, with a view to a principle springing from the deed. The Lord is the giver of fruits (BG 7.21-22) and the causal agent making one do good and evil acts (KauS 3.8). The Lord is the only cause of all creation, and he creates creatures in forms and conditions according to (the merits of) their former actions since the Lord acts by taking into account the efforts made by creatures.

Chapter 3.3: Cognitions (Vidyas) of Brahman

*[1] What is understood (*vijnana*) by all Vedantic texts is identical since there can be no difference in the injunctions and so forth.*

Objection: If Brahman is free of all distinctions, it is pointless to ask whether all cognitions of Brahman (i.e., meditations or their results) are separate or are only one cognition. If the cognitions were different, then only one cognition could be correct.

Response: The discussion of difference and nondifference of cognitions relates to Brahman with attributes, Prana, and so forth. Like ritual actions, meditations (*upasanas*) have seen and unseen results, and some must lead by stages to perfect knowledge and liberation. The cognitions are determined by the objects mediated upon. Scripture teaches that ritual actions have various results, but the Vedas declare all cognitions (of the same meditative object) to be identical.

[2] Objection: Meditative knowledge is not all the same because of the difference (in meditative practices). Response: There may be differences (in practices) for even the same (cognition). [3] For example, different ritual practices. Restrictions are analogous to various offerings.

Secondary matters account for differences, but the cognition is the same. Different sacrifices and meditative practices do not change the actual knowledge.

[4] And scripture declares that Brahman knowledge is one. [5] Meditative knowledge of Brahman being one and the same, all the properties from different practices should be combined because of the unity of purpose, like the subsidiary practices of an injunction. [6] Objection: The cognition is different in the Brihadaranyaka and the Chandogya Upanishads because the authoritative texts are different. Response: The resulting knowledge is not different.

If cognitions of Brahman were different, the Vedas would restrict them to each cognition.

[7] There is difference here due to the difference in subject-matter — one subject is "great" and the other is the "greater than great."

One subject is OM and the other is life-breath. Features of two different cognitions are not to be combined.

[8] Objection: Yet the names are the same. Response: That has already

been explained. And the same name is found where the practices are different.
[9] And since meditating on Brahman pervades all Vedic practices, this
differentiation of different practices is appropriate.

For example, meditation on "OM" is part of more general practices.

[10] Since all knowledge of Prana is nondifferent, these characteristics
found in one place can be asserted elsewhere.

Properties mentioned in one text for purposes of meditation (*dhyana*)
can be inserted in other texts where nothing is said about them. Properties
belonging to the same subject have to be combined wherever that subject is
referred to even if they may be expressed in only one place.

[11] Bliss and other properties of the principal subject (Brahman) are to be
combined in all mentions of Brahman.

Properties from different passages such as being bliss, a single mass of
knowledge, all-pervading, and the atman of all things are to be combined
whenever Brahman is spoken of.

[12] But some properties, such as joy being the head of the Atman, are not
to be added everywhere since they vary and their increase and decrease occur
only in the realm of differentiations.

Properties that can be distinguished by degree belong to the qualified
Brahman, not to the highest Brahman that is above all qualifications. Different characteristics are not to be added to meditations that differ in context.

[13] But other properties apply in all contexts since their purpose is the
same in every context.

Such properties as bliss are mentioned concerning the nature of
Brahman for the attainment of knowledge of Brahman, not meditation.

[14] Properties mentioned in Katha Upanishad 3.10-11 and elsewhere are
for the purpose of deep meditation on the Atman. They have no other purpose.

"Sense-objects are higher than the senses; the mind is higher than sense-
objects; the intellect (*buddhi*) is higher than the mind; the great one (*mahat*
in Samkhya theory) is higher than the intellect. Higher than the great one is
the unmanifest (*avyakta*); higher than the unmanifest is the Person (*purusha*,
i.e., the atman); nothing whatsoever is higher than the Person. That is the
goal, the highest state" (KaU 3.10-11). This teaches that the Atman is higher
than anything for purposes of knowledge. The next aphorism states that the
Atman is hidden in all beings. The other items are listed only for the purpose
of contemplating the Atman. "Deep meditation" means that meditation is an
antecedent means for realizing reality — it is not an end in itself.

[15] This is so because of the use of the word "Atman" in Katha 3.12.

The enumeration of the senses and so forth is for the realization of the Atman. "This Atman is hidden in all beings and does not shine forth. But it can be seen by keen people with a superior and sharp intellect" (KaU 3.12). Thus, the Person is hard to know but is reached only with a purified mind. Meditation on the Atman is prescribed: "a wise man should merge his speech into his mind, merge his mind into the atman of knowledge (*jnana*), merge that atman into the great one (*mahat*), and merge the great one into the tranquil Atman" (KaU 1.13). Speech here means all the sense-organs. The main purpose of scripture is realizing the highest Atman and nothing else.

[16] The word "atman" in the Aitareya Aranyaka 2.4.1 is to be understood as referring to the highest Atman, as in the other texts about creation, because of the subsequent specifications. [17] Objection: From the context of the passage as a whole, the Atman is not meant. Response: There is the clear statement that only the Atman existed in the beginning.

[18] Since the ritual of rinsing the mouth is mentioned as a recognized duty in one context, it can occur in another context in connection to a new injunction (i.e., to meditate on the vital organs).

In the passages in question, the rinsing of the mouth is enjoined in the ritual and only the cognition that water is the dress of the organs.

[19] And the cognitions are the same since the object of meditation is not different (i.e., Brahman).

The object of meditation constitutes the character of the meditation, and as long as there is no difference in character there, no difference in the cognitions can be established. The particulars of different passages about the same cognition have to be combined into one whole.

[20] The meditative cognitions are the same because of the connection in different contexts of the same reality in meditation.

The secret names (*upanishads*) may be different, but they apply to the same reality (*satya*), i.e., Brahman (BU 5.5).

[21] Or the secret names are different because of the differences of the objects that are meditated upon (e.g., Brahman located the sun or in the eye). [22] Scripture also declares that.

Different properties for qualified Brahman may lead to different names.

[23] For the same reason, different properties of Brahman such as possession of the sole power of support or pervading the heavens are not to be combined with other meditations. [24] So too, the properties of "knowledge of the Cosmic Person" meditations of the Chandogya Upanishad are not to be combined in the meditation of the same name in the Taittiriya Upanishad

because they have not been recited in other schools. [25] The "piercing the heart" meditation and so forth are not to be combined with other meditations because they have different purposes.

[26] When shaking off good and bad karmic acts (by the enlightened) is mentioned, that (the unenlightened) receive good and bad karmic effects is also implied since it is connected with the related term, as in the case of related ritual terms. This has been stated by Jaimini.

[27] At the time of departing from the body by the enlightened at death, all action is left behind since there remains nothing to be attained. Followers of other schools also declare this doctrine.

When a man with knowledge of Brahman has departed his body and is about to reach Brahman, there is nothing to be reached through deeds. The karmic results of all good and evil deeds are contrary to the result of knowledge of Brahman and are destroyed by the power of that knowledge. The enlightened are delivered from all their deeds.

[28] And since there can be no contradiction between two texts concerning cause and effect, the destruction of all karma, good and bad, must be by voluntary practices.

The destruction of all karma must occur while the enlightened are still embodied and thus have the means to destroy it by self-restraint, regulated conduct, pursuit of knowledge, and so forth while they were on the path.

[29] The two paths of a person at death differ: the unenlightened travel one path to the world of the gods, and the enlightened travel the other. Otherwise, there would be a contradiction in scripture.

The enlightened at death do not travel anywhere — being free of desire, they are not moving at all. The highest oneness with Brahman (MunU 3.1.3) is not reached by transporting a person to another location.

[30] This position on a twofold path is justified because indications of the difference are met with (in scripture), as well as in the world.

The first path has nothing to do with perfect knowledge of the unquali-fied Brahman. Those who have risen to the realization of the Atman's oneness, all wishes have been fulfilled and all potentiality of suffering has ended. They have nothing to expect except the dissolution of the body, which is the abode of actions and the enjoyment of prior deeds. There would be no point in traveling the path of the gods (see BG 8.26).

[31] The journey of unenlightened individuals along the path of the gods is not restricted by any form of meditation. This involves no contradiction since it is known in both scripture and traditional texts.

Meditative cognitions of the qualified Brahman lead to the path of the gods and is not restricted to only some forms of meditation (CU 5.10.1). The path cannot be attained by faith and austerities alone, unaided by knowledge (i.e., meditation); thus, "faith and austerities" must also indicate meditations. But all of these cognitions are the same, and so cognitions are not limited to only the type of cognition actually mentioned in a given passage.

[32] *For people with a special assignment to be accomplished in this world, the cycle of rebirths continues as long as the mission requires it.*

Even those who have knowledge of Brahman may be reborn (by order of the Lord for a special mission), but in all cases they will reach liberation from rebirths once their assignment is completed.

Some sages (*rishis*) have succumbed to the lure of worldly powers (*siddhis*) resulting from cognitions, but later when they become aware that such powers decay they turn from them and fix their minds on knowledge of the highest Atman and attain liberation. At the dissolution at the end of a world-cycle, those with knowledge (of qualified Brahman) with purified minds enter into the state of liberation with the highest Atman.

But the effect of knowledge of Brahman is an immediate experience (BU 3.4.1). Being immediate, there can be no doubt of missing its fruit. Fruit of actions is not immediate. "You are that" (CU 6.8.7) cannot be construed to mean that you will *become* "that" (i.e., Brahman) after death. Becoming identical with Brahman occurs immediately with the rise of perfect illumination. Thus, liberation (*moksha*) is inevitable for one who knows.

[33] *But conceptions of the imperishable (BU 2.8.8) (expressed negatively) must be included in all meditative practices (just as must those conceptions expressed positively) because of the similarity of its defining nature and because the object of meditation is the same in all practices. It is just as with the mantras of the Upasad sacrifice, as has already been stated by Jaimini.* [34] *The conceptions are the same in different Upanishads despite differences in wording because of the mention of the same limit in the different passages.*

This is so even if the conceptions must (ultimately) be denied.

There is no difference between the highest Atman and the inner atman, and so there are no difference in the cognitions — all cognitions of the Atman are identical. The reference to a *jiva-atman* is made, not to refer to a different entity, but to speak of the person being identical to the Atman.

[35] *Thus, one's own essence (atman) is the innermost essence of all beings since the aggregate of all elements has one essence hidden in it.*

"He is the one god (*deva*), hidden in all beings, pervading all the world, the inner atman (*antar-atma*) of all beings" (SU 6.11). Texts that declare the Atman to be within everything must be construed as presenting the same knowledge. (And so all cognitions of an atman are the same.)

[36] Objection: Unless the conceptions are different, the scriptural passages cannot be justified. Response: There are different instructions leading to the same knowledge.

Both texts declare the highest Atman (*sva-atman*) to be within all things, and thus there must be only one cognition. Two atmans cannot be the innermost atman in the same body. Only one atman can be within every-thing. In the body, the element of water is inside the element of earth, and the element of fire inside the element of water, and so on, but each is the innermost only in a relative sense (i.e., relative to one body), not literally the innermost atman of everything. And since the entity to be known is one, the cognition is also only one.

[37] There is reciprocity between conceptions in different meditations since practitioners of different meditations clearly recite so in the case of other properties, [38] since the same truth/reality and so forth is in all cognitions.

Scripture specifies a reciprocal relation between the transmigrating *jiva-atman* and the Atman only for purposes of meditation. In fact, they are identical. There is only one knowledge of the truth/reality (*satya*), not two. Thus, the oneness of cognitions on it is well established.

[39] Effective desires (satya-kamas) and other properties are to be combined in other practices and vice versa because the abode of the properties and so forth are the same.

Again, the knowledge is the same despite differences in the passages.

[40] Because of the respect given to it in scripture, the Agnihotra ritual cannot be omitted. [41] It is to be performed from the food that is present, since scripture declares it. [42] There is no restriction about that (i.e., that medita-tions must be connected to rituals) since the ritual is seen in scripture that there is separate fruit from the rituals and from meditation. Thus, meditation does not hinder the rituals.

Meditation on the ritual is not part of the ritual. But meditations are actions and thus subject to injunctions, and special results may be enjoined for those meditations based on sacrificial acts.

[43] This is so for offerings to the gods. That has been stated by Jaimini.

In the scripture Agni and Vayu are taught separately, and so they are separate objects of meditation that should be meditated upon separately.

[44] Because of the abundance of characteristic marks (lingas), such an

indication is more powerful for establishing a meaning than the context of a discussion of a ritual. This also has been stated by Jaimini. [45] But because of context, mental fires are an alternative to ritual fires. They constitute a ritual (karma) like the mental imaginary drinking of Soma. [46] And this position is supported by the extended similarities seen between the mind and fire. [47] But mental fires indeed constitute a cognition (vidya) as is seen from scripture [48] and in the indicating marks in aphorism 44. [49] Because of the greater authority of express statements in scripture, this cannot be refuted.

[50] The mental fires are independent of the ritual fires because they are connected with the mind and for other reasons, in the same way that other cognitions are separate. And it is also seen as another instance of a withdrawal from general matters. This too has been stated by Jaimini. [51] The mental fires are not connected to the ritual fires even on the grounds of similarity, for they are learned only on the grounds of scripture, and they serve a different function at the time of death. Nor does the world become fire based on some similarities to fire. [52] And from the subsequent Brahmana text, it follows that scripture has an injunction to meditate in view, and the connection of fire occurs because of the abundance of parallels to fire in the mental state.

[53] Materialists' (Lokayatikas) objection: *We deny the existence of an atman independent of the body — the atman exists (only) where the body does.*

Response: If there were no atman different from the body, liberation would not be possible, and Vedic injunctions would have no purpose. Nor could Brahman be one's atman. When a statement of a refutation comes after stating a doubt, it gives the firm conviction like driving a spike (into firm ground rather than sand).

Materialists' objection: The atman is in the body and consciousness (*chaitanya*) only appears when material elements are shaped into the form of a body enabling it to emerge. Consciousness is analogous to intoxication (in that both occur only when certain material elements are mixed in a special way). In sum, man is only a material body qualified by consciousness. No immaterial self (atman) exists independently of the body that could go to a heaven or attain liberation. Since consciousness does not appear anywhere except in a body, we must conclude that it is only a property of the body, just as light and heat are properties only of fire. Nor can the body be proven to be the "abode" of an independent self. Thus, life, activity, consciousness, memory, and so forth are not properties of a (separate) self but only of the material body. Therefore, the self is not different from the body.

[54] Response: *There is a distinction between the atman and the body*

because consciousness may not exist when the body does, as with attaining
Brahman (in a state beyond the body).

The body may exist when the properties of the atman (i.e., consciousness, bliss, and so forth) are not present. Life does not exist in death, but the
body continues to exist. The properties of the body can be observed by
others, but not the properties of the atman such as consciousness and
memory. We can ascertain those properties when the body exists, but we
cannot ascertain their nonexistence when the body does not exist — at death
it is possible that these properties may pass over into another body.

Materialists must also explain the nature of a consciousness arising from
(nonconscious) material elements alone. If consciousness were a property of
matter, it would be contradictory to say that consciousness could be aware
of those elements since nothing can act on itself any more than fire can burn
itself or an acrobat can stand on his own shoulders. One property of matter
does not make another (e.g., form does not make color), but you say the
elements are made into objects of the senses by consciousness.

Thus, we must admit that perceptive consciousness is separate from the
elements and their products. And as consciousness constitutes the nature of
our atman, it follows that the atman must be distinct from the body. That
consciousness is permanent follows from the uniformity of its nature and
from the fact that the atman recognizes itself as a conscious agent — a
recognition expressed in judgments such as "I saw this" — and from memory
and so forth. In addition, perception takes place only where there are certain
auxiliaries such as lamps without making perception a property of the lamp.
By analogy, that perception only occurs where there is a body does not mean
that it is a property of the body. Nor is the body always needed as an auxiliary
since dreaming occurs when the body is motionless.

[55] The meditations connected with the limbs of rituals are not confined
to particular Vedic schools but are applicable in all the schools of the Vedas,
[56] as in the case of mantras and so forth. Thus, there is no contradiction.

Cognitions from these meditations are valid everywhere.

[57] Meditation on the abundance of reality is superior to meditation on
lesser objects, just as with sacrifices. So scripture declares.

[58] The meditations differ because of differences in words, and so forth.

Even when the object of cognition is the same (e.g., the Lord or Prana),
the cognitions are considered different because of differences in the words
employed in the injunctions to mediate— e.g., "he meditates" or "let him
meditate" — that cannot be combined. "And so forth" means that attributes

of the meditative object and other things make a difference in the cognition.

[59] There are options to choose among meditations because they are indistinguishable in their results.

There must be a choice between meditations, not a combination. Each meditation has the same fruit: the realization of the object meditated upon — the Lord. Once the Lord has been realized through one meditation, a second meditation would be purposeless. In addition, combining different meditations into one would not produce the realization but would only cause one's attention to be confused. That the fruit of a cognition is to be brought about through realization is declared by scripture (CU 3.14.4, BU 4.1.3) and traditional texts (BG 8.6). One thus has to select one meditation and remain fixed upon it until through a realization the fruit of the cognition is obtained.

[60] But meditations connected to fulfilling worldly desires may be combined or not, as one wishes, because they have distinguishable results.

[61] Mimamsa objection: Meditations connected to the parts of rituals are as important as the parts themselves. [62] The meditations can be combined also because they are enjoined by scripture. [63] And because some meditations rectify deficiencies in other meditations, just as some rituals rectify deficiencies in other rituals. [64] And also because scripture declares a property of cognition to be common to all the Vedas.

The abodes of the meditations (i.e., different parts of the rituals) go together, and so the meditations abiding in them should also be combined.

[65] Response: The meditations connected to parts of a ritual are not to be combined because scripture does not mention this [66] and in fact declares the opposite.

The parts of the rituals go together to serve the sacrifice, while the meditations on the ritual, although resting on the parts of the ritual, serve man. No direct scriptural declaration can be constructed from putting various meditations together. Nor are meditations caused by what they rest upon, and thus that the meditations are founded upon the parts of rituals does not mean that they too must be combined. And there are no direct scriptural declarations for the need to combine meditations. In fact, scripture declares that meditations should not be combined (CU 4.17.10). But, according to one's choice, these meditations may either be collectively or separately.

Chapter 3.4: Injunctions and Knowledge of Brahman

Introduction. Is the knowledge (*vidya*) of the Atman that is derived from the

Upanishads connected with ritual work, or is it a means independent of rituals to accomplish the highest goal of man (*purusha-artha*)?

[1] Badarayana says that scripture states that the goal of man (i.e., liberation from rebirth) is achieved by knowledge of the Atman.

Badarayana claims that only through the knowledge from the Vedantic texts is the purpose of man achieved. (Its fruit is separate from the fruit attained through the ritual.) This is based on scripture (CU 3.4.1, 8.7.1; MunU 3.2.9; TU 2.1; BU 4.5.6-15).

[2] Mimamsa objection: *But Jaimini claims that since knowledge is subordinate to ritual action, statements about the fruit of knowledge of the Atman are merely for the praise of the person acting in the ritual, as in other cases of praise.*

Knowledge of the Atman cannot produce any results in this world. It only supports the action of ritual sacrifices that does produce such results. Passages that appear to suggest that knowledge does produce fruits actually are only praise of it as an instrument supporting ritual action.

Response: Scripture does not state that knowledge of the Atman is connected to rituals through the agent of the sacrifice.

Objection: Knowledge of the inner atman enters into ritual action through the meditation of the officiating priest.

Response: Such knowledge of Brahman is different than the body cannot be employed in a ritual.

Objection: According to the Vedas, no activity for works that manifest their fruit after the death of the body would be possible without knowledge of an atman separate from the body. Knowledge of an atman that is distinct from the body is of no use in this world except in the ritual.

Response: The Upanishads refer to an atman that is free of stain, and that is the Atman that stands outside the cycle of rebirths and therefore is not to any worldly activity.

Objection: The Upanishads teach that the object of knowledge is the transmigrating individual person (BU 2.4.5). Properties such as "free of stain" aim only to praise the Atman. But the Upanishads teach that Brahman, the cause of the world, constitutes the reality of the transmigrating person.

Response: True, but to establish that, objections have been refuted concerning the question of the fruit of knowledge of the Atman.

[3] Mimamsa objection: *Our position is confirmed by the actions of the enlightened (connected to rituals) in scripture (BU 3.1.1, CU 5.11.5). [4] Also because scripture declares that (liberation is not attained by knowledge alone)*

(CU 1.1.10), [5] the knowledge and religious action work together (BU 4.4.2), [6] scripture enjoins rituals for one who has Vedic knowledge (CU 8.15.1), [7] and because of the restrictive rules in the texts (IU 2).

If liberation can be achieved only by knowledge, why are their accounts of the enlightened fulfilling holder duties requiring strenuous effort?

[8] Response: But scripture teaches that there is one greater than the individual agent of the ritual (i.e., Brahman, the Lord). Thus, Badarayana's position stands as it is, for this is revealed in scripture.

The transmigrating embodied atman is the actor and enjoyer of the karmic fruits of actions. What Vedantic texts teach as the object of knowledge is something different from the embodied atman: the non-transmigrating Lord who is free of all properties of the transmigrating person (e.g., agency) and free of stain — the highest Atman. Knowledge of that does not promote action but undercuts all action (see aphorism 16 below). The Lord is superior to the embodied atman (MunU 1.1.9, TU 2.8, KaU 6.2, BU 3.8.9, CU 6.2.3). There are passages that refer to the embodied atman as the object of knowledge, but they are complemented with passages about the Lord being the object of knowledge. This means that the texts do not teach the two selves as being completely different, and so there is no contradictions — the atman of the Lord is the real nature of the embodied atman (CU 6.8.7, BU 3.8.11). The state of being embodied is due only to limiting adjuncts.

[9] There are scriptural declarations equally supporting our position (contra aphorism 3).

There are scriptural passages of equal weight stating that knowledge is not complementary to action (e.g., BU 3.5.1, 4.5.15). Texts may declare that a cognition of Brahman as limited by adjuncts is accomplished by deeds, but the knowledge nevertheless is not subordinated to those deeds.

[10] The scriptural declaration (supporting aphorism 4) is not universally applicable.

The passage does not refer to all knowledge but only to a ritual.

[11] Knowledge and religious actions are to be divided like dividing one hundred coins into two lots (contra aphorism 5). [12] Religious actions are for one who has merely read and recited the Vedas (contra aphorism 6).

Knowledge of the Atman has an independent purpose and is not merely a means to generate competence for performing ritual deeds.

[13] And the restrictive rules do not apply to the enlightened since the restrictions do not explicitly say so (contra aphorism 7). [14] Rather, the consent for the enlightened to perform religious acts is for the praise of knowl-

edge (contra aphorism 2). [15] And some refrain from performing religious acts.

The meaning of the complete passage is that to a knower of Brahman, no deed will cling (i.e., produce a karmic effect) because of that knowledge, even if he performed religious deeds his whole life. Some who have realized the fruit of the knowledge of Brahman express the uselessness of the means to any other fruit (such as rituals, and so they abandon those actions).

[16] The destruction of all karmic effects comes from knowledge.

Scripture teaches that the inherent nature (*svarupa*) of the world of actions, actors, and karmic results which is the means for all religious work springs from root-ignorance — this world (*prapancha*) is destroyed by the power of knowledge (and thus knowledge cannot be subordinate to action).

[17] Scripture declares that knowledge belongs to those in the celibate renouncer stage of life.

The stages of life are intimated in the Vedas — e.g., those in the forest who practice austerity (CU 2.23.1, CU 5.10.1, MunU 1.2.11). Scripture and tradi-tional texts tell us that one need not have been a householder to enter the ascetic renouncer stage (*sannyasa*).

[18] According to Jaimini, scripture merely alludes to the stages of life involving renunciation and there are no injunctions to lead that life because the scripture condemns renunciation. [19] But according to Badarayana, the renouncer stage is also be practiced because scripture treats all stages equally. [20] Or reference to that stage is an injunction, like holding fuel for a ritual.

References in the Vedas either glorify the renouncer stage or enjoin its practice. For one who is grounded in Brahman (*brahmasamstha*), no works are required (MunU 3.2.6, BG 5.17). Such a state is impossible for a student, householder, or forest-dweller (who still must perform stage-of-life duties). But a wandering mendicant (*samnyasin*) does not achieve liberation simply by adopting the renouncer life since renunciation is still an action, not knowledge.

[21] Objection: The reference to parts of the ritual is only praise since the parts have only a supporting role. Response: No. Because of the unprecedented nature of what is being taught, it must be a genuine injunction. [22] In addition, they are injunctions because they are expressed as injunctions.

For example, "Let him meditate on the ritual" (CU 1.1.1).

[23] Objection: Certain stories in the Upanishads) are meant only for ritual purposes, not to imply that the renouncer stage of life is to be followed. Response: That is so only for the specified stories and not for the Upanishads as a whole. [24] And because the stories are connected with meditations and

are part of one idea in that way. [25] For that very reason, the renouncer has
no need to light the ritual fire and so forth.

The stories were not meant simply to be told as part of a ritual. The
stories do not serve the ritual but bring us closer to understanding the
cognitions. In this way, they are seen to form connected wholes. Rituals need
not be observed by renouncers because actions do not lead to knowledge.

[26] But as for the unenlightened, all religious actions are necessary, as
prescribed by scripture, just as a horse requires a harness and so forth.

Rituals are a means leading toward attaining knowledge. Once knowledge is attained, it does not depend on any other factor to produce its fruit.

[27] But one intent on attaining enlightenment must possess calmness,
control of the senses, and so forth, since they are enjoined as subsidiaries for
attaining that knowledge and thus necessarily must be practiced.

Possessing a calm mind and so forth are enjoined as means for attaining
knowledge (BU 4.4.23). They are a direct means to knowledge, while rituals
are only indirect means and needed on the path.

[28] Scripture declares that it is permissible to eat any type of food when
one's life is in danger. [29] In this way, scripture on restrictions of types of food
are not contradicted. [30] The traditional texts also concur. [31] This is also
consistent with the scriptural passage concerning license.

[32] The duties of the stages of life are also to be performed by those not
seeking enlightenment since these are enjoined by scripture. [33] And because
their performance are co-generators of knowledge along with meditation.

Works of permanent (*nitya*) duties are to be performed by all (prior to
liberation), even those not desiring liberation, because they are enjoined by
scripture and conducive to enlightenment. But they do not *produce* knowledge — no act does. Knowledge is not the subject of an injunction. The
connection of permanent acts to their results is fixed, and knowledge is not
a fruit of duties. Non-permanent actions (e.g., reciting the Vedas) may aid in
attaining knowledge.

[34] In either case, the same duties are to be performed either to fulfill the
Vedic duties of the three earlier stages of life or to aid in attaining knowledge
(in the renouncer stage). [35] In addition, scripture declares that one leading
the renouncer life is not overpowered by passions and other afflictions.

[36] One standing between two stages of life is qualified for knowledge of
Brahman since such cases are encountered in scripture (CU 4.1, BU 3.6.8). [37]
Traditional texts also record instances. [38] In those cases, special acts (e.g.,
fasting, repetition of mantras, or adoration of gods) favor knowledge.

The quest for knowledge can be helped by meritorious deeds performed in different stages of life in previous lives through mental impressions (*samskaras*) acquired in past lives (BG 6.45). So too, the absence of obstructions is enough to qualify a seeker to undertake hearing the Upanishadic doctrines and so forth since knowledge has a directly perceptible result. Thus, widowers and others qualify for pursuing knowledge.

[39] But scripture indicates that being in a stage of life is better than not being in one.

Some people between stages of life have become great yogins. For widowers and others, the favor of knowledge is also possible through special religious acts such as praying or fasting repetition of mantras, or adoration of gods. Also acts performed in previous lives may promote knowledge. (Such people are qualified to receive the teaching about knowledge, but all acts are preparatory — no action can force the realization of knowledge.)

[40] But Jaimini states that for one who has become a renouncer, there is no return from it to the other stages of life because of scriptural restrictions and the absence of scriptural sanction for such a return and the absence of good precedence. [41] In addition, even a lapse from celibacy is not available for the renouncer since his fall is known from traditional texts to be without remedy, and thus he must have no connection with (any expiatory ritual). [42] But some consider this to be a minor transgression and claim that it can be expiated, as in the case of eating forbidden food. So it is explained by Jaimini. [43] But (whether the transgression is minor or major) those (who violate celibacy are to be kept) outside of a monastic community in accordance with traditional texts and the actions of the celibate.

[44] The teacher Atreya states that meditation on parts of a ritual is to be practiced only by the sponsor of a sacrifice who meditates, not the priest who performs it, because scripture speaks of the fruits of that meditation (belonging to the meditator). [45] But the teacher Audulomi states that it is the duty of the priest of the sacrifice to engage in meditation because he is paid for that (work). [46] Scripture confirms this (Shatapatha Brahmana 1.3, 1.26; CU 1.7.8).

[47] An injunction is implied to practice other auxiliary activity of meditation as a third activity in addition to learning (panditya) and being child-like for one who seeks knowledge, just as with the principal injunction requiring the practice's subsidiary actions.

Scripture enjoins becoming a silent meditator (*muni*) (BU 3.5) — which is a means to knowledge — just as it enjoins being learned to be child-like.

[48] But since knowledge is included in all stages of life, scripture ends

with the householder life in some passages. [49] Thus, there is an injunction to practice the other stages of life in addition to the stage of the silent one.

[50] The passage on being child-like (BU 3.5.1) means not displaying one's knowledge since that meaning fits the context of the entire passage.

By "child-like" is meant the absence of strong sensuality and so forth. One should be free of deceit, pride, and so forth, and not invite notice by a display of knowledge, learning, virtuosity, and so forth, just as a child does. As in a traditional text: "He whom no one knows to be either noble or ignoble, learned or ignorant, well-conducted or ill-conducted — he is a (true) Brahmin. Quietly devoted to duty, let the wise roam through life unknown. Let him travel this earth as if he were blind, unconscious, and deaf." He is "with hidden nature, hidden conduct."

[51] Knowledge may arise in this life if there is no obstruction to the means adopted for attaining knowledge. That is seen in scripture.

If there are obstructions in this life, knowledge may arise in the next from practices in a previous life.

[52] There is no rule concerning the fruit of final liberation because that state has been definitely ascertained to be the same as knowledge itself.

The Vedas state that there is only one type of liberation: it is nothing but Brahman, and so it has only one nature (BU 3.8.8, 3.9.26, 2.4.6, 4.4.25. 4.5.15; CU 8.24.1; MunU 2.2.11). The phenomenal means of correct knowledge may produce a high degree of knowledge but not the result of (perfect, complete) knowledge — liberation. Again, liberation is not something that is brought about but something whose nature is permanently established and is only reached through knowledge. Nor does knowledge have lower or higher degrees since it has only one nature — highest knowledge. It would not be knowledge at all if it were lower. So too, the result of knowledge — liberation — cannot be distinguished by a higher or lower degree. But for cognitions having the qualified Brahman (i.e., the Lord) as their object, a difference in practice is possible according to the property meditated upon and thus a difference in results is possible — unlike the meditation on Brahman without properties, which leads only to liberation.

Book 4
Chapter 1: The Fruits of Meditation

Introduction. Book 3 dealt mainly with the means of knowledge relating to cognitions of higher and lower Brahman. Book 4 continues this and then deals mainly with the fruit of knowledge.

[1] Repetition of the Vedantic teaching "You are that" is required because the teaching is repeated in scripture and [2] because there are indications in scripture of the need for repetition for the teaching to sink in.

The Atman is to be heard (about from teachers), thought about, and reflected upon (in meditation) (BU 2.4.5, 4.4.21; CU 8.7.1). Scripture gives repeated instruction, and thus repetition is required. All these mental activities have the realization of Brahman for their objective. In some texts knowing is listed first and then meditating (e.g., CU 4.1.4) and in other texts meditating is listed first (CU 3.18.1).

Objection: What is the point of repetition? If "You are that" does not generate knowledge upon its first hearing, repetition will not help. Reasoning about it will help, but that needs to be gone through only once.

Response: Repetition is not needed for those who realize "You are that" upon hearing it only once. But it is needed for the realization of Brahman by those who do not realize the true nature of Brahman upon the first hearing. We observe the need repetition again and again the world. "You are that" means that what is denoted by "you" is identical to what is denoted by "that." The reality denoted by "that" is free of properties of transmigratory existence and has consciousness as its atman and is called "Brahman." Brahman is not produced, not observable, not subject to death, and "knowledge" denotes that the light of consciousness constitutes its nature. "You" denotes the inner atman (*pratyag-atman*) that is the agent of seeing and hearing and is apprehended as the inmost atman inhabiting the various sheaths starting with the visible body and is realized as consciousness itself. "That" denotes Brahman which is by nature conscious and radiant and free of all worldly attributes.

And although the object to be known (i.e., the Atman) is partless, people wrongly superimpose upon it the properties of a being made up of many parts — the body, the senses, the mind (*manas*), the intellect (*buddhi*) — and objects of the senses. By one act of attention, we may discard one of these parts, and by another act another part. So a progressive succession of cognitions may take place. But this would be merely an antecedent to the true knowledge of the Atman (which does not come in stages). (Comprehending "You are that" intellectually is not enough.)

Persons for whom the meaning of the two terms "you" and "that" is obstructed by root-ignorance, doubt, and misconception, the sentence "You are that" cannot produce right knowledge of its sense upon only one hearing since the knowledge of the sense of the sentence depends on knowledge of the sense of the words. Thus, repetition of scriptural texts and reasoning about them is needed. But the quick-witted in whose mind the sense of the words "you" and "that" are not obstructed by root-ignorance or doubt can realize the sense of "You are that" upon the first hearing, and thus repetition is not required for them. For once the knowledge of the Atman has sprung forth, ignorance is dispelled once and for all.

Objection: The sense that the Atman is subject to pain is strong in us — no one realizes the total absence of pain.

Response: The error that the Atman is subject to pain is as wrong as the error of the body being the Atman. The error is in identifying one's atman with the body — "I am in pain." The condition of being subject to pain is external to consciousness. (Once you realize "You are that," the pain still may occur, but it is not seen as part of Brahman.) It is not present in dreamless sleep (BU 4.3.22).

Once we know "I am the Atman," no action remains (to be done) (BU 4.4.22, BG 3.12). But for those who have not reached this realization (on one hearing), repetition is required to bring about the realization. Reasoning and contemplation on the texts may be needed to fortify their understanding. Moreover, one who repeats the texts only out of a sense of duty, the true of meaning of "You are that" is not found, but they think that they have a claim on knowledge of the Atman as an agent (and thus remain deluded).

[3] But scripture acknowledges Brahman as the Atman (i.e., the one ontic essence of everything) and causes this identity (of Brahman with the essence) to be so understood.

Objection: The Lord and the individual person (*jiva-atman*) are different — e.g., the person is subject to rebirth and is not free of stain, unlike the Lord. If the Lord were subject to rebirth, scripture would have no meaning. Thus, the Lord is not the real atman of the transmigrating individual.

Response: Scripture states that the Lord is the person (*jiva-atman*) (e.g., BU 1.4.10, 3.7.3; CU 6.8.7). Meditating on "You are that" differs from when scripture states to meditate upon a finite symbol such as the mind as the Lord (CU 3.18.1), and the latter statements must also be understood to be teaching nondifference since the texts expressly forbid any view of duality (e.g., BU 1.4.10, 4.4.19, 2.4.6). Conflicting properties are not being taught.

Scripture teaches that the atman is the Lord by denying that the Atman in any sense could transmigrate. The nondual Atman is free of all taint, and anything contrary in the individual is illusory. the Before knowledge arises, the transmigrating individual is still in the realm where perceptions and actions operate, but as soon as knowledge springs forth means of correct knowledge such as perception cease to be valid (as indicators of objects distinct from Brahman) (BU 2.4.14). Indeed, once knowledge arises, scripture itself ceases to be valid for the knower of Brahman — the Vedas cease to be Vedas (BU 4.3.22). This also disposes of the objection that nonduality cannot be established because the Atman is affected with duality by root-ignorance. (For the enlightened, all duality disappears.)

Question: Well then, to whom does root-ignorance belong — Brahman or the individual?

Response: It belongs to you who are asking the question! If you realize that you are the Lord, then there is no one without that knowledge. The Atman does not become associated with some second reality because of root-ignorance. Thus, one should fix your mind on the Lord being your atman.

[4] The meditator should not project himself into a symbol (of Brahman utilized for meditation) because the symbol is not the highest Atman.

One can meditate upon symbols when the Atman is apprehended in them — the mind or space (CU 3.18.1) or the sun (CU 3.19.1) or name (CU 7.1.5) as Brahman. But do not attach the nature of these symbols to Brahman as its nature — symbols are non-existent (limiting adjuncts). The individual character of those effects of Brahman are subrated (by the knowledge of Brahman). How then can the symbols be mistaken to be Brahman? And then how can Brahman be apprehended in them? So too, meditation on only symbols does not do away with the meditator's agency and other features of individuality. Thus, there is no apprehension of the Atman in those symbols even though the meditator is the same (in nature) as the symbol (i.e., limited by adjuncts) — the symbol cannot be looked upon as the essence (atman). (The meditator is the same as the highest Atman, not a name-and–form.) Objects made of gold are identical with each other only insofar as gold constitutes the atman of all of them (but are separate as phenomena in the world). From the oneness of Brahman being the atman of everything, it follows that the symbols do not exist (as independently existing individual realities, and thus the meditator cannot be one with the phenomenon meditated upon as symbols of Brahman).

[5] But the symbol should be looked upon as Brahman because of the exaltation of the symbol (not vice versa). [6] And symbols as a subsidiary part of a ritual are to be looked upon as Brahman. That is justified.

The idea of Brahman is superimposed on the symbol for meditation, just as Vishnu or another god is superimposed on a symbol for worship. (One meditates on the symbol as Brahman, not vice versa.)

[7] One should meditate in a sitting posture since meditation is (only) possible in that position. [8] Also because of the possibility of deep meditation (dhyana) in that position. [9] And for maintaining motionlessness. [10] This is also mentioned in traditional texts (e.g., BG 6.11).

By meditation (*upasana*) we understand the steadfast focusing upon a single apprehension. This should be done sitting. Such fixing of the mind cannot be done when walking or running or standing erect since these activities distract the mind. Lying down leads to sleeping. But by sitting one can avoid these problems. "Deep meditation" describes a mind concentrated on an object when their vision is fixed and their limbs move only very slightly. This is easy for one who sits steady as the unmoving earth (CU 7.6.1). The Yoga treatises speak of the lotus position.

[11] Wherever attaining one-pointed concentration (ekagrata) is possible, there one should meditate because no particular place is specified in scripture.

One can meditate at any place, in any direction, and at any time.

[12] Meditation should be performed even up to the moment of death, for this is seen in scripture and traditional texts.

Objection: Once knowledge of Brahman is attained, meditation need not be continued.

Response: Meditations should be repeated until death to destroy the potentials in the karmic fruit that is manifested after enlightenment. (After enlightenment, no karmic effects are produced by one's new actions because, with their knowledge of reality corrected, the enlightened have no the personal desires that drive rebirth. Meditation is to destroy earlier seeds that had begun to be manifested.)

[13] On attaining knowledge of Brahman, scripture declares that all future and past transgressions are destroyed and that they no longer cling (to the enlightened). [14] In the same way, meritorious deeds do not cling. But liberation from rebirth comes only when the body falls away at death.

Upon attaining knowledge of Brahman, prior evil deeds do not cling to the enlightened. The karmic fruit of past acts that has not yet begun to ripen does not cling to one who knows (CU 4.14.3). Prior evil deeds are destroyed (CU 5.24.3, MunU 2.2.8). This is not to deny the fruit-producing power of deeds, but that power is counteracted by knowledge. The karmic effects of good deeds connected to religious duties as well as the karmic effect of bad deeds are also destroyed by knowledge of Brahman (BU 4.4.22, MunU 2.2.8, CU 8.4.1). (Thus, the fruit of prior meritorious and demeritorious deeds that would otherwise cause rebirth are ended by knowledge of Brahman.)

[15] But only those deeds committed prior to enlightenment that have not yet begun to bear fruit are destroyed upon attaining knowledge. Deeds that have begun to bear fruit last until the limit of death.

The above only applies to karmic effects that have not yet began to occur before the rise of knowledge of Brahman. Karmic results that have already begun to occur in the life of the enlightened (*prarabdha-karma*) are not destroyed by the knowledge (CU 6.14.2). Otherwise, the enlightened would gain liberation and die immediately upon gaining enlightenment. Liberation only occurs with the death of the body after all karmic effects are exhausted.

Objection: Why aren't all karmic effects destroyed by knowledge?

Response: The rise of knowledge cannot occur without the dependence on the aggregate of prior works (that produce a body) whose effects have already begun to occur, and, this being so, then like a potter's spinning wheel once the motion has started in that medium it will continue until it is exhausted. Knowledge that the Atman does not perform any actions refutes wrong knowledge (*ajnana*) and thereby destroys all actions. But wrong knowledge persists for a while as the result of past impressions (*vasanas*), just as the appearance of a double moon continues (for those with defective vision) after its has been refuted because of the impression it has made.

That one who realizes the knowledge of Brahman can continue in a body in this world is not even a matter for discussion. For since the realization of Brahman belongs to a person alone, how can another person dispute the realization of one who feels in his heart that he possesses knowledge of Brahman and yet continues to retain a body for a time?

[16] But scripture shows that the fire ritual and so forth lead toward the effect of enlightenment. [17] According to both Badarayana and Jaimini and others, there are actions other than these that certainly also have this result.

Rituals undertaken for the fulfillment of some special desire (e.g., to gain merit for others) do not contribute toward the arising of true knowledge of Brahman. But rituals undertaken without a view of reward may lead to contact with knowledge. Rituals performed with a view of liberation indirectly lead to the extinction of the karmic effects of evil deeds, and thus they are means to purifying the mind and an (indirect) cause of liberation. They operate toward the same effect as (unenlightened) knowledge of Brahman. Knowledge is not the object of any injunction, and once enlightened, a knower of Brahman need not perform any ritual since one who realizes the oneness of the atman and Brahman is no longer a subject of scriptures. But the unenlightened who are meditating on Brahman with attributes still has a sense of being an agent and so may perform the rituals. The rituals may then be associated with a meditation that is performed disinterestedly (i.e., without any motive for enlightenment or other attachment).

[18] *For scripture states that whatever is done (including actions outside of the rituals) with knowledge is free of karmic effects.*

From scripture, we know that works accompanied by knowledge have a greater capacity to help in the rise of knowledge and thus are superior to those works without knowledge. All works of religious obligation that are performed before knowledge arises by someone desiring liberation are a means for the destruction of demerit, which obstructs knowledge, and thus are a cause of attaining knowledge. But such works are only an indirect cause of liberation, serving the immediate causes of hearing and reflecting on scripture, faith, meditation, devotion to the Lord, and so forth. In this way, ritual acts operate toward the same effect as knowledge of Brahman.

[19] *But exhausting pre-enlightenment good and bad karmic actions by experiencing their fruit in this life, the knower of Brahman becomes one (sampadyate) with Brahman upon death (CU 6.14.2, BU 4.4.6).*

The knower has to remain in this world until the karmic effect of pre-enlightened actions are exhausted. After death, there is no reason for the continuation of a sense of apparent multiplicity, as it had for the enlightened before death, because the seeds of it (from root-ignorance) are destroyed. Actions depend on false knowledge (*mithya-jnana*), and false knowledge has been destroyed by perfect knowledge (*samyag-jnana*). Thus, after death the enlightened are in a state of perfect oneness (*kaivalya*) with Brahman (or "isolation" from karma and the realm of transmigration, or).

Chapter 4.2

Introduction. This chapter deals with what happens to the unenlightened and enlightened individuals at death.

[1] *(In the process of rebirth,) speech merges with the mind at death. This is seen, and also scripture declares it. [2] And for the same reason, all the senses follow speech into the mind. [3] That mind then merges with the life-breath, as declared in scripture. [4] That life-breath then merges with the ruler (i.e., the jiva-atman) because it approaches it (at death) and for other reasons.*

It is the capacity of each sense, not its organ (*prana*), that merges with the mind (*manas*). The capacity is only figuratively referred to as the organ itself. So too, it is the capacity of the mind that merges with Prana (the life-breath). In the process of departure and rebirth, the individual atman is the chief agent, not Prana, and is identified with the intellect (*buddhi*), since it plays the dominant role.

[5] *Scripture declares that the individual person then abides among the elements.* [6] *The person does not join only one element. Both scripture and traditional texts show that.*

The individual now joined by life-breath (and thus the mind and senses) takes its abode in the subtle (i.e., unobservable) elements that accompany the element heat and form the seed for the new body. But at the time of passing over into a new body, the individual does not abide only in the element heat but all four elements (CU 5.3.3, BU 4.4.5, Laws of Manu 1.27) — earth, water, fire, and air. One is bound to rebirth by the sense organs and objects determined by past actions.

[7] *The departure from the body for the knower of qualified Brahman and unenlightened begins the same way up to the beginning of the path to the moon. Embodied immortality is attained while the remaining root-ignorance is not burned up.* [8] *Scripture declares that the aggregate of elements consti-tuting a body continues until the liberation from the cycle of rebirths.*

The embodied immortality is not the true immorality of liberation since root-ignorance is not totally burned away (BU 4.2.7) (but is life in this world). It results from lower knowledge (i.e., knowledge of Brahman with properties). Although Brahman is the substance of the elements, at the time of death individuals are merged with reality (*sat*) in a way that they continue to exist (as distinct individuals) but only in an inactive potential condition, as in deep sleep and at the dissolution of the world. Otherwise, the limiting adjuncts of every individual would be (automatically) extinguished at the time of death, and the individual would enter the absoluteness oneness of Brahman and not return. The injunctions of scripture would then be pointless.

[9] *The unobservable subtle body (that emerges at death) is minute in size. That is grasped in experience.* [10] *Thus, the subtle body is not destroyed with the destruction of the observable body.* [11] *The warmth of the living body is due to the subtle body. That is justified.*

[12] Objection: *The departure of the subtle body of the enlightened from the cycle of rebirths is denied in scripture.* Response: *What is denied is the separation of sense functions from the embodied individual person (BU 4.4.6).* [13] *In one recension of scripture, this is clear.* [14] *And traditional texts also say so.* [15] *Scripture declares that the mind and other senses of the enlightened*

merge upon death into the highest Atman and [16] that the two are then not distinct (avibhaga).

(The atman of the enlightened *jiva-atman* does not depart the body because the atman is already really the Atman.) The ordinary view is that the elements of the body merge into the subtle elements, but the view of one who knows Brahman is that the whole aggregate of the parts (i.e., the capacities of the mind and senses and Prana) of one who knows Brahman is merged totally in Brahman. But the parts are due to root-ignorance and dissolved by knowledge. Names and forms are dissolved, and one becomes without parts. Only the remainder (i.e., Brahman, the only reality) is left.

[17] *When the atman of one who knows only the qualified Brahman with properties is about to depart the body, there occurs an illumination at the top of its abode (i.e., in the heart [BU 4.4.1-2]). The embodied atman goes through a door that is illuminated by the light of Brahman. And by the power of knowledge and by the proper effect of constant meditation* (yoga) *on the way that is part of that knowledge, the enlightened individual departs through the hundred and first vein in the heart (CU 8.6.5) under the favor of the one who resides in the heart (i.e., the Lord). [18] The atman of the enlightened then proceeds by following the rays of the sun. [19] Objection: There is no progress for the atman departing at night because then the person cannot follow the rays of the sun (CU 8.6.2, CU 8.6.5). Response: There is a connection between the veins and the sun's rays as long as the body lasts. Scripture also declares this. [20] So too, for the enlightened who die during the southern course of the sun (i.e., the inauspicious months of the year). [21] And this is mentioned concerning yogins and in the texts of both Samkhya and Yoga.*

The Lord will be there whatever time a yogin dies (BG 8.23).

Chapter 4.3

[1] *The departed who know the qualified Brahman with properties travel along the path beginning with light of Brahman. This is well-known. [2] The departed go from the year (CU 5.10.1) which is between the months and the sun to the god Vayu (wind), following the absence and presence of specifics of the path according to different scriptural passages. [3] The departed then reach the god Varuna who is beyond lightning because of his connection to water in the clouds. [4] Certain gods are indicated in scripture to be guides (for the departed). [5] They are established as guides because both the travelers and the path are nonconscious and thus need guides. [6] From the world of Varuna and*

other gods, knowers of the qualified Brahman are guided by Varuna, for so states scripture.

The knower of the qualified Brahman with properties (i.e., the Lord) takes the path of the gods (*deva-yana*).

*[7] The teacher Badari asserts only that the travelers are led to the effect (*karya) that can be justified, [8] since there is the specific mention of this.*"

The knower of the lower, qualified Brahman is guided to the world of Brahma (the Lord or qualified Brahman) (BU 6.2.15, BU 4.4.23) ruled over by the god Hiranyagarbha. On the other hand, we cannot connect "one who goes" or "an objective gone to" or "an act of going" with the highest Brahman since that Brahman is present everywhere and is the inner atman of all.

Objection: The goal is the higher, unqualified Brahman since that is the cause of the origin of the entire world. Otherwise, the word "Brahman" is not appropriate.

[9] Response: *Qualified Brahman is designated here because of its nearness to unqualified Brahman.*

When the supreme Brahman is described for the purpose of meditation as having certain properties (e.g., mind) that depend on a connection to nothing but limiting adjuncts, we call it the lower Brahman.

Objection: That does not comport with what scripture states about individuals who are not reborn: there is no permanence anywhere apart from the highest Brahman, and scripture declares that those who set out on the path of the gods do not return (CU 4.15.6, BU 6.2.15, CU 8.6.5).

[10] Response: On the dissolution of the world of the qualified Brahman (loka-brahma), the enlightened, along with the Ruler of the world, attain the supreme (the unqualified Brahman) that is beyond the qualified form of Brahman. So scripture declares. [11] The traditional texts concur.

If one becomes enlightened in the heavenly world of the lower Brahman, one attains liberation at that time. Liberation by successive steps is accepted on the basis of scripture's declarations of the non-return of persons since the highest Atman cannot be reached by any acts, such as the "act of going."

[12] Objection: *Jaimini asserts that the knower of qualified Brahman attains the highest (i.e., unqualified Brahman) because that is the plain meaning of the word "Brahman," [13] and because scripture states that (KaU 2.14). [14] In addition, the firm resolution concerning knowing Brahman is not for the*

" "*Karya*" means "effect" or an object caused by Brahman. This works for Badarayana's emergentism but not for Shankara's nondualistic view of Brahman. For Shankara, lower Brahman is the form of Brahman that is seen only through root-ignorance.

effect (i.e., qualified Brahman) but for the highest itself.

Response: All scriptural passages about movement are connected to the lower Brahman, not the highest. So too, scripture negates the claim that Brahman has any distinctions (SU 6.19; MunU 2.1.2; BU 3.8.8, 4.4.25, 3.9.26).

Opponent: Brahman has different powers. The scriptures show that it has the power of creating, sustaining, and destroying the world. The texts cannot be interpreted any other way.

Response: Such passages are only to establish that Brahman is one without a second. Passages such as the analogy of Brahman to the clay of all clay objects teach the absolute oneness of Brahman and unreality of the modifications, and so do not teach the reality of the origin and so forth of the world (as a second reality). Passages about the negation of differences take priority over passages about creation since only the former bring about the cessation of all curiosity (about origin and so forth of the world) — when the absolute oneness, permanence, and purity of the Atman has been apprehended, the highest goal of man has been achieved, and thus no further desires are even conceivable (IU 7, BU 4.2.4, TU 2.9). Those who know Brahman achieve contentment, but one who sees differences in this world goes from rebirth to rebirth (KaU 4.10).

The object of knowledge is only Brahman, the root of the world (being) (CU 6.8.3, TU 3.1). Since these passages teach oneness of the Atman, Brahman cannot be viewed as having multiple powers — the passages in the Upanishads denying these cannot be interpreted in any other way. Again, "going to" Brahman is impossible (since Brahman is already present as the inner atman of all things). Nor does Brahman have parts or activity, and so it cannot have a special relation to a particular time or place. Since Brahman is partless, it is improper to think of it as having parts or being whole (since a whole is made up of parts). The individual (*jiva-atman*) is not a part or effect of Brahman. Since Brahman is without parts or effects, it is completely unchanging and could not enter into the cycle of rebirths.

If the individual atman were other than Brahman, then the atman must be infinitesimal, infinite, or something in between in size (see 2.3.19-26). If it is infinitesimal, then sensation could not extend all over the body. If it is infinite, it could not move. If it is in between, it could not be permanent. And if it is different from Brahman, texts such as "You are that" are without a point. So too, if different, the individual could not attain liberation since the oneness of the atman with the cycle of rebirths could never be eradicated and it would never lose its innate nature (and be one with Brahman).

Objection: Rituals of permanent obligation and rituals to be performed on special occasions do not produce harmful karmic effects. If rituals for special desires (to reach a heaven or to avoid the hells) are not performed, and the fruit of other rituals come to fruition in this life, then after the death of the present body, there is no cause for rebirth and the atman will abide in its own nature (and not be re-embodied). Thus, the atman will become identical with Brahman's atman even without knowledge of Brahman.

Response: There is no evidence that this is so. Nothing in scripture teaches this. Just because the cycle of rebirths depends upon works does not mean it will cease without works — the absence of another possible cause cannot be discerned. Nor can we know if the actions from past lives have been exhausted in this life. Good works of permanent obligation performed in this life cannot wipe out similar good works from past lives. Good works of permanent obligation may destroy the karmic effects of evil deeds, but good works may supply a cause for a new rebirth, and we do not know if all past evil deeds have in fact been extinguished. And anyone who has not reached perfect knowledge may commit an error (that propels a new birth).

If the individual's oneness with Brahman is denied, then the individual, who is essentially an actor and enjoyer, cannot even desire a blissful state isolated (from karmic effects and the realm of rebirths) since a being cannot divorce itself from its essential nature, any more than fire can cease to be hot. As long as the potential for action is present, it will at some point produce action since the necessary causes are permanently connected (within the individual). Thus, if the essence of the individual is acting and enjoying, it cannot possess a fundamental oneness with Brahman that could be realized by knowledge, and so there is no possibility of attaining liberation. Scripture also denies that there is any way to liberation except by knowledge (SU 3.8).

Objection: But if the Atman is not different from Brahman, all practical existence comes to an end since perception and the other means of correct knowledge have no application.

Response: Practical life will still have its place, just as dream-life holds its place up until the dreamer awakes up. Scripture states that the means of correct knowledge are operative in the sphere of those who have not achieved correct knowledge of Brahman (BU 4.5.15), and it goes on to show that those means do not exist for those who possess that knowledge (since there is no distinct objects to know by perception and so forth). For the knower of Brahman, any cognition of something to be "gone to" (i.e., a separate reality) is obliterated, and so his "going" is not possible.

Objection: Then what sphere do scriptural passages about the individual atman's "going" belong to?

Response: These are for meditations on the sphere of the qualified Brahman (CU 5.3-10, KsU 1, CU 5.11-24). No passage speaks of the Atman's going to the highest Brahman, and it is specially denied. Passages with the verb "to reach" that have the sense of going must be understood analogously, like the text "Being Brahman, he enters into Brahman" (BU 4.4.6). Language in scripture of "movement" only refers to knowledge of qualified Brahman. Only because the distinction of higher and lower Brahman is not discerned are statements about "going to" that apply to the lower Brahman wrongly connected to the higher Brahman. "Attaining Brahman" (TU 2.1) by realizing one's own nature does not mean any movement but only that the individual has dissolved the names and forms that he imposed upon Brahman through root-ignorance. The culmination that is established in one's atman is brought about by knowledge of Brahman and is directly self-evident to the knower. Knowledge does not produce any result but merely presents liberation as an ever-present accomplished reality.

Opponent: So there are two Brahmans?

Response: Yes — scripture distinguishes the higher and lower (forms of) Brahman (Prashna Up. 5.2, BU 2.3.1). The higher (form of) Brahman is spoken of in texts negating all distinctions founded upon name-and-form, and so forth presented by root-ignorance. It is invisible (while the qualified Brahman is visible in its effects, i.e., the phenomenal world.) The lower (form of) Brahman is qualified by some distinction depending on name-and-form (CU 3.14.2) and so forth that are imposed on the higher Brahman for purposes of devout meditation.

Opponent: Then nondualism is contradicted.

Response: Names and forms are adjuncts created by root-ignorance. The fruit of meditation on the lower Brahman is lordship over the worlds, a fruit falling within the sphere of rebirth since root-ignorance has not yet been cast aside. Although the Atman is all-pervading, the atman is seen as going to Brahman because of its connection to the mind and its other adjuncts, just as general space is seen as entering into contact with jars (see 2.3.29 above).

[15] Badarayana says that the gods lead those who do not focus on the symbols themselves (in meditation but focus on Brahman). There is no fault in accepting this twofold division, and one becomes what one resolves to become (i.e., what one meditates upon — i.e., either the qualified or unqualified Brahman). [16] Scripture shows this differentiation (of the fruits of meditation).

One becomes what one meditates upon. But those who meditate on the symbol itself (rather than what is being symbolized, i.e., Brahman) do not go to the world of Brahman. Those whose attention is fixed on Brahman reaches lordship (of the qualified Brahman) pursuant to the scriptural claim that in whatever form one meditates on him, that is what one becomes. But when the focus is only on the symbol, meditation is not fixed on Brahman and the meditator goes to only the symbol.

Chapter 4.4: The Nature of Liberation

[1] Once the light of Brahman is attained, the true nature of the individual person is manifested (CU 8.12.3). This is so because scripture uses the phrase "its own (sva)."

The nature of the individual is manifested only through the atman, not through a property (i.e., a limiting adjunct of the individual).

[2] According to the declaration made in scripture, this is liberation.

The individual atman is liberated from rebirth and abides in its own purity in the highest Atman. Previously, it was stained by the three embodied states of consciousness — waking, dreaming, and dreamless sleep.

[3] The light that the individual person enters into is the highest Atman, as is clear from the context of the scriptural passage.

Light denotes Brahman (BU 4.4.16). See aphorism 1.3.40 above.

[4] In the liberated state, the person's atman abides in a condition of unseparatedness from the highest Atman, as is seen from scripture.

Scripture teaches "You are that" (CU 6.8.7) and "I am Brahman" (BU 1.1.10) and non-division (i.e., the identity of all of reality) (BU 4.3.23). The fruit is knowledge (see 4.3.15 above). "As pure water poured into pure water becomes the very same, so does the atman of a discerning silent sage become (one with Brahman and has the same pure nature)" (KaU 4.15). The purpose of such passages is to describe the liberation of the individual atman from rebirth — they declare that there is no separation, like the comparisons to rivers flowing into the ocean (MunU 3.2.8). Even passages expressing separation (e.g., "abode" and what "abides") are explained as expressing non-separation in a secondary way (as only figurative) (e.g., CU 7.24.1, 7.25.2).

[5] Jaimini asserts, based on scriptural references and so forth, that the liberated person attains properties like those of Brahman (CU 8.7.1, 8.1.6) (such as omniscience and omnipotence). [6] The teacher Audulomi asserts that the liberated person attains pure consciousness (chitta) alone, that being its real

nature (BU 4.5.13). *[7] Badarayana asserts that there is no conflict between Audulomi and Jaimini since the earlier nature of the atman as consciousness persists in the liberated state according to scripture.*

Even though scripture indicates that attributes such as being free from taints are separate, in fact such attributes have their origin only in false conceptions arising from speech. The attributes indicate merely the absence of taints and so forth — Brahman's (positive) nature consists of only pure consciousness. That is the true nature (*sva*) of the Atman (and so the true nature of any atman). But the powers of its lordship (i.e., the creative and ruling properties of qualified Brahman) are not rejected from the worldly point of view. But love, play, and so forth (CU 7.25.2) cannot actually be ascribed to the Atman because these require a second reality and there is only one.

[8] Scripture states that a liberated person attains all his desires through will alone (CU 8.2.1). [9] And also for this reason the liberated person is without a lord to rule over him.

For the liberated, there is freedom in all worlds (CU 8.1.6).

[10] Objection: The teacher Badari asserts that those who reach Brahman have no body or organs because scripture states so.

The liberated have an inner organ (i.e., the mind) by which they can exercise their will (CU 8.12.5) but no body or sense-organs.

[11] Jaimini asserts that those who reach Brahman have a body and organs because scripture speaks of the liberated being manifold (i.e., able to manifest many bodies).

But the power to multiple oneself (CU 7.26.2) is only a fruit of knowledge of the lower Brahman.

[12] Response: Badarayana holds that the liberated are of both kinds (i.e., with or without bodies), just as the Dvadashaha sacrifice can be of different types according to the will of the sacrificer. [13] In the absence of a body, the fulfillment of wishes is still justified, as in dreams. [14] When the body and organs exist, the fulfillment of wishes occurs as in the waking state.

The liberated can appear either with a body or without one, as they wish. When they are without a body, liberated have wishes granted, like wishes being granted in the dream state where the objects are not real. And when the liberated are embodied, the fulfillment may have real objects, as in the waking state.

[15] Thus, the entrance of a liberated person into many different bodies (CU 7.26.2) through divine power is possible, just like the same flame lighting many different lamps, since scripture shows this to be so.

The inner atman and the one mind (*manas*) of a liberated individual can be connected to more than one body because the Atman has the power to create other bodies with minds that conformable to the original mind and to give each an atman. Yoga texts explain now one soul can be attached to several bodies.

[16] What scripture states about the absence of all cognition (BU 2.4.14, 4.3.30, 4.3.32) is made) from the point of view of either of two states — dreamless sleep or entering Brahman. That is made clear in scripture.

The phrase "Entering into one's own atman (*sva-apyaya*)" refers to dreamless sleep (CU 6.8.1) and "oneness" refers to merging into Brahman and being isolated (from any embodied state) (BU 4.4.6). The absence of cognitions of diversity means one of those two states. Having departed the individual person, there is no more (worldly) knowledge (BU 2.4.12, 4.5.15, 4.3.19) (nor any powers over the world). Passages on "lordly power" (gained by meditation on the qualified Brahman) refer to an altogether different condition: an abode, like a heavenly world, where knowledge of qualified Brahman produces results.

[17] The liberated gain all the powers of the Lord of the universe except the power of creating, sustaining, and dissolving the universe. This is known from the context of scriptural passages about Brahman and from the individual person not being close to matters of the creation of the universe, and so forth.

Through meditation on the qualified Brahman, the embodied atman attains oneness with the Lord and possesses all the lordly paranormal powers except creating, sustaining, and dissolving the phenomenal universe since scripture only talks about the highest Lord running the world. The highest Lord alone is appointed to do all work concerning the world as a whole. Scripture shows that the lordly work of others has a beginning (within the world) because it depends upon striving for and knowing the Lord. Individual minds might conflict over the issue of preserving or destroying the world (at a given time), and so such work must be consigned to the Lord alone. All the embodied atmans depend upon the will of the highest Lord.

[18] Objection: But the liberated person does have such unlimited powers according to direct scriptural teachings. Response: Scripture speaks of the one who appoints the lords of the different spheres and who resides in those spheres and the individual person cannot do that.

The individual's attainment of rulership (TU 1.6) depends on the highest Lord. The individual reaches the Lord of all minds (TU 1.6) and becomes the lord of speech, sight, hearing, and understanding. Thus, the lordly powers of individuals depend upon the eternally perfect Lord.

[19] And scripture declares that there is (a reality) that does not abide in the effect (i.e., not within the created realm).

There is a form of the highest Lord that is eternally free and does not abide in effects (beyond the qualified Brahman). It is not the form of the ruling Atman that lies within the realm of effects (as the inner controller of all persons and things) and is perceptible in its effects (i.e., the phenomenal world). Thus, the Lord abides in a twofold form (CU 3.12.6). And the higher unmodified form cannot be reached by those who put their trust in the other form (i.e., the qualified Brahman) since their minds are not set upon the higher. Those who do not reach the form that is separated from all properties stop at the qualified form that is distinguished by properties, and so they are unable to reach the unlimited paranormal powers of the higher form but remain within the lower form with only limited lordly powers.

[20] Both direct experience and inference show this to be so.

Direct experience (*pratyaksha*, i.e., scripture) and inference (*anumana*, i.e., in traditional texts) declare that the highest light does not abide in created effects (MunU 2.2.10, BG 15.6) but is beyond all changing things.

[21] And it is known from the characteristic mark in scripture that the liberated person and the highest Brahman share equality only in enjoyment (i.e., the liberated do not gain the cosmic powers of the qualified Brahman) (KsU 1.7; BU 1.5.30, 1.5.23).

[22] Scripture states that there is no return to the cycle of rebirths for the liberated. Indeed, there is no return because scripture states that to be so.

(Those with knowledge of the highest Brahman are released upon their death and do not return to the cycle of rebirths. However, those who have knowledge only of the qualified Brahman are) liberated but follow the path of the gods through the vein and the ray of the sun on which light is the first stage reach the world of Brahman (CU 8.5.3). They do not return to the cycle of rebirths after having finished the enjoyment there of the fruit of their actions (BU 6.2.15; CU 4.15.6, 8.6.6, 8.15.1; also see aphorism 4.3.10 above). It is settled that those who have dispelled all mental darkness by means of perfect knowledge and are devoted to the eternally perfect *nirvana* (i.e., *moksha*, liberation) do not return. Even those who rely only on knowledge of the qualified Brahman eventually reach *nirvana* (at the end of the world-cycle) and do not return.

* * *

II. Essays

~ *The Theology of the Brahma Sutra* ~

The *Brahma Sutra* is the earliest surviving attempt to harmonize the apparently conflicting doctrines of the Upanishads. It mentions earlier teachers and their doctrines, but this may be the world's oldest "theology" — i.e., the attempt to systematize the doctrines of an allegedly revealed source. It is not concerned with the ritual portion of the Vedas (the *karma-kanda*) but is devoted to trying to explicate Brahman and its relation to the world and to individual persons in the Upanishads (the *jnana-kanda*). The text is attributed to Badarayana (despite the text referring to him by name [e.g., 3.2.41, 4.3.15]). It probably was edited over several centuries and reached its final form probably around 200-450 CE, although major portions are no doubt much older.[12] (Badarayana himself may have live before 200 CE.) It is also known as the "*Vedanta Sutra*" and by other names. Shankara called it the "*Shariraka Mimamsa*" and the "*Vedanta Mimamsa*." It consists of 555 aphorisms (*sutras*, "verses") — incomplete shorthand memorization aids whose meanings are to be expounded orally by a teacher. The text remains highly orthodox with its insistence that the Vedas are the final authority for issues of creation and related topics. It became, along with the Upanishads and the *Bhagavad-gita*, one of the three pillars of all Vedanta schools.

The text does not attempt to summarize all the doctrines in the Upanishads or even cite all of the principal Upanishads — in fact, it relies on very few passages. Rather, it mainly attempts to harmonize the Upanishads' conflicting passages concerning Brahman and release from the cycle of rebirths. The first book discusses the nature of Brahman. The second book attempts to refute orthodox theories (e.g., Samkhya's doctrine of a nonconscious matter as a cosmic principle and Vaisheshika's pluralistic atomism) that compete with its understanding of Brahman and also to refute heterodox theories (Buddhist, Jaina, and materialist). The third book discusses knowledge (*vidya/jnana*) and the path (*sadhana*, "means") to enlightenment, including karma and free will, and the role of meditation to attain knowledge of Brahman. And the last book continues the discussion of meditation and

---

[12] It may be simply the literary style to refer to oneself in the third person, but the text probably had multiple authors. Notice that the *Brahma Sutra* does not always accept Badarayana's position.

discusses the soteriological fruit (*phala*) of enlightenment.

The text is traditionally divided into 189 topics (*adhikaranas*), each presenting a claim from the Upanishads, a reason why there is an issue with it, a statement of an objection, an established conclusion (*siddhanta*), and a connection between the sections. No appeal is made to mystical experiences. Some arguments are philosophical in nature is common, chiefly with the use of analogies or apply to common experience. But most arguments end up being based on scripture (*shruti*) as the unquestioned authority because Brahman is known from scripture alone (2.1.27). This makes the text theological in nature. The text asserts that reasons are valid only if they comport with scripture. Thus, what is justifiable (*upapatti*) may refer only to what the Upanishads establish (according to the text) rather than abstract reasoning. Passages in the traditional but not revealed literature (*smriti*) such as the *Bhagavad-gita* are accepted only if they are seen as agreeing with the Vedas (*shruti*). The text asserts that we must accept scripture on some points regardless of philosophical problems it may have (2.1.27). The text's exegesis of an Upanishadic passage includes looking that the larger context of the passage and invoking other scriptural passages. Sometimes the text relies simply on the authority of teachers. And some positions are presented without any supporting arguments — e.g., it is simply assumed that references to the creator and sustainer of the phenomenal world must be to Brahman.

Understanding the Text

It is important to realize that the *Brahma Sutra* is not a work in the *Advaita* school of Vedanta — Shankara had to interpret it to fit his theory. A dualistic theistic interpretation that takes into account both oneness and difference is a better understanding of the work than Shankara's nondualism. The Upanishads are not uniform in their doctrines but have varying and conflicting doctrines, and this allowed different interpretations. So too, the text's aphorisms are so condensed and incomplete that they are open to very different understandings: the author(s) chose brevity for memorization over clarity. Many of the aphorisms (especially in the first book) are less than five words long — three are only one word. It is not always clear where one aphorism ends and another begins or whether an opponent or the advocate of a doctrine is speaking. And aphorisms often end "and so forth" suggesting that more was left for teachers to expound or something known to the students. Its arguments are short and must be filled out.

Once writing became prevalent, the text was the subject of multiple commentaries. One medieval commentator in Ramanuja's school stated that he had seen twenty-one commentaries. Some may well be older than Shankara's, but only three of these have survived — Shankara's, Ramanuja's, and Madhva's. The commentaries are always more complex than the *Brahma Sutra's* broad statements. More than a few scholars argue that the text has no the meaning independent of different schools' interpretations. But the text is not totally unintelligible — doctrines of its own are discernable.

At the time of the composition of the *Brahma Sutra* the most prominent Vedanta school espoused a doctrine of "difference-and-nondifference" (*bheda-abheda*) of Brahman and the world (see Nicholson n.d.). So too for a person. That is, individuals (*jivas*) are both *not different* from the one reality underlying the world (Brahman/Atman) in their substance and yet *different* from it in their properties. The phenomenal self is nothing but Brahman and thus is not substantively different from it, but it is not identical to it either since there is more to Brahman than just one individual or other phenomenon, and Brahman has features that the *jivas* do not and vice versa.

Brahman

Advaita rejects the "difference" prong of that school: all of realty is *one* and so is *nondifferent*, and it does not *change* in any way. But the *Brahma Sutra* espouses a version of the difference-and-nondifference theory in the relation of Brahman to the world. The text accepts an *emanationism*: the phenomenal world is emanated (*srishti*, "emitted") from Brahman as its "radiance," like the rays of light emitted from the sun. The world also merges into Brahman at the end of each world-cycle. Thus, the emanated "effect" is both different and nondifferent from the "cause," as with milk and cream. Nothing real exists independently of Brahman: Brahman is the world's only cause and substance. But Brahman still transcends the phenomenal world — when this world disappears at the end of each world-cycle, Brahman remains unaffected.[13]

---

[13] The issue of creation in Indian philosophy is framed in terms of "causation" and "cause and effect," but here causation is not efficient causation (like one billiard ball causing another to move) but more like Aristotelian *material causation* (e.g., cream being in milk, a seed becoming a sprout, or the relation of formless clay to a clay pot) or *emergence* of something apparently from something else. When Shankara speaks of the nondifference of cause and effect, it is the nondifference of the *substance* of the cause and the *substance* of the effect, not the efficient cause and the structure or properties of the effect.

Thus, the world is considered a real transformation (*parinama*) of Brahman itself (1.4.26) — not an illusion of a transformation (*vivarta*) — since it is Brahman's radiance. Thus, the text espouses a form of realism concerning the world and individuals: with the world, Brahman becomes extended reality that is then both one (as the transcendent source) and many (in the multiple phenomenal manifestations). The "dreamer" is not observable, but its "dream" is. This may have been the prevailing view with Vedanta at the time.

In sum, the world is not *identical to* Brahman nor *different from* it: Brahman is the world's transcendent source and thus the world is different from it, but Brahman is also immanent in the world as its sustainer and inner controller and thus the world is nondifferent from it. The "highest essence (Atman)" is formless (*arupa*) (3.2.14), but a creator god emanates out of it (3.2): the supreme Lord (*ishvara*), i.e., Brahman with attributes (*saguna-brahman*). The highest essence is conscious, not the nonconscious matter (*pradhana/prakriti*) of Samkhya theory (1.1.5). It is more personal in nature than in Shankara's works: it is the highest person (*parama-atman*), but unlike an Abrahamic god, it is not concerned with people — it does not love nor is it compassionate. It is the source of all happiness (*sukha*) (1.1.14, 1.2.2), but nonpersonal features are stressed: it is unbounded and omnipresent (3.2.37), endless (3.2.11) but without parts (2.1.26), and undifferentiated (3.2.11). It is uncreated but self-luminous (*svaprakasha*) and also imperishable and thus eternal (1.3.10, 3.3.33). The text has no devotional (*bhakti*) elements (unlike the Upanishads), but theistic Hindus had no trouble giving the text a fully theistic reading.

Brahman's role as a transcendent creator is especially important — both as the material and the efficient cause (1.4.23-27): Brahman is that from which the origin, sustaining, and dissolution of everything proceeds (1.1.2). It is the womb (*yoni*) of the world (1.4.27). It is without form(3.2.14), but it takes different forms, like light assuming the form of things it contacts (3.2.15). Brahman is reality (*sat*) itself (2.3.9), and nothing is distinct from it (1.3.10). As the common support (*ayatana*) of all things (1.3.1), it can be called the totality of all things (1.1.23). Negative theology does not play a major role, but Brahman is contrasted in its properties from the phenomenal in a dualism of creator and created. The emanated "effect" (the world) is within the "cause" (Brahman) (2.1.7) — they are nondifferent (*an-anya*) (2.1.14). The world exists as potentials prior to creation (2.1.6). Creation is just the natural activity of Brahman done for no purpose or goal — thus, it is like our play (*lila*) (2.1.33).

The World

The world is *real* (*sat*) and not an illusion because it is the radiance of Brahman. (The *Brahma Sutra* uses the word "*maya*" only once, while discussing dreams [3.2.3].) The world is also eternal just as the transcendent Brahman is. Sense-experiences are in general veridical (2.2.28-30) since they involve something real. The Lord creates an objective world at the beginning of each world-cycle. But he is constrained by the karmic effects of beings' actions from the past (2.1.34), and since the cycle of rebirths is beginningless (2.1.35) there has always been prior karmic actions having effects. Karma is also used to explain the suffering and evil we experience (2.1.21-36). Thus, the creator is not seen as arbitrary, unjust, or inflicting suffering.

The Person

Although the text is called the *Brahma Sutra*, the word "Brahman" is actually used only three times as a stand-alone term (1.1.1., 4.1.5, 4.4.5). "Atman" is its preferred term. It is used to refer to the "essence" of all things. The text also espouses the difference-and-nondifference theory for the relation of Brahman to the individual person (*jiva-atman*). A person is considered a part (*amsha*) of Brahman (2.3.43) even though Brahman is considered to be without parts (*niravayava*) (2.1.26).[14] The Lord possesses powers of creation of the world that individual persons do not (4.4.17-18) even when liberated, and this distinguishes the "highest person" from *jivas*, and so there is no identity of the two, although they are substantively nondifferent. Because of the difference, Brahman does not experience the pain or pleasure that individuals do (1.2.8-9, 2.1.13, 2.3.46). An individual's atman is minuscule while the Atman is not (2.3.17-23). (The text is constantly claiming that passages that seem to indicate a *jiva* or matter are actually referring to Atman.) Brahman resides in the heart (1.2.7-8, 1.3.14-21) of each individual (along with the individual atman [1.2.11]) and is the inner controller (*antaryamin*) of actions (1.2.20).

Enlightenment

Vedanta stands in the Indian tradition that has ending our suffering by ending our rebirths in the phenomenal realm as its soteriological goal. The

---

[14] It may be that two different senses of "part" are intended: on the analogy of the dreamer and dream, Brahman resides in its entirety in each part and yet is partless.

Brahma Sutra does not directly state this, but it can be safely implied by how it deals with enlightenment. Direct knowledge of Brahman is the only means of liberation (*moksha*) from rebirth (3.4). Certain practices are mentioned as the means of clearing the mind for this knowledge. Book 3 and the beginning of Book 4 set forth the practices (*sadhanas*) leading to liberation. Ritual actions cannot accomplish this and at best are only help in preparing the mind for meditation (3.4.25-27, 4.1.16). Actions related to calming the mind are discussed. Brahman is not an object perceivable by sense-organs (2.3.29, 3.2.23) but is experienceable in meditative perception (*ikshati*) (1.3.13). Deep meditation (*dhyana*) is required (4.1.8). One-pointed concentration (*ekagrata*) (4.1.11) is needed for attaining this knowledge since Brahman is realized only in a fully concentrated meditative state of the mind (*samradhana*) (3.2.24). Choices of method are permitted (3.3.58-60), but one is warned not to identify with the symbol used for Brahman in meditation (4.1.4-5).

The end is knowledge (*vidya/jnana*) of Brahman. It is the sole means of liberation. By realizing that Brahman is nondifferentiated even though it appears dual, the individual person enters into oneness with the infinite (3.2.25-26). One enters into union (*yoga*) with Brahman (1.1.19). One's true nature (*svarupa*) is revealed (1.3.19). One-pointedness of mind is to maintained until death (4.1.11-12). The need for mental preparation shows that enlightening knowledge is not simply learning a new fact but is a mystical "knowledge by participation" in what is known. But ultimately, liberation depends on Brahman (3.2.25), not any actions by the person. Rituals are no longer needed (4.1.25) since the enlightened are beyond all karmic actions (4.1.13-14). But karmic effects of deeds performed before enlightenment that have begun to bear fruit will continue until the fruits is exhausted (4.1.15). The bodily aggregate remains until then (4.2.8), but the liberated do not return (4.4.22). The liberated also gain paranormal powers (e.g., 4.4.15).

Upon death, one is liberated from the cycle of rebirths in most circumstances (4.1.19), and so the individual's atman is re-absorbed and does not re-emerge from Brahman again. (But one who knows only the Lord, i.e., "Brahman with attributes" gains only an embodied liberation until all root-ignorance is expunged [4.2.7]). Thus, one's atman becomes one with Brahman (4.1.19) — they are non-separate (*avibhaga*) (4.2.16) — although the enlightened person still has different properties (1.1.19-21) resulting from the atman's embodiment in this world (4.2.-15-16). Of course, prior to enlightenment, the person was already substantively one with Brahman. But now one shares the same bliss as Brahman (4.4.21).

~ Shankara, His Texts, and His Development ~

The next essays will attempt to aid readers in understanding Shankara's commentary on the *Brahma Sutra* and will correct some misunderstanding. The first such misunderstanding is that Shankara founded the Advaita branch of Vedanta — he refers to his tradition (*sampradaya*) at the beginning of his commentary on the *Brihadaranyaka Up.* and refers to earlier teachers who espoused nondualism. Many of the *Sannyasa Upanisads* are clearly more nondualistic than the earlier classical Upanishads. The grammarian Bhartrihari (5th century CE) had a nondualistic framework. How many of his ideas came from earlier Advaitins cannot be established. Hajime Nakamura argued that most of the characteristics of his thought were advocated before him (1983: 678). Some names are known, but there are no extant texts before the *Gaudapada-karikas*. In the BSB, Shankara referred to one unnamed teacher as "the commentator" (*vrittikara*), and some of the ideas in his commentary may have come from that person. Daniel Ingalls also suggested that "[m]uch of Samkara's commentaries must be simply repeated from what teachers had written down before him" (1952: 8). For example, in the first book the BSB Shankara interprets eight aphorisms on bliss in accordance with Bhaskara's theory before criticizing it (ibid.: 10). Extensive quotations from earlier material would help explain the massive quantity of writings at least attributed to Shankara.

Shankara flourished early in the 8th century CE. (Most scholars reject his traditional dates of 788-820 CE as too late.) He was probably born into a Shaiva Brahmin family in the small village of Kaladi in Kerala in South India and traveled extensively. He is said to have established four great monasteries (although the historical record does not mention them in his time). His followers saw him as an incarnation of Shiva, but he may have been a Vaishnava (Potter 1981: 119). He is said to have died at age 32 in the Himalayas. Gaudapada is said to have been the teacher of his teacher (Govinda). Some scholars argue that he was a follower of Bhaskara's "difference-and-nondifference" school or the Yoga school before converting to Advaita after being introduced to the *Gaudapada-karikas* (ibid.: 118). (For more details about his life and more legends, see Potter 1981: 14-16.) He may also have been directly influenced by Vijnanavada (Yogachara) Buddhism.

The *Brahma Sutra* is the earliest surviving attempt at a "Vedanta" — a systematic understanding of the Upanishads — and it does not advocate Advaita's nondualism. The earliest school advocated the "difference-and-non-difference" of Brahman and the individual person noted in the first essay. Samkhya's dualism in which reality consists of non-conscious, inert matter (*prakriti, pradhana*) and multiple transcendent, eternal conscious persons (*purushas*) was also popular. The Vaisheshika's pluralism of real nonconscious atoms also had to be considered. The Advaita school espouses nonduality (*advaya, advaita*) of reality and thus rejects both Samkhya's dualism and Vaisheshika's pluralism. So too, it rejects the "difference" prong of the "difference-and-non-difference" school (2.1.14, 2.1.27) and instead advances an absolute oneness of reality: there is only one reality — one ontic core of being to all phenomena — and the Vedas teach "difference" only for things in the "dream" realm (3.2.29). For all Advaitins, Brahman is "one without a second" (*a-dvaita*) (2.1.26).[1] Brahman is not made up of a collection of essences (*atmans*) — there is only one ontic essence (Atman) common to all phenomena. Shankara goes further in dismissing the apparent reality to the phenomena as illusory.

The earliest known Advaita work is the *Gaudapada-karikas* (Dasgupta 1922-23: 1: 422) and was discussed in Volume 1. That work generated interest in the nondualist thread of the Upanishads. The Gaudapada school may have been the first Advaita school. But Shankara helped make nondualism popular and turned the school away from the realism of the *Brahma Sutra*. To do this, he had to distort the plain meaning of passages in the *Brahma Sutra* (e.g., 2.3.3). He had to dismiss even some clear statements in the Upanishads as statements of "indirect meaning" (*gauna*) (e.g., 1.1.17) that needed to be interpreted in light of the Upanishads' true nondualistic intent. But his nondualism conveys only a partial picture of the Upanishads. In particular, he relied upon two Upanishadic "great sayings" (*mahavakyas*) as the cornerstone for understanding all of the Upanishads: "You are that" (CU 6.8-16) and "I am Brahman" (BU 1.4.10). Related ones include "The essence (atman) is Brahman" (ManU 2), "Brahman is knowledge (*prajna*)" (Aitareya Up. 3.3), and "Brahman is reality, consciousness, and nonfinite (TU 2.1). But the Upanishads do not have one uniform doctrine running through all of passages (see Jones 2014a),

---

[1] Advaitins did not adopt the word "monism" — e.g., "*ekatvavada*" — possibly because that would suggest that Brahman has the phenomenal attribute of oneness or that the phenomenal realm is fully real. Indeed, Brahman cannot be said to be one or many since numbering occurs only in the phenomenal realm of diversity, and "nondualism" conveys the idea of "one reality without a second" without that.

and other schools interpreted these saying differently. Most scholars agree that Shankara's approach skews many of the teachings of the Upanisads in trying to make them sound nondualistic. In particular, there is a line of thought affirming some genuine reality to the world and individuals as creations of Brahman or God. Shankara also restricted the importance of the rituals portion of the Vedas: he did not consider any action, including rituals, to be a means to enlightenment — only knowledge is — and rituals were not binding for the enlightened.

It is difficult to tell which of the huge number of texts attributed to Shankara he actually wrote. Each text has some variations in doctrines and terminology, making it difficult to be certain if Shankara is in fact the author. But most scholars believe that the author of the *Brahma Sutra* commentary attributed to Shankara also wrote the commentaries attributed to him on the *Gaudapada-karikas* (probably written early in his career), the *Bhagavad-gita*, the *Chandogya Upanishad*, the *Taittiriya Upanishad*, the *Brihadaranyaka Upanishad*, and the *Kena Upanishad*. One text where he was not constrained by being a commentator on another text is also mostly by him — *Upadesha-sahasri*. That text was assembled (probably by his disciple Sureshvara) from his earlier and later teachings; some of it may not be by Shankara.

Shankara did not claim to be an innovator but only a commentator on the Upanishads and other texts simply explicating what he saw as the true meaning of those texts. But as discussed below, he was very much an innovator when it came to the *Brahma Sutra* and the *Gaudapada-karikas*, and had to interpret the authoritative Upanishads themselves to fit his doctrines. But Shankara's thought developed over time, as he moved away from the emanationism of the *Gaudapada-karikas* in which the phenomenal world is treated as real. He also directed more attention to the nature of *knowledge*. The ontology in the *Upadeshahasri* is more "realistic" than his later illusionism concerning the phenomenal realm in the BSB (although as will be discussed he treated the phenomenal realm as if it had some reality).

And as Karl Potter states, "[i]t is safe to say that [Shankara's commentary on the *Brahma Sutra*] is the single most influential philosophical text in India today" (1981: 119). Shankara also was the most influential figure in medieval Indian philosophy — accept him or reject him, other thinkers had to respond to his positions. But he did not immediately take the Advaita school by storm. His contemporary, Mandana Mishra, was more influential until the tenth century when Vacapati Mishra harmonized the teachings of the two teachers (Halbfass 1995: 30). Shankara's own students felt free to diverge from him in their elaborations of his writings. Indeed, what became standard classical Advaita doctrines (let alone Neo-Vedanta's) often diverge from Shankara's teachings.

Thus, Shankara's teachings should be looked in their own right rather than understood in light of later Advaita positions. The following essay will focus his commentary on the *Brahma Sutra* since that is generally considered to contain his mature positions. The introduction to his commentary is the closest Shankara comes to a stand-alone essay on his philosophy. He does not cite the Upanishads or any other authority there. The rest of his commentary is not systematized — different points crop up in different places.

Shankara's commentary on an aphorism usually begins with an opponent's doubt or issue. He then relied on reasoning and ultimately on the authority of the reveal nature of the Vedas to defend a nondualistic interpretation the Upanishads' doctrines of Brahman/Atman against other orthodox and unorthodox schools — the Mimamsa, Yoga, Vaisheshika, three schools of Buddhism, Jainism, materialism (Lokayata, Charvaka), and in particular Samkhya. He argued that each of the orthodox schools could not be defended on the basis of the Vedas. But all Indian schools adopt elements of the other schools and Shankara's Advaita is no exception — e.g., it had elements of Samkhya's psychology, although it vigorously rejected Samkhya's premise of a duality of conscious beings and inert matter (Potter 1981: 20).[2] So too, he incorporated enough from Madhyamaka and Yogachara (Vijnanavada) Buddhism on the unreality of phenomena entities, two levels of truth, and vocabulary connected to consciousness (ibid.: 20-21) that some later Vedantins such as Ramanuja accused him of being a crypto-Buddhist (*pracchannabauddha*), despite his affirmation of a transcendent self as the only reality and his vigorous attack on the three prominent Buddhist schools of the time.[3] Indeed, Shankara viewed Buddhism "as one of the worst of heresies" (ibid.: 13) and saved "some of his choicest disrespectful language for the Buddhists" (ibid.: 20). Other Vedanta schools were theistic and accepted some distinction between the individual atman and the Lord and treated Brahman as ultimately having personal qualities. But Shankara also rejected theism as merely another product of the unenlightened dualistic point of view.

---

[2] The BSB presupposes much that common to various Indian traditions. In particular, Shankara does not discuss the soteriological goal of ending suffering by ending rebirths, but ending rebirths is mentioned occasionally while discussing other topics.

[3] Buddhism was dying as an intellectual force in India by the 8th century CE (Ingalls 1952: 13).

~ *Shankara's Philosophy* ~

A TV producer once said that the answer to every question in Hollywood is "Money." Well, for Shankara the answer to every question is this:

> *"Reality is nondual: there is only one reality — Brahman — and all appearance of multiple things and change is actually an illusion due to a lost-lasting root-ignorance."*

That is his philosophy in a nutshell, and that is the only point that Shankara wants to defend. Whatever question about a topic in the Upanishads is raised it leads ultimately to that claim. This ontology could not be simpler. Everything is either real or unreal. It is all or nothing — there is no third category. This makes the changing world a problem. But for him, all apparent diversity is only an illusion with no reality whatsoever, like the snake in the rope/snake analogy. There is no duality of subject and object or multiple objects. His goal is to help us realize that our essence (*atman*) is the same one ontological essence of all things and thus that there is no second reality (CU 6.2-7).[1] There is no reality but a nonpersonal consciousness transcending the dream. That reality is present in our subjectivity. There is no object of consciousness set against the subject or a plurality of objects but only that consciousness. In sum, the metaphysical substance of everything, including each person, is only the consciousness transcending the dream. That knowledge ends our rebirth in the root-ignorance's realm with its suffering. He used the *Brahma Sutra's* claims as a springboard to get to the answer he wanted.

But Shankara's single-mindedness in getting to that claim from the questions that are initially asked about something else makes his works confusing — and sometimes inconsistent. Add to this his imprecision in the use of terminology. And his lack of interest in any other question leaves unaddressed many issues that we would like answers to — in particular, why there is the apparent diversity in the first place. All he does is attack the idea that there is more than one reality and does not explain the phenomenal

---

[1] "Nonduality" for him means that there is only a single ontic essence to reality — *no second reality* (*a-dvaita*) (2.1.26). It is not about a *oneness* of Brahman and the (illusory) realm or a *union* of different essences (*atmans*) with Brahman.

realm. All we have is his ontological monism and his philosophy of illusion-ism (i.e., the unreality of the apparent independence, multiplicity, and impermanence of the phenomenal realm) that is necessary to defend the ruthless logic of his monism. But disentangling different ontological and epistemological strands makes the picture clearer.

The Criterion for Reality

First, Shankara's criterion for what is *real* needs to be set forth: reality is only what is eternal and unchanging. This criterion is adopted from the Upanishads. What is real cannot be created since something eternal and unchanging cannot arise from something else or from nothing. So too, creation would be a change. Nor can what is real be affected in any way since that would also be a change. Nor can it be destroyed since that too would be a change. Nor can its nature (*svarupa*) be altered. Thus, what is real must be uncreated, unchanging, and therefore eternal. Any type of "becoming" cannot be real — only unconditioned "being" is.[2] Nor is the real ever negated (*badha*, "subrated") by any experience, unlike illusions generated by root-ignorance.[3]

Buddhists, employing the same criterion of reality as Shankara, take our lack of experience of permanence in our everyday life as requiring the denial of the reality of conceptualized entities in the phenomenal realm. But most people would instead reject the premise that to be real something must be permanent and unchanging — too much of our experience simply conflicts with that premise. However, Advaitins (and the Greek Parmenides) take the opposite tack and instead reject *observed changes as being real*. Shankara had to invoke illusionism to explain this: the changes that we apparently see are no more real than changes that happen in dreams. That is, something must be real to be able to change, but the real does not change, and thus, in the final analysis no change is genuine but only an illusion. Nor can the illusory affect what is real. So no real creation or change occurs in the eternal, changeless reality. Thus, scriptural passages that suggest that Brahman changes are not meant literally (e.g., 2.1.27). Even Gaudapada's emanationism

---

[2] Anything that is created has a beginning and so does not exist eternally in the past. And since it is created, it is perishable and so will not exist eternally into the future. Conversely, anything that has an end is not eternal and so must have a beginning.

[3] If Shankara used the criterion that to be real something must have causal power, he could still argue that the phenomenal world is not real because the content has no power — only Brahman in the form of Ishvara acts.

would introduce change and diversity into Brahman, and so Shankara rejected it as too dualistic.

So too, there is no real birth, change, or becoming within the phenomenal realm. (If the apparent differences we see in the phenomenal world were in fact *real*, knowledge of Brahman could not remove them: what is real is intractable and thus could not be altered — but these differences are only imaginary and so can be removed by knowledge but not by action.) Each phenomenal person (*jiva*) is not a real character in a "dream." (Today we could use the example of movie characters on the screen.) Thus, there is no solipsism here: any character within a dream is not the substance or cause of the dream itself. The phenomenal realm is Ishvara's dream, not ours. (The role of the creator Ishvara will be discussed below.) Indeed, Advaita metaphysics is the opposite of solipsism since no individual subject exists — there is only the one undifferentiated consciousness. Nor is one *jiva* identical to any other *jiva* or any object in the phenomenal realm or the cause of any actions. The witnessing consciousness of a dream character is actually the consciousness constituting Brahman, but it is not divided up into separate entities. It is possible that there could be multiple permanent, eternal, unchanging conscious realities (as with the Samkhya's "selves" [*purushas*]), but according to Shankara the Upanishads teach that there is only one. And coupled with his illusionism, one reality does account for the apparent diversity, and so only one reality is needed and there is no reason to postulate more realities.

Shankara was a "realist" in the broadest sense: something exists independently of our conceptions. Indeed, we only consider something to be *not real* by knowing something that we deem *real*. That is, we can negate something as real only by reference to something else that is real (2.2.6, 3.2.22) — we can negate the snake when a rope is misperceived only by affirming the existence of the rope. Thus, phenomena in the waking world can be negated only if there is a further reality behind them, which Shankara affirmed — Brahman cannot be negated because it is the basis for all erroneous superimpositions (3.2.22). In sum, denial is possible only if something is left (3.2.22). Thus, he considered Madhyamaka Buddhists to be nihilists since they affirm no eternal reality but only impermanent phenomena empty of self-existence (*shunyata*) (2.2.31) (but see Jones 2020) — they deny the reality of phenomena without affirming another reality. He dismissed them in a few sentences — they do not warrant even their own aphorism in the *Brahma Sutra* — and spent more time on Buddhist "realists" and "idealists."

Brahman

With this criterion of what is real, Shankara took the simplest possible ontology: there is only one reality — Brahman. Like the *Brahma Sutra*, Shankara used "real" (*sat*) only in reference to Brahman. Brahman is the only reality, and what is not Brahman is totally nonexistent — the illusory world of change has no more reality than the snake in the rope/snake analogy. For him, there is no middle category between being eternally real (*sat*) and being utterly unreal (*asat*) like the child of a barren woman (2.1.18) or the horns of a hare (2.2.26). So too, Brahman is not an "absolute" underlying or producing other realties — it is all there is. There is no pantheism since the phenomenal realm is ultimately an illusion and so what is real (Brahman) is not in it: Brahman cannot be immanent to the illusory world since what is real cannot be connected to the unreal nonexistent (*asat*) (2.1.18). The apparent connection of the highest Atman to our body or to limiting adjuncts is only a product of root-ignorance (2.3.30, 2.3.38-39, 2.3.46, 3.2.22, 4.3.14). Nor is Brahman transformed into the world since that would involve a change (2.1.27). So too, Brahman is not an object and so is not observable by the senses (1.1.1, 1.1.3, 1.1.4, 2.1.6, 2.1.27, 2.3.7, 2.3.29, 3.2.23).[4]

Unlike in the *Brahma Sutra* (1.1.2), Brahman is not a reality from which phenomena arise: it is not the "ground," "source," or "substratum" (*adhisthana*) of phenomena — Brahman is the only reality, and so there is no duality of "ultimate reality" and "contingent reality" or "creation." There is no "derivative" or "dependent" things having a lesser degree of reality. No second reality of any degree exists. Nothing (the snake) is superimposed on a substratum (the rope).[5] All there is is Brahman and our misperception of the nature of an illusory world that has no reality. Thus, Shankara has no category for the illusory phenomenal realm that appears to exist. Later Advaitins accepted some degree of reality to the phenomenal realm and described its ontological status as "indefinable" or "indescribable" (*anirvachaniya*) as either "real" or "unreal." But Shankara's ontology admits degrees of reality or levels

---

[4] To call Brahman "invisible" would suggest it is object that could be seen but is not.

[5] Shankara adopted the idea of superimposition (*adhyasa*) of the subject on the object and vice versa from Gaudapada (who may have gotten it from Yogachara [Vijnanavada] Buddhism). But the idea does not really fit with a metaphysics of only one reality since it is an inherently dualistic concept and there is nothing real to superimpose on the one reality. The concept is not mentioned much after the introduction in the BSB and lost importance after Shankara.

of reality — it's all or nothing. And thus the changing phenomenal world is nothing — it has no degree or type of reality.[6]

Brahman is the Atman (4.1.3). It is not the modification of another reality (2.3.6). It transcends the phenomenal world, as a dreamer transcends a dream — it would continue to exist even if all persons and other phenomena disappeared. Time, space, and causality do not apply to it since they apply only within the dream. Nor do any other phenomenal characteristics. Brahman is unchanging and unaffected by what happens in the illusory world, just as the magician is unaffected by his act of magic (2.1.9) or the sun is unaffected by its reflection in the water (2.3.46) or the rope by the illusory snake (1.4.6). So too, the highest Atman is unaffected by the waking, dreaming, and dreamless consciousness of the embodied atman (2.1.9). It is "infinite" (*ananta*) in the sense of being "non-finite," i.e., unlike anything phenomenal — not an infinite amount of what is phenomenal. It is self-existent (1.4.26), and so it is unborn and uncreated or self-created. It is self-sufficient. It is self-luminous (*svaprakasha*) and perceived by another reality (1.3.22). It undergoes no changes whatsoever and so is unmodified (2.1.27). So too, it can never end since that too would be a change. Its nature is eternally pure (*shudda*), conscious (*buddha*) and liberated (*mukta*) (3.2.22). The *Taittiriya Upanishad* 2.1.1 characterizes it as real (*satya*), conscious (*jnana*, "knowing"), and non-finite. Brahman is all-knowing. It is without parts and without any form (*rupa*) (2.3.43, 3.2.14, TU 2.7). It can also can be characterized as bliss (*ananda*) — Shankara accepted this (1.1.12), but he did not think it is the essence of Brahman (1.1.19). But he did not emphasize bliss since that is more of an experience or feeling, and he did not associate these with Brahman. (Nor does he say that Ishvara is bliss.) In general, Shankara did accept these characteristics (e.g., 3.3.11) but did not define Brahman as anything but reality (*sat/satya/satta*).

But Shankara did characterize Brahman as an all-knowing inactive consciousness (*chit*, *chitta*) or awareness/knowing (*jnana*). The highest Atman has consciousness as its nature and is eternal because consciousness is eternal (2.3.18). Brahman is consciousness only (*chaitanya-matra*) (3.2.16, 18). Or Brahman is a "mass of knowledge" (1.4.22). But for Shankara knowledge, being (*sat*), and consciousness are all the same thing (3.2.21) since there is only one reality. He mentions this characterization very little in the BSB,

---

[6] Shankara did not use "*anirvachaniya*," but he did state that name-and-form cannot be discerned (*anupakhya*) as either being (*tattva*) nor something distinct from being (2.1.14) or as either identical to Ishvara or not (1.1.4) which amounts to the same thing.

unlike later Advaitins — here it is only to dismiss the idea that Samkhya's insentient matter is the true reality. Consciousness is not a product of the body since corpses are not conscious. Rather, there is a "light within us" (4.3.7) that is the "unmodified highest Brahman" (2.3.18). This centrality of consciousness is not the core teaching of the Upanishads — there "atman" refers to any essence of any object, and phenomena may not be conscious. Although Brahman is consciousness, there is no panpsychism within the phenomenal realm since that realm is an illusion and in no way connected to what is real — Brahman does not permeate what is not real. For example, when the father taught his son about the essence by which he lived (CU 6.1-13), there is no mention of consciousness being the essence of a banyan tree. The pure and unmanifest transcendent consciousness is eternally present (1.1.1) even in deep sleep in a latent state (2.3.31) since we have memories after we wake up of what occurred before the sleep — the continuity could be explained only if consciousness was continuous. But this transcendent consciousness is separate from the content of the psychological complex of our personal "subjective" mind (the *manas* or "inner organ" [*antahkarana*]) that thinks and feels. Our sense of self (*ahamkara*) is in fact only the product of consciousness being "yoked" to the limiting adjuncts (*upadhis*) of mind and body and thus is only an illusion.[7] From the dualistic root-ignorance perspective, we can say that the Atman illuminates the dualizing subjective mind. Our basic error is identifying with this individual subjectivity, our body, and our social roles — no individual "I" exists. But consciousness is inactive, unlike our mind, and transcends the three states of waking, dreaming, and dreamless sleep. It is not affected by what occurs in any of those states (2.1.9). Our own subjectivity is as much a part of the phenomenal world as the illusory objects that we think are sensed.

In sum, Shankara postulates a consciousness transcending our finite mind and having no personal traits as the sole reality — everything else is an illusion. It is not subjective in the sense of a brain-generated activity but is reality (*sat*) itself. This consciousness is a ever-present inner light (*antar-jyotis*) (BUB 4.3.7, 1.1.23) that continuously illuminates our mind and our awareness. It is described as a searchlight-like "witnessing" consciousness (*sakshin*) (BSB intro.) distinct from mental activity and free of distinctions

---

[7] Shankara appeared to endorse the general Samkhya position that mental activity (apart from a searchlight-like consciousness) is *material* in nature. Buddhists agree that there is no real individual phenomenal self (*atman*) since none is ever an object of our experience, but they deny a permanent transcendent consciousness.

that is constantly on, but technically it is not that since there is nothing real to witness. Just as we normally do not see the light but the illuminated objects, so too we normally do not see consciousness. But Brahman is not a "subject" since there are not "objects" to see. We cannot see the seer of seeing or the knower of knowing (BU 1.4.7). Any thought or other mental act is a modification (*vritti*) of something within the dream. Brahman is never spoken of as an object (1.1.4), and it cannot even know itself as an object since it is permanently in the "knowing" mode, and such knowledge would also make the inactive reality an agent of an act — either would set up a duality, and Shankara rejects all ontological dualities since Brahman is the only reality. It can be known only from within, never as an (illusory) object.

Two Forms of Brahman

For Shankara, Brahman ultimately is undifferentiated and featureless. It is consciousness (*chitta*) and no more (3.2.16). It cannot be sensed or grasped by our conceptualizing mind (*manas*) — Brahman is undifferentiated and formless, and all language differentiates. Thus, speech cannot reach it (KeU 1.3; TU 2.4 2.9; MunU 1.1.5). It has no characteristic mark (*linga*)(3.2.11) or phenomenal attributes (*visheshas, gunas*) to express in language. Only what can be presented to the dualizing mind as an object can be comprehended and expressed. This presents a problem for discussing Brahman: no words, which arise in the realm of duality, apply literally. Even metaphors and analogies (e.g., the rope/snake or the dream/dreamer) all must come from the "dream" realm and retain a dualistic point of view — they are products of root-ignorance and so are limited and problematic. Shankara claimed that Brahman is unspeakable (*avachya*) and inexpressible (*anirukta*) (TUB 2.7.1). All statements are made with limiting adjuncts from the point of view of root-ignorance and not reflect Brahman's true nature. Even the language of direct meaning (*svartha*) in the Vedas is not literally accurate and is only meant for the unenlightened (4.1.3). Even the words "Atman" and "Brahman" are only superimposed onto what is real (BUB 2.3.6) — the idea of Brahman as an entity is superimposed on the name "Brahman" (3.3.9). Names and all other words are in the domain of the mind (*manas*), not consciousness (*chitta*), and thus do not apply to Brahman.[8] Even the three positive designations of Brahman — real, knowledge, and nonfinite (TU 2.1) — are

---

[8] Our mind (*manas*) is considered just another product of root-ignorance and thus is nonconscious (*achitta*) (1.2.12). It is simply another sense-organ — the inner organ.

only said in order to remove other attributes.[9] Each negates the other two: Brahman cannot be the agent of "knowing" since that requires change, and so "knowledge" only negates nonconscious "reality" and "nonfinity"; "knowledge" negates "materiality"; and "reality" and "nonfinity" negate subjective "knowledge" (TUB 2.1.). All terms used in connection with Brahman are only meant to negate their opposite without affirming something positive. Thus, in the end reality must be "not this, not that" (*neti neti*, literally "no so, not so") (BU 2.3.6, 3.9.26, 4.2.4, 4.4.22, 4.5.15).[10] Anything said of Brahman must be qualified as "as it were" or "so to speak" (*iti*) (1.4.7) — it is only a "manner of speaking" and is not truly accurate. Language does not describe Brahman but only indirectly applies and only directs our attention away from the illusory realm toward Brahman (3.2.21, TUB 2.4.1). Language on Brahman's transcendence does not apply but only *implies* its existence (3.2.22).

Thus, from the highest point of view, Brahman's true nature (*svarupa*) is a reality *without form* (*arupa*) (1.1.20, 2.1.6, 1.3.19, 3.2.14; TU 2.7). Nevertheless, the unenlightened need guidance toward enlightenment, and so from our point of view within the realm of root-ignorance (*avidya-vishaya*), we can conceive of Brahman in two forms (*rupas*) to guide us toward realizing it (1.1.11): Brahman with attributes (*saguna*) as the god Ishvara ("the highest Lord"), and as Brahman denying all attributes (*nirguna*). Brahman can be spoken of as qualified by limiting adjuncts or unqualified (e.g., 4.3.8-14). So too, the Vedas teach Brahman has a form only for purposes of meditation (3.2.21). But Brahman takes on forms only by contact with limiting adjuncts (3.2.14). It is not that Brahman is bifurcated into two entities or that Brahman with form emanates from Brahman without form like an active God from an inactive Godhead, although from the dualistic point of view we can say that the highest Atman divides himself into forms (2.2.42). Still, from the correct point of view, this is a matter only of our *misconceptions* of the one Brahman: the lower Brahman *is* the higher Brahman seen through limiting adjuncts (4.3.9). Brahman is not two-fold (3.2.11). It has no characteristics (except being consciousness) (3.2.11.) We objectify Brahman and introduces duality, but the entire idea of a creator being is subrated upon enlightenment. Brahman is also nonpersonal, although this means only that it is not personal

---

[9] I am using "nonfinite" rather than "infinite" or "limitless" because the latter suggests merely an infinite amount of phenomenal substance. Rather, the term is meant to convey that Brahman has no attributes connected to the finite phenomenal realm.

[10] Shankara also states that "*neti neti*" only negates *phenomenal features* and leaves Brahman as being permanent, pure, conscious, and free (3.2.22).

in nature and does not denote anything positive about its nature — any characterization *and its opposite* must both be negated. (Brahman is a neuter noun, while Ishvara, Atman, Brahma, and *purusha* are all masculine.) We misconceive Brahman as a god that is personal in nature and the creator, sustainer, and destroyer of the phenomenal realm (2.1.14) and the source of the order manifested in the phenomenal realm because we think in terms of persons and causation.

But all of this is from a dualistic point of view: in reality, Brahman has no personal features and takes no actions, and there is no actual creation (2.1.14). Sometimes Shankara used "Ishvara" as a name for Brahman, and then it indicates *nirguna* Brahman; but when it is used in connection to creation, which is illusory, Ishvara is also illusory. Shankara ultimately treats Ishvara "as much an expression of the linguistic imagination as any other thought of the unliberated mind" (Forsthoeffel 2002: 215). In short, God is as unreal as any other entity seen from the unenlightened point ov view. The idea of "creation" or any other type of "causation" is a misreading of the one action-less reality. Ishavara does not have any power to create anything real. So too, Ishvara is not only the creator of the (illusory) world but the inner controller who controls all transformations within it (2.3.13) and actually performs all the actions occurring in the phenomenal realm.[11] (Of course, the division of inner controller and body [*sharira*] is another dualism that is illusory [1.2.20].) Indeed, Ishvara is the only thing in the phenomenal world that is conscious

---

[11] This presents problems: if only God acts, then we have no free will, and God is responsible for the evil in the phenomenal world. But God "acting" means only that he *powers* the actions determined by our good or bad acts (2.3.41-42) — he does not determine our acts of will. Individual *jivas* are illusory, and so it is God who actually ever acts in any of "our" actions. (But how could an illusory *jiva* have any acts of will?) So too the fruit of action (*karma*) comes from the Lord (3.2.39), not a natural causa-tion. So of course God does the liberating action since *jivas* perform no real acts (2.3.41) — "grace" (*prasada*, "favor") does not mean God chooses which *jivas* to liberate, but only that through God actually performing the actions are we liberated once we attain knowledge since God is the power that implements all events including the actions that we choose including the liberation coming from realizing Brahman (contra Malkovsky 2001). Becoming liberated is not different in this regard than any other event. So too, Ishvara's act of creation is constrained by creatures' prior acts (3.2.41). The problem of evil is dealt with in BSB 2.1.32-36: evil is only phenomenal, and it so does not attach to Brahman. For the same reason, suffering does not attach to Brahman (2.2.10, 2.3.46). Thus, evil and suffering are of no further concern to Shankara. Of course, this is all from the faulty dualistic point of view of root-ignorance — in reality, Ishvara is featureless Brahman misseen dualistically, and Brahman does not act.

(1.3.19, 2.3.30) — it alone is the subject of knowing (1.1.17) since he is actually Brahman.[12] Ishvara creates without Brahman changing its nature (2.1.27) like a dreamer has dreams without changing his or her nature.

But all talk of a creator and creation is also only seen from a deluded dualistic point of view (1.2.20): there is no change in what is real (Brahman), and so no creation, and without creation there is no creator. All talk of "creation" is about the illusory phenomena realm (2.1.33, 2.3.16) — no real change occurs. The Lord arose only after creation and so is not its cause (2.2.37). All passages about Brahman undergoing change are of indirect meaning (2.1.27), but from our unenlightened dualistic point of view, we see Brahman as a creator god, the world as a creation, superimposition on a substratum, and realization as a union of our self with Brahman. But all must be rejected from the ultimately correct point of view: any dualistic terminology can be applied to what is actually real (Brahman) only figuratively (*upachara*) or in a secondary sense (*lakshartha, bhakta, gauna*) and must be qualified "as it were." (The *Brahma Sutra* also distinguishes direct and indirect senses of a descriptive word.) That Atman is seen as an acting agent is only the result of Brahman's association with limiting adjuncts (2.1.14, 2.3.33). Only when a division of ruler and ruled is made (3.2.28) or Ishvara is called illusory (2.1.14) did Shankara say that the distinction of Ishvara and Brahman does not really apply to Brahman (Hacker 1995: 91).

Thus, Ishvara is as much a part of the realm of illusion as phenomenal objects. But speaking of the "highest Brahman" as the rejection of all attributes also arises only from within our dualistic point of view. Even calling it "Brahman without attributes" (*nirguna*) is a product of root-ignorance — a concept devised in contrast to "Brahman with attributes" (*saguna*) that still

---

[12] With this inclusion of Ishvara, Shankara may have been trying to accommodate the growing Bhakti devotion in India at the time, although nothing in the BSB suggests such devotion. (But hymns were ascribed to him.) The growing Muslim presence was also monotheistic. So too, he is commenting on a basically theistic text (the BS) for the benefit of the unenlightened, and so his language is sometimes theistic. Some Christians take Shankara's talk of the Lord as indicating that he was really a theist (e.g., Malkovsky 2001). But these theologians can do this only by taking his language voicing a root-ignorance-infected point of view of dualities as Shankara's final word. But Shankara explicitly insisted that from the ultimately correct point of view Brahman does not act or create or change in any way. Nor does a world exist in any way that is dependent upon Brahman. Nor is Brahman personal in nature. Nor is it concerned with persons (*jivas*) in the phenomenal world. Nor is it portrayed as loving, caring, or compassionate in any way. Nor can we love the Atman since love requires a second reality to love and there is only one (4.4.5). (See Mahadevan 1985: 18-19.)

makes Brahman into a mental object of thought. What is real is beyond all concepts. The conception of "*nirguna brahman*" does reflect enlightened knowledge in a term that reflects dualisms, but for us still under the sway of root-ignorance it is only another misguided conception made with limiting adjuncts arising from our root-ignorance — rejecting dualistic attributes is as much a dualistic action as accepting them. Thus, talk of "two forms" also falls under the rule of "*neti neti*" (3.2.22 on BU 2.3.6). Indeed, the very distinction of two forms of Brahman is a dualism made only from within the "dream." That Brahman is actually without form and qualities — *only nirguna brahman* and *not also saguna brahman* — may be Shankara's "most original philosophical contribution" (Ingalls 1952: 12).

But not all false claims are equal: some are more helpful in leading us toward ending dualistic conceptions and thus toward enlightenment. The identity of cause and effect is better than their differentiation. Samkhya's dualistic metaphysics is better than naturalistic materialism. Talk of a creator god is better than Samkhya's metaphysics. But any dualistic conception involving in a god must also be stripped away in favor of nondualism. In the BSB, Shankara referred to the Lord or "highest person" (*parama-purusha*) more often than to the featureless *nirguna brahman*, but this can be explained by the facts that the text that he is commenting on — the *Brahma Sutra* — is more theistic in outlook and that the first step away from materialism for most people normally involves an anthropomorphic conception even if it is more dualistic than its rejection. The "two forms" approach accommodates a personal god, but a god reflects root-ignorance more than does its denial since Ishvara is connected to limiting adjuncts more than is *nirguna brahman*.[13] None of that changes Shankara's final view: Brahman is not personal in nature, does not act, has no phenomenal features, and is without any form. Meditating on Brahman "with attributes" does not lead to liberation from rebirths but only paranormal powers; meditating on Brahman "without attributes" leads to negating all distinctions based on names and forms (1.1.11, 4.3.14, 4.3.17). Neither form of Brahman is an object of the senses (1.1.1) and so cannot be perceived by the senses, but the empty depth-mystical experience (*anubhava*) subrates the idea of a personal being. No experience

---

[13] The two forms of Brahman may be taken as two ways of experiencing the same reality through different altered states of consciousness: introvertive experiences with differentiated contents and those without. However, Advaitins take the ASC without differentiated content to be epistemologically more fundamental and more insightful for what is real since it, like the criterion of reality, is changeless.

can subrate the idea of a formless Brahman. That idea cannot be contradicted (*abadhya*).

In the end, Shankara used "Brahman," "Atman," "Brahma," "Ishvara," and "highest person" pretty much interchangeably when referring to Brahman because he saw none of them conflicting with his ontology of the oneness of reality. Ishavara and its opposite — *nirguna brahman* — are merely Brahman misseen through the eyes of *avidya* as a being and its opposite. (Ishvara was mentioned less by his students and later Advaitins.)

Atman, Atmans, and the Individual Person

What is the relation of Brahman to the individual person (*jiva*)? This brings up the topic of what Shankara meant by "*atman*." (He uses that term as much as "Brahman.") In the Upanishads, "*atman*" meant the essence of a phenomenon — what give a phenomenon its being. In effect, "Brahman" refers to the cosmic ontological essence in general and "*atman*" refers to that essence when discussing an individual phenomenon: each term is only a different name for the "Real of the real" (*satyasya satya*)(BU 2.1.20) since phenomena of the world are also deemed *real*. But for Shankara, there is only the one reality (Brahman), and the phenomena of the world are deemed *illusory*: only one's being — one's ontological essence — is real. Indeed, the dualism of "essence" and "phenomenon" is false: there is no "essence" or ontological "core" to phenomena because phenomena are not real — there is only reality and illusion. Nothing generated by root-ignorance has an "essence" (atman) but is simply not real. But Brahman can be called an "individual atman" figuratively because of its connection with limiting adjuncts (3.2.9). Thus, the one Atman appears multiple because of the adjuncts (3.2.9). Only the highest Atman is permanent, not the reflected knowing atman of an individual person or the atman of a god (1.2.17). Thus, Shankara eliminated the category of "individual persons (*jivas*)" from his ontology (2.2.10-20) — they are not reduced to another reality but are dismissed as nonexistent illusions. (Shankara did state that some in his school believe the individual person is real as an entity [1.3.19].)

Thus, from the ontologically correct point of view, there is only Brahman, the highest Atman. "Brahman" and "*atman*" are simply two different names for the same thing. The difference is in the point of view: "Brahman" is the name of the reality when looking at all things collectively, and "*atman*" is the name of the same reality when looking at the ontic essence of some particular thing (the "breath" animating that thing). The term "Brahman" accents the universality of the ontic principle, and each *atman* is identified with it. It is eternally pure, conscious, free, not in contact with anything, and devoid of form (1.3.19).

But Shankara also adopted the dualistic point of view arising from root-ignorance for discussing phenomena within the dream. From that perspective, subjects and objects are distinct, and our changing individual subjectivity and unchanging transcendent consciousness are different but connected (MunU 3.1.1). So too, Brahman then is the unmanifested universal, all-pervading essence (1.2.7, 3.2.37) underlying the illusory phenomenal world and person.[14] Scripture does speak of the difference in properties of the inner atman and the highest Atman (2.1.22, 2.3.43), but in the final analysis there is no difference — the differences are from speech alone (2.1.23). But this enables Shankara to speak dualistically of the essence within us being the same as the essence within other phenomena. From this point of view, each *jiva* and all other phenomena are all not different from Brahman which the inner atman of everything (e.g., 1.4.22, 2.1.15) — *jiva-atmans* are qualified as living (jiva) only because of their contact with limiting adjuncts but are really nondifferent from the highest Atman (2.4.21). However, from the correct point of view, even nondifference (*ananya, abheda*) must be rejected — only one reality exists, and the appearance of multiplicity only involves an illusion (2.1.27).[15] So too, our understanding of the Upanishadic "great sayings" of "You are that" and "I am Brahman" is still infected with root-ignorance if we are still thinking of ourselves as realities.[16] The sayings apply only to the highest Atman, not lower atmans (1.3.19). "Advaita" means "no second reality" — not that "your essence [atman] is nondifferent from Brahman" even though that

---

[14] Later some Advaitins held the view that there is only one *jiva* in the illusory realm (*eka-jiva*). There are not multiple atmans but only one essence since multiple *jivas* and objects are illusions, and so there is no multiplicity of (illusory) entities with essences but only the one consciousness that is Brahman.

[15] Shankara uses the language of both "identity" and "nondifference." Nondifference highlights that it is impossible to say if name-and-form is either the same or different from Brahman (1.1.5). Name-and-form in both its undeveloped and manifested states cannot be defined as the same or different from Brahman (2.1.27). But in this way Advaita is the opposite of the *bheda-abheda* school: the latter affirms that the world or individual is *both* the same and different from Brahman, while Shankara claims we *cannot specify* that they are the same or different.

[16] We could conventionally say "I am aware that I don't exist" when what is meant is "There is the awareness, but no concrete center of awareness exists."

is true. Any talk of "nondifference" still represents a dualistic way of thinking even though Shankara utilizes it: there is only one reality — "Brahman" and "Atman" are simply two names for the same reality from two different perspectives.

Also from the root-ignorance perspective, Shankara spoke of different essences (atmans) in the phenomenal world — each phenomenon and person has its own atman. And within a single phenomenon there may be different essences, with Atman being the "highest atman" (*para-atma*) (e.g., 1.1.11-12). (This follows TU 2 on the five essences or sheaths [*koshas*], each one deeper than the one before.) Similarly, there are different lords with Brahman being the highest. So too, he spoke of the individual person as an embodied atman (*jiva-atman, sharira*) (e.g., 1.2.20) within the phenomenal realm, each with its separate karmic stream that continues after this life. (Thus, although this may sound confusing, the highest Atman is the inner atman of the embodied *jiva-atmans*.) But Atman is not subject to root-ignorance. So too, Atman does not suffer when we suffer (2.2.10, 2.3.46).[17] For Shankara, it is the *essences* that are nondifferent, not *the phenomenal world and Brahman*. The individual atman is a reflection (*pratibimba*), as it were, in the mind of the Atman resulting from limiting adjuncts (2.3.50). But this is only from its association with the nonreal limiting adjuncts (1.1.4, 1.3.18) — i.e., our identifying ourselves with our waking, dreaming, and dreamless states of consciousness (2.1.9).[18] There is no self-contained individual entity within us.

For persons, our essence is directly known to be the transcendent consciousness of Brahman (1.4.15, 3.3.34). But our essence is not the material mental "inner organ" (*antahkarana, manas*) that is the seat of our dualistic thinking and feeling that through root-ignorance that we normally identify with (1.2.1). Nor does Atman in any way have the nature of a person. (That is why translating "Atman" as "self" can be misleading — it psychologizes the

---

[17] That the individuals believe they themselves are subject to suffering is only the result of a delusion (*bhrama*) (2.3.46) — only the body in the dream is affected.

[18] Shankara recognized only four states of consciousness: awaking, dreaming, dreamless sleep, and the "fourth" (*turiya*) (3.2.1-9; ManU 3-7). The senses and internal organ are active in the waking state; only the internal organ is active in dream sleep; no limiting adjuncts are active in dreamless sleep. The "fourth" is the permanent consciousness constituting Brahman. Dreamless sleep is constituted by Brahman but in an unmanifested state (1.3.8) since the dreamer is not aware of that because there is no distinction of knower and known without limiting adjuncts (2.3.40, 3.2.7, 4.4.16). Other altered states of consciousness are not considered, although there was a debate on whether "swooning" constituted a distinct state (3.2.10).

nonpersonal Brahman. No vestiges of an individual's personality or psyche transfer to the Atman even when it is embodied.) "You are that" means that our inner atman (*pratyag-atman*) is the highest Atman (4.1.2). All atmans are nondifferent and one with the highest Atman; the apparent difference is due only to root-ignorance (3.2.26, 3.2.6). Brahman is our most inner essence, and cognition (*vijnana*) is our highest essence below Brahman. But again, from the point of view of knowledge, there are no multiple essences or beings having essences but only one reality. "Living person" (*jiva*) and the inner "atman" are used virtually interchangeably (e.g., 2.3.17). (Shankara sometimes treated "*vijnana*" as a term for the consciousness of Brahman and other times as a transient act.)

So too, from the root-ignorance point of view, we can speak of "uniting" our atman with a transcendent Brahman, but from the ontologically correct point of view, there is nothing to unite and no union — only Brahman/Atman exists, and the two terms identify the same reality. Nor (contra the *Brahma Sutra*) does Brahman have parts (*amshas*) — it only has parts "as it were" (*iti*) (2.3.43). Brahman is not divided but only seems so because of limiting adjuncts (2.3.17). All distinctions are unreal — there is a oneness without multiplicity. Thus, there is an identity of Brahman and what we conventionally see as the essence of an individual (*jiva*) (2.3.17). There are no real individual atmans (2.3.30), and Brahman is only figuratively a "*jiva-atman*" because of connections with limiting adjuncts (3.2.9). All atmans are nondifferent from the highest Atman (1.4.6, 2.4.10, 3.2.26). The two epistemological points of view can lead to apparent contradictions. For example, the embodied atman is both identical to the highest Atman (1.3.19, 1.4.22) and different from it (2.1.22), or it is either *in* an individual (1.2.26) or *is* an individual (1.2.20). Or it is analogous to a snake and its coils: viewed as a whole, the snake is one and nondifferent, but an element of difference appears when we look at its parts (3.2.27). So too, the "atman of bliss (*ananda*)" is said to be the innermost atman (1.1.12, 1.1.15), but then that is said to be only meant figuratively (1.1.19). But in the end, there is only one reality that appears to include differences.

In fact, Shankara could accept that there is no real self (*jiva* or *Atman*) in the phenomenal world, just as Buddhists do with their *anatman* theory. This claim only sounds startling to modern readers because we are so accustomed to the term "*atman*" being translated as "the Self." But Shankara too accepted that the phenomenal "self" (*jiva-atman*) is only a constantly changing illusion devoid of reality (*sat*) — there are no self-contained realities in the "dream." The essence (*atman*) in us is not a phenomenal "self."

All in all, "atman" can mean several different things. The term arose merely as a reflexive pronoun to refer to oneself — i.e., "oneself" with no metaphysical implication of "one's Self." But philosophical usages arose early on, and Shankara used the term to refer to the highest essence (Atman with a capital "A") and thus equivalent to Brahman, from a dualistic perspective the inner essence (atman) of a person, or merely the living person (the Atman embodied as a *jiva-atman*). These differing uses may be confusing (and Shankara was not always consistent) since there is only one reality.

The Phenomenal World

For Shankara, neither form of Brahman is an object of the senses (1.1.1), and so all we ever see is the illusory world, not Brahman — the phenomenal world (*jagat*) is not Brahman in any sense but its opposite — a baseless illusion.[19] Brahman cannot be connected to anything that is not real. (Again, nondualism means the absence of a second reality, not the identity of Brahman and the phenomenal world — the phenomenal world is an illusion and Brahman has no connection to an illusion.) This illusion does not "conceal" or "veil" Brahman in the sense that removing the illusion reveals the world to be Brahman. Brahman is devoid of form and not perceptible (2.1.6) and so is never sensed in observations even by the enlightened. Appearances are not appearances of underlying realities or substratum but only illusions. Since phenomena change, the phenomenal world is in no way real (*sat*). Nevertheless, there is something there and so it is not unreal (*asat*) either. The waking world seems more real than a dream world (3.2.4) and is to be taken to be real until we awaken from it (2.1.14), just as a dream world seems real to those in the dream. But then again the world is nondifferent from Brahman and has an undefinable status (2.1.14). From our dualistic point of view, the Vedas show that Brahman is the efficient cause and material cause of the world (2.1.6, 2.1.30) or transforms itself into the world (1.4.26, 2.1.24). From that point of view, Brahman has all powers (2.1.30).

The entire apparent world of actions, actors, and karmic results springs from root-ignorance (3.4.16). This appearance is beginningless (2.1.36) and thus co-temporal with Brahman. So too, transmigration is beginning less

---

[19] In Shankara's commentary on the *Gaudapada-karikas*, the illusion is distinguishing objects from the subject. In his commentary on the *Brahma Sutra*, the illusion is the idea that the world and its contents have a reality of their own.

(2.1.35). Some believe that the phenomenal realm will end when the transmigrating (illusory) individuals within it have been released, for then the Lord will have nothing to rule (2.2.41). Space also is beginningless (2.3.1-4).[20] With our dualistic consciousness, we see the world as real: the creation of Ishvara or as arising from Brahman or as Brahman wishing to be many (CU 6.2.3, TU 2.6). From the dualistic point of view, Brahman modifies itself (1.4.26). And Shankara freely adopted the realist language of emanation and creation (e.g., 3.2.31) from the Upanishads and the *Brahma Sutra* even though ultimately he rejected those concepts (e.g., 1.4.22, 2.2.42) or any action by Brahman and the idea that something real could be created.[21] Brahman seen as Ishvara does not have the power to create anything real. Nor would it have any motive, desire, or need to create something that is other than itself (1.2.2).

Shankara stated that Brahman does not undergo modification into the form of the world (2.1.14), but soon thereafter he spoke of Brahman transforming and creating (2.1.24). However, he is not being inconsistent: he can do that when speaking of how the world looks from the unenlightened conventional, dualistic point of view versus the ontologically correct point of view supplied by Brahman knowledge. For the point of view grounded in root-ignorance, all of Brahman is in each part of the imagined phenomenal realm, just as the mind of the dreamer is fully in each part of a dream and not divided up into segments. It is an extreme form of the "cause" being in the "effect" — one cause is all effects. But from the knowledge point of view Brahman is not the source of the world, nor is it transformed into it (2.1.27) — the world is illusory, and what is real cannot be connected to what is not real.[22] Unchanging Brahman is never in different states. An "origin" arises only from speech (2.1.14).[23] In reality, nothing exists but Brahman (2.1.14).

----

[20] Shankara used space's eternality as an analogy for Brahman and had to explain scriptural texts of the creation of space as claims of only indirect meaning (2.3.1-5).

[21] The Sanskrit word normally translated as "creation" — "*srishti*" — more literally means "to let go" or "to spring forth." It is a matter of emanation or emission.

[22] The language of the mere appearance of change (*vivarta*) to contrast with a real transformation or modification of Brahman (*parinama*) had not yet taken hold. Shankara did not use the term in that regard. Since Shankara saw change as illusory, he did not have to posit any causes within Brahman to account for changes.

[23] There is a danger in seeing this as an instance of linguistic philosophy: for Shankara, transcending "speech" is shorthand for transcending all the bodily organs and their functions (*pranas*). Thus, this includes hearing, touching, and so forth. Here he may be referring only to bodily limiting adjuncts.

Indeed, for Shankara all effects and all "names and forms" of the realm of the root-ignorance arise entirely from speech (2.1.23, 2.1.27, 2.2.10).

All of this world is ultimately false: the world is not a projection of Brahman, as Gaudapada held, but an illusion — it is ultimately no more real than the snake in the rope/snake analogy. Nor does the illusory realm affect Brahman any more than the snake affects the rope (1.4.6). There is no genuine motion: Ishvara is only erroneously connected with motion in the realm presented by root-ignorance (2.2.2). Apparent motions are likened to immobile trees seeming to move when viewed from a moving boat (BGB 4.18) — Brahman is not moving, only our mind (*manas*) is. (Today we would use the example of the sun apparently arising and moving across the sky when in fact the apparent motion is caused by the earth turning.) Or Ishvara is unmoving but only seems to move like the seeming movement of the unmoving sun appearing from its reflection in moving phenomena (2.3.46). So too for the proliferation of multiplicity (*prapancha*). The consciousness of Brahman is all that is real and one but only seems to proliferate.[24]

But Shankara is not as world-denying as the use of "illusion" suggests. The world is not an illusory projection of an individual *jiva's* mind but of Ishvara and survives the disappearance of individual *jivas*. Ishvara projects and then enters the dream realm to guide and control it. (That Ishvara as an illusory form of Brahman is *part of the illusion* is a problem.) Ishvara "creates" the world and the objects (*vastus*) within it (3.2.1-6). The "seeds" of the world and individuals from the previous world-cycle survive and are somehow in Ishvara. From them, Ishvara creates the world in each rollout of a world-cycle but is constrained to set the circumstances for each person (*jiva*) that are dictated by their karmic acts in the earlier cycle (1.3.30, 2.1.34). From our unenlightened point of view, Brahman is both the efficient cause and its material (1.4.23). But the world is only as real as the illusory Ishvara is. Thus, "creation" has the same nature or status as a dream — an illusion.

The world is the "play" (*lila*) of Brahman — i.e., it has no further end and does not fulfill any necessity or desire or goal. Why the world appears has no further explanation or reason or purpose (2.1.33). Manifesting the world is done without intent — it is just what Ishvara does naturally and without an act of will, like breathing is for us. But for Shankara, the phenomenal world is not a real creation or emanation of Brahman in any sense — there is no

---

[24] One may argue that even though the *content* of the "dream" world is not real but changing, at least the *consciousness* of dreaming producing the illusion is itself real. But Shankara does not go that far in giving the phenomenal world any reality.

cause or effect — but only an illusion. Our root-ignorance distorts its ontological nature so that we think it is independent of Brahman and diverse. Ultimately, even calling the universe the "play" of Brahman is wrong since the world is not in any way a product of Brahman or a state of Brahman.[25]

However, the world is "objective" in the sense that it does not depend in any way on the subjectivity of individuals within it (except Ishvara's), and it should be treated as "real" by the illusory persons within the dream until they are enlightened. Part of the illusion is conscious and part nonconscious (2.1.6), and matter should be treated as inert even if the consciousness of Brahman is all that is real. Shankara started his discussion of root-ignorance in his BSB with the distinction of subjects (*vishayins*) and objects (*vishayas*). He also railed against Yogachara Buddhism's alleged denial of an external world (2.2.28-31) and generally defends the externality of Ishvara's "creation" even if ultimately there is no creation and only undifferentiated consciousness — things "exist" in the dream even though they are not "real" in the ultimate sense. Perceptions in the waking state are grounds to subrate the idea that any dream experience is real because veridical sense-experiences correspond to external objects in the phenomenal world (2.2.28, 3.2.4). Individual (illusory) persons and objects remain distinct (4.1.4), and the terms "objective" and "subjective" remain applicable to phenomena in the phenomenal realm. The cycle of rebirths for the persons is beginningless even if it is illusory. The phenomenal dream realm is also stable, ordered, and governed by laws such as karma. (Shankara uses the order of the phenomenal realm to dismiss Samkhya's nonconscious matter [*pradana*] as the world's ultimate cause — consciousness must have been involved in its creation.) The Vedas have no authority in such worldly matters — a hundred scriptural verses saying fire is cold would not make it so (BGB 18.66). So too, there are optical illusions within the cosmic illusion — some perceptions are veridical but some are delusions.

In addition, the phenomenal world persists after enlightenment: the enlightened *see* diverse phenomena in the world, despite knowing better, just as persons with an eye disorder continue to see two moons even though they know there is only one (BSB intro., 4.1.15) — the *delusion* (*branti*) that the realm is *real and diverse* vanishes, but the *illusion* remains. It is like ordinary optical illusions that persist even after we know better. The enlightened

---

[25] But the BSB also refers to Ishvara having put in "profound thought" before creation (2.1.13), as if he had a plan. However, this may refer only to his constraint in setting up conditions for individuals.

merely have the correct knowledge of the world's ontological nature, but the knowledge does not remove the illusion — Ishvara's "creation" is still there and looks the same, but it is now seen for what it is. The "snake" does not disappear. Enlightening knowledge displaces the delusion, and yet wrong knowledge (*ajnana*) in that sense persists (4.1.15). So too, karma has the power to keep even the enlightened in the realm of illusion until the karmic fruit of actions that had begun to ripen before enlightenment expires.

Shankara also spoke from a dualistic point of view of "cause" and "effect" among phenomena within the dream realm even though ultimately there is no real change. "Causation" is illusory, just another product of root-ignorance: there is only one reality, and so the "effect" is not real and does not really exist.[26] The cause and effect are substantively nondifferent (2.1.9, 2.1.13) in the dream world — a pot is simply clay in a particular impermanent state. Such distinctions in our ordinary experience do not actually exist: modifications are only names arising only from speech — the clay alone is real (2.1.14). There is no real diversity but only Brahman; otherwise, it would not be possible to know what is real about all things by knowing only one thing (2.1.14). But phenomenal within the "dream" are not identical to each other (2.1.13, 4.1.4): one object is not *in* another — the sun and the moon are not in us or united to us — but the same one *being* (*sat*) is everything.

Shankara's used various labels for the "substance" of the phenomenal realm in its unmanifested and undeveloped primal state (*prag-avastha*) (1.4.2-3) — "illusion (*maya*)," "matter (*prakriti*)," "undeveloped or unmanifested (*avyakta*)," "imperishable (*akshara*)," "seed-potency (*bija-shakti*)" of rebirth and the world (1.2.22, 2.1.14), and "root-ignorance (*avidya*)."[27] But his preferred

---

[26] "Causation" in Indian philosophy is seen as an ontological issue of *substances*: is a pot pre-exist in the unformed clay, or is it something new? Are evolutes the same or different from their source? Any answer does not fit the situation and leads to both positions seeming partially correct and partially wrong. Thus, the idea of substance only confuses the question of "difference" and "nondifference" and makes the "emergence" of cream from milk or a pot from clay seem problematic or impossible.

[27] Shankara seldom used the word "*maya*," and for him it had no one meaning (e.g., 1.1.5, 1.1.20, 2.1.27; Hacker 1995: 78-81, 114). Only once did he use it to refer to Ishvara's activity (2.2.7). Later Advaitins employed the term more, with the usual later Indian meaning of a power to create the illusion of a world, and distinguished it more clearly from root-ignorance. Like a magician trick (*maya*), the phenomenal realm is both dependent upon the magician and its ontological nature is easily misleading. The term rarely occurred before Advaita (e.g., SU 4.10, BG 7.14) where it meant God's or Brahman's power to produce the phenomenal world, with no connotations of *illusion*. It can also mean simply magic (e.g., RV 10.177).

term for the developed state was "name-and-form" (*nama-rupa*), a term from the Upanishads (CU 8.14.1-2, BU 1.4.7) and popular in Buddhism (see Hacker 1995: 67-78). For Shankara, there are both undeveloped names and forms and manifested ones. The undeveloped names and forms are eternal, not created by human beings: the imperishable has the seed (*bija*) of name-and-forms in it (1.2.22). Name-and-form in the undeveloped state is Ishvara himself, as it were (2.1.14), and is his divine power (*daivi shakti*) (1.4.9). Ishvara is the substratum (*ashraya*) of name-and-form (1.2.22) and also the agent who unfurls unmanifested name-and-form (1.3.41, 2.4.4, 2.4.20), but he must also conform to that name-and-form (*anurodhin*) (2.1.14). Thus, name and form come from Ishvara (2.4.20), not created or imposed by individuals.[28]

Plurality (*prapancha*), with the properties of name-and-form, is a fiction of root-ignorance (2.1.27). The distinctions characterized by names and forms are only imagined through root-ignorance (2.1.27) — the very process of naming produces the idea of separate realities and diversity. Name-and-form is the seed of both rebirth and of the entire expanse of the phenomenal world (*prapancha*) that is called the Lord's power (*shakti*) of illusion (*maya*) or nature (*prakriti*) (2.1.14). The developed, manifested name-and-form is in the phenomenal world (1.1.22, 1.2.14, 1.4.2, 2.4.20). Both the undeveloped and developed distinctions of names and forms cannot be defined as either the same as Brahman or as different from it (1.1.5, 2.1.27) but are only products of root-ignorance. By this plurality, Brahman appears to be the basis of this whole apparent world of changes by modification through these distinctions, but its real nature always remains unmodified and beyond all change — the fiction of names and forms arises entirely from speech alone (2.1.14), and thus this does not mean that Brahman has parts (2.1.27) or in any way make a genuine creation. The manifest world developed by name-and-form or into name-and-form (1.1.5, 1.3.41, 1.4.14, 2.1.17). But manifest names and forms are merely limiting adjuncts (BUB 2.4.10). Conversely, the limiting adjuncts of the embodied atman (the body and mind) that differentiate Atman and embodied atman are made out of name-and-form (1.4.22, 2.1.14, 2.1.22, 2.3.43, 3.2.6). And so name-and-form is an illusion (*maya*) (2.2.2).

---

[28] Shankara's unusual use of unmanifested and unevolved "names-and-forms" in Brahman was dropped by later Advaitins, including his immediate students. It would seem to give forms a reality. In Madhyamaka Buddhism, names and forms veil the phenomenal realm as it truly is (*tattva*). Enlightenment for Buddhists ends our conceptual projections of discrete entities and changes our perceptions, not merely our knowledge. Early Buddhist ontologies dealt only with the phenomenal realm, while Shankara dealt with a reality transcending the (illusory) phenomenal realm.

In sum, the phenomenal world is an illusion, not in the sense of being a figment of our individual minds, but in appearing to be a reality independent of Brahman and consisting of separate real subjects and objects. But Shankara did not treat the phenomenal world frivolously or as something to be treated as a dream: its ultimate ontological status is as a dream, but the structured "creation" of Ishvara (Brahman misperceived as a being) cannot be ignored — even after one is enlightened, the world does not disappear like the snake does once we realize there is only a rope.[29] Rather, the world still remains and looks the same. The mother-of-pearl shell still looks silver (BSB intro.). Even if we know that only Brahman exists, the illusory world is still there. With the delusion that it is a second reality other than Brahman ended, one now sees Ishvara's "creation" for what it really is.

Root-Ignorance (Avidya)

The entire realm of name-and-form is falsely projected by root-ignorance (2.1.33).[30] Name-and-form has root-ignorance as its essential nature (*avidya-atmaka*) (2.1.14).[31] Any results of root-ignorance have no objectivity or reality. Root-ignorance is more fundamental than *maya* and name-and-form: it gives rise to the limiting adjuncts that are superimposed upon on the idea of Brahman and vice versa. That is, superimposition is the mental transference of properties of what is not the Atman to the Atman and vice versa. The Atman remains unaffected. Connecting the subject and body in thinking "I am this" is a basic example (BSB intro.). The unenlightened have a general awareness of Brahman through self-awareness (BSB Intro.) and they see Ishvara's creation. That is the ground enabling such superimpositions (see 1.1.2). Superimposition, is sum, is simply root-ignorance (BSB intro.). It is based on memories: it is the presentation to the mind of some quality (*dharma*) previously observed in something else that is remembered and then

---

[29] The snake does not *go anywhere* once it is subrated by the idea that there is only a rope since it was not real to begin with but was only a nonexistent illusion.

[30] We may want to say that *avidya* is Ishvara's *power*, but what is real — Brahman — cannot be connected with nonreality.

[31] This gives *avidya* an *ontological* dimension, but Shankara gave it this function only when he mentioned various names for the phenomenal realm in lists. Other times it remained an *epistemological* concept. Referring to the "realm of *avidya*" does not make it into an entity — it is only where *avidya* operates. Later Advaitins made *avidya* into the *substance* of the phenomenal world or a creative *power* (*shakti*).

transferred to the content of a new cognition. Since the cycle of rebirths is without beginning, there is always some prior observation giving us material to superimpose later.

Unlike *maya*, Shankara made *avidya* a central concept. He introduced his commentary with a discussion of it. Root-ignorance is not merely the lack of knowledge (not knowing some fact) or mistakes in knowledge (*mithya-jnana*) but a fundamental error made by our discursive mind (*manas*) that affects our perception and understanding (and thus how we feel and live) — a *root* ignorance (*mula-avidya*). *Avidya* is not merely part of the "dream" but responsible for it. Reducing the Atman to "the life of individuated consciousness" is the "primal epistemic error" (Forsthoeffel 2002: 217). It is the impediment that interferes with true knowledge of Brahman manifesting itself in us. Through root-ignorance, we misperceive the entire dualistic phenomenal world as a second reality independent of Brahman. That is the basic delusion — a world of distinct and independent persons (*jivas*) and objects that has an existence of its own. It is innate in the psychology of everyone in the realm of name-and-form. But Shankara never said it was not beginningless, unlike that realm (Hacker 1995: 65).[32] It can be destroyed only through knowledge, not any ritual or other action or experience.

What is superimposed on Brahman needs to be negated by discriminating the real (*sat*) — i.e., the transcendent consciousness — from the unreal. Subration (*badha*) is an intellectual judgment that denies the alleged reality of something experienced. The content of dreams seems real when we are having the dream, but our waking experiences cause us to subrate the content of dream experiences (2.1.14), and veridical sense-experiences lead us to subrate the reality of hallucinations (2.2.29). (This also means that veridical waking experiences subrating hallucinations and dreams is a case of something not real subrating something else that is not real.) Ideas and practices based on them (3.2.27) are subratable. Thus, the *idea* that the world is a distinct reality is subrated, but the world (i.e., Ishvara's apparent "creation") is not (3.2.21, 4.1.15). Enlightening knowledge (*vidya*) that reality is one and the resulting experience (*anubhava*) lead us to subrate the alleged reality of the entire phenomenal realm but the phenomena realm itself. But that enlightened knowledge cannot be subrated by any experience.

---

[32] If *avidya* were beginningless, it would have no cause and would be *real*, although one can still ask why it is there. The phenomenal world has no beginning but is made by Ishvara — of course, the "world" and a process of "creation" are really illusions. Ishavara arose after the formation of the phenomenal world (2.2.37).

Knowledge of Brahman

For Shankara, the only way to remove the impediment of root-ignorance is through knowledge of Brahman (*brahma-vidya, brahma-jnana*).[33] The individual person's (*jiva-atman*) is concealed by limiting adjuncts (3.2.6). Brahman is knowable (1.1.1), but it is not an object observable in the elements or space (2.3.7) and thus is not open to the senses or knowable through reasoning by the conceptualizing mind (*manas*) (1.1.3, 2.1.31). It is directly experienceable as the inner consciousness that is our essence (atman) (1.3.13). Liberation from rebirth depends upon this knowledge alone, not action or a combination of knowledge and action. No mental act is itself the knowledge since the knowledge is not produced but is eternal: no temporary experience, ritual, merit, meditation, or any other action can produce something (knowledge) that is eternal and permanent (1.1.4).[34] Actions (*kriyas*) are only the result of root-ignorance and thus cannot remove that root — no finite human effort could attain the infinite. Actions are dualistic in nature, unlike knowledge of Brahman. Knowledge of Brahman is dependent upon its object (Brahman) and nothing else (1.1.4). Nor is there a real "agent" to act, phenomenal or real. (From a dualistic point of view, we may think of pure consciousness as Ishvara granting knowledge to us through his favor [*prasada*] [2.3.41].) Ordinary knowledge within the domain of root-ignorance is inherently dualistic, unlike the knowledge that is itself Brahman. Knowledge of Brahman is an "objective" state of consciousness, not the "subjective" states under the sway of root-ignorance. The unchanging consciousness, and hence the knowledge by participation, is Brahman itself.

This knowledge is realizing that Brahman is the only reality — only the dreamer is real and not the dream.[35] This insight cannot be subrated by any

---

[33] Shankara accepted the Upanishadic doctrine of two types of knowledge — higher (*paravidya*) and lower (*aparavidya*) (1.2.21). In the Upanishads, lower truths are truths concerning rituals, grammar, astronomy, and so forth, while higher truths relate to Brahman. But for Shankara, all lower "truths" are infected with root-ignorance even though they are not dismissed in the Upanishads as ultimately untrue. His basic point is the contrast between the standpoint of knowledge and the standpoint of root-ignorance (e.g., 1.1.1). He may have gotten the idea from Buddhism.

[34] Shankara had trouble with the *Bhagavad-gita's* emphasis on the "path of action" (*karma-yoga*), even as he accepted the text as authoritative.

[35] It should go without saying that Self-knowledge is not self-knowledge in the ordinary sense of psychology. It is knowledge of the essence of reality, not what is in one's individual psyche (which ultimately is only an illusion).

experience and thus is the final claim. All meditative cognitions (*vidyas*) of unqualified Brahman are the same (3.3.1).[36] With the illumination of nonduality, we finally understand the great sayings of the Upanishads "You are that" and "I am Brahman" properly. Following the Upanishadic principles, one *becomes* what one knows (see Jones 2014a: 173-77), but since we already are Brahman, knowledge merely vanquishes the root-ignorance obscuring this fact. Nothing changes with attaining knowledge: what is real is unchanging. It is not a matter of a "union" or "merger" of one's essence (atman) or consciousness with Brahman since we already *are* Brahman (although Shankara employed terms of union in discussing enlightenment from an unenlightened dualistic point of view, e.g., 1.1.9) — the essence (atman) within us is already identical to the highest Brahman (BSS 4.3.9). In short. one's atman already is Brahman and no action is necessary. Nor is it uniting with other nonreal phenomena of the "dream": distinctions are valid within the phenomenal world — nondifference of cause and effect applies for the true status of the world (2.1.14). We simply now know our proper status and have the omniscience of knowing what Brahman knows.[37]

In sum, enlightenment is merely coming to realize what has always been the case: there is only one reality and no separate *atmans* or independent objects. Enlightenment thus is a matter of discriminating the real from the unreal and negating the nonreal objects of root-ignorance. It is a matter of unchanging knowledge and not of any particular experience. But by realizing that there is only the dreamer and that we are not independently existing characters in the dream, nothing new is gained — *avidya* and wrong knowledge (*ajnana*) are merely overcome.[38] The illusion of multiple realities is not "removed" since it was never real, just the "snake" does not actual "vanish" upon seeing the rope correctly. Nothing real is attained or accomplished, but the knower is released from suffering (1.4.6, 4.1.2).

This knowledge is propositional — realizing "I am Brahman." No higher truths are revealed in mystical experiences. Shankara maintained that we

---

[36] Cognitions (*vidyas*) in meditation may not be the knowledge (*vidya*) of Brahman but any cognition gained there. "*Vidyas*" can also refer to the meditations themselves.

[37] "Omniscience" means knowing the *being* (*sat*) of everything — not all the facts of the illusory realm. That is, one knows all clay pots and dishes by knowing what constitutes them (the clay), but one does not know each individual clay object (the modifications of names and forms). Only in that sense of knowing what constitutes all things do the enlightened know all things (1.4.23, 2.1.14, 2.3.6; CU 6.1.4, MunU 1.1.3).

[38] "*Ajnana*" can mean merely the absence of true knowledge or wrong knowledge.

only have to hear, understand, and concentrate on the Upanishadic "great sayings" (BU 2.4.5). Teachers and the accurate transmission of the tradition's teachings are vital to this process. His classic example is that of a group of ten boys crossing a river; after they get across, the leader counts only nine and is worried one was lost until one of the boys points out that he had not counted himself — with hearing that, he gains the knowledge (TUB 2.1.1; Upad 1.12.3). No special experience or state of consciousness is involved to realize the truth of that claim, nor any actions. No mental exercises are needed if you can understand the claims without such preparation. It is merely an intellectual matter requiring the instrumentality of limiting adjuncts to learn.

Does this mean that no *mystical experiences* are involved in gaining enlightening knowledge? Is it like accepting any ordinary knowledge-claim? Is intellectual acceptance of the claim "You are that" enough? The issue is that we can understand the claims that Brahman is the only reality and that we are Brahman in our ordinary dualistic consciousness infected by our root-ignorance (thinking in terms of the experiencer *and* Brahman). But all our dualistic understanding is defective, including our understanding of the claims about Brahman. Enlightenment needs to get beyond such dualistic understanding since if simply understanding and accepting those knowledge-claims dualistically is all that is needed, then enlightenment would be fairly simple. But if we need to realize it nondualistically, an *experience* that "I am Brahman" is needed. To use a Buddhist example, it is the difference between accepting the claim "Water quenches thirst" and actually *drinking water* (*Samyutta Nikaya* 2.115). Only after drinking the water is one certain, and only then is the claim "self-evident" and not in need of any proof. So too, we need the actual experiential conviction of nonduality to truly see the world that way and thus be enlightened. (Also see Jones 2014a: 173-85, 2014b: 137-41.)

The Anubhava Experience

Comprehending "I am Brahman" while still in a dualistic frame of mind in the "dream" is a "false knowledge" (to use a contradictory phrase) — a claim still permeated by root-ignorance even if we accept that we should not identify with a character within the "dream" realm.[39] Any *idea* that the world is

---

[39] Thinking "I am Brahman" can involve a dualism of "I" and "Brahman" — any sense that you are experiencing Brahman shows that you are not experiencing Brahman. Brahman cannot know itself since this would contradict its unity (BU 3.9.28). No separate knower is present during the awareness of Brahman. There is no distinction

consciousness and free of dual realities remains a matter only of our dualistic imagination. Shankara was adamant that no *experience* equals the enlightening knowledge since any experience is temporary, conditioned, and compatible with *avidya*, while knowledge of Brahman is not. He separated enlightening knowledge from a subsequent direct experience (*anubhava*) of Brahman that is the consequence of the inquiry into Brahman (1.1.2). It is an experience resulting from knowledge rather than vice versa. Realizing that we are Brahman breaks our dualistic root-ignorance mind, and the experience of Brahman results. One is not aware of Brahman in that state since there is no distinction of knower and what is known without the presence of limiting adjuncts (3.2.7). If the phenomenal mind (*manas*) were involved in the experience of Brahman, the state of *anubhava* would be a temporary mental modification (*vritti*) and thus would have to be classified as an "experience" even if it is of eternal Brahman. But if the experience bypasses all the phenomenal dualistic features of the activity of the *manas*, Shankara would not classify it as an "experience."

Enlightenment itself still remains propositional, and no new propositions are revealed in the *anubhava* experience of Brahman. But if enlightenment were merely acceptance of a metaphysical proposition in ordinary consciousness, it could not be *lost* — we would merely have to be reminded of the proposition that "Reality is one." Once the conception of duality is uprooted, it can never arise again (1.1.4). The "snake" would never reappear once you know it is a rope. But if enlightenment involves an *altered state of consciousness*, that state can be lost even though the enlightening knowledge is permanent. It is maintained through meditation (BUB 1.4.7).[40]

For Shankara, *anubhava* is not an action, any more than realizing who the tenth boy is — nothing is done, only root-ignorance vanishes. And it is easy to see why he would not consider *anubhava* an *experience*: for him, all experiences involve the *duality* of experiencer and experienced object, and realizing Brahman does not involve any duality — we *are* Brahman. This could be called "participatory knowledge" or better, "knowledge by identity" since we already *are* Brahman. (It is like self-awareness without being aware of an object, but there is no individuated consciousness.) The knowledge is itself Brahman (1.1.5, 1.3.19). It can only be attained in a realm of illusion by figuratively exiting the realm through a total mental disconnection from the

---

of knower, object known, and the act of knowing — there is only Brahman.

[40] The enlightened must also meditate to destroy the potentials in the karmic fruit that is manifested after enlightenment (4.1.12).

realm — ceasing all action and being unawareness of the "dream." It is an action only in the way that waking up from a dream is an action.

One's mind must be emptied of anything other than Brahman. This must alter our consciousness from a state driven by a sense of a separate self, not merely accepting a new factual claim. The mind (*manas*) infected with root-ignorance does not operate here for there is no object for the mind to sense. It has representations of Brahman but no access to it, and its representations are as fictitious as any other representations. Brahman is without qualities (*nirguna*) and thus has no visible form to be the object of the senses or the mind. (The "inner organ" is considered simply a sixth sense with ideas as its sense-objects [1.1.3].) Nor is enlightenment a dualistic knowledge requiring an agent (a knower). Brahman is never an object that can be sensed or known as an object (1.1.4) — the "light" of Brahman cannot turn back upon itself and make itself a cognizable object. We cannot dualistically know the knower of knowing (BU 3.4.2). But the featureless, undifferentiated pure consciousness that is Brahman can fill our awareness, and we can know from within even if the correct understanding is only provided by the Vedas before and after the experience. We realize that our essence (atman) is consciousness and that that is Brahman and that we have always been Brahman.

Thus, knowledge of Brahman is wholly different in nature from claims grounded in root-ignorance experiences. For Shankara, the revealed Vedas (*shruti*) are the only "means to correct knowledge" (*pramana*) for true knowledge of Brahman. The *pramanas* depend on the object involved as when seeing the rope correctly dispels the snake. Shankara did not analyze the *pramanas*, nor does he defend the claims that the Vedas are eternal and authorless (2.2.38) and are the only *pramana* for matters related to Brahman.[41] He accepts that the Vedic "seers" (*rishis*) heard Ishvara repeat the eternal teachings of the Vedas at the beginning of each world-cycle. No experiences, including *anubhava*, validate Brahman-knowledge (1.1.1-2): the seers' direct experience (*pratyaksha*) of hearing the texts and no other experiences validate the texts. In his BSB, Shankara mentioned direct experience (*pratyaksha*) and inference (*anumana*) concerning sense-objects. He

---

[41] Shankara stated that the low caste *shudras* are not permitted to study the Vedas but could study the enlightening knowledge through traditional texts such as the *Bhagavad-gita* or they may have studied the Vedas in a previous life (1.3.38, 4.1.3). But the Vedas still remain the ultimate source and authority for knowledge of Brahman. Nor does this mean that *anubhava* is an alternative means to knowledge or a *pramana*. But directly studying the Vedas may not be the only way to enlightenment.

holds these as valid for the phenomenal realm (4.3.14). But for him only the testimony (*shabda*) of the revealed Vedas give the correct understanding of Brahman since Brahman is not an object of dualistic knowledge (1.1.4) and thus is not open to any other *pramana* (2.1.16, 4.3.14). The *pramana* of perception cannot apply since Brahman is not a visible object, nor is there any basis for an inference (2.1.11). Reason alone is incapable of demonstrating the nature of reality, as all the conflicting theories reveal, although reasoning in accord with the Vedas may prove useful (2.1.1). Nor can Brahman be known by reason (2.1.31). All orthodox Hindu simply assume the Vedas' authority.

But the *pramanas* — including the Vedas — operate only within the realm of root-ignorance. The phenomenal world is "real enough" that *pramanas* can apply, but they only apply within the "dream." But even the Vedas are instances of dualistic root-ignorance — all passages of even direct meaning must be negated in the end because nothing literal can be said of Brahman.[42] Thus, the Vedas are authoritative for ultimate matters only for *those who have not experienced Brahman* — for the enlightened, the Vedas cease to be Vedas (4.1.3). The enlightened do not need any such authority or validation: knowledge of Brahman is self-established (*svatah-siddha*) (2.3.7) — like Brahman, it is self-luminous — and thus is not in need of any further proof or justification and not open to error. This may seem to destroy the foundation of his entire "inquiry into the nature of Brahman," but the inquiry is from within the realm of root-ignorance for the unenlightened. Mastering Vedic knowledge still remains the only means leading to enlightenment and validating knowledge of Brahman. It is a case of some false claims being better than others: the claims are only provisional truths, but they are of instrumental value since they lead us away from the illusory distinctions arising from root-ignorance, and thus lead the unenlightened toward enlightening knowledge of nonduality and toward an experience of Brahman.

No longer identifying with the individual *jiva* cracks root-ignorance. The inquiry into Brahman results in nondual knowledge but actually culminates (*avasana*) in an *experience* (*anubhava*) of Brahman (1.1.2) — the presence of Brahman in a person's mind. The Vedas are part of the path out of the realm of root-ignorance and vouchsafe the knowledge given in the *anubhava* experience: the Upanishads provide the correct understanding of the content of this mystical experience, even though no understanding may be present

---

[42] How a product of the realm of nescience (the Vedas) can provide the proper *understanding* of the Brahman-experience is not clear. The Vedas would reflect or even shape the knowledge of Brahman given in the enlightening experience.

during the experience. *Anubhava* is a direct, unmediated awareness of Brahman, and thus this knowledge is utterly unlike accepting dualistic knowledge-claims. Since Brahman is not an object of the senses (1.1.4), it is not experienced through the senses during an *anubhava* experience or after the experience in the enlightened person's new extrovertive mystical experience of the phenomenal world.[43] Brahman is only experienced inwardly. During the introvertive *anubhava* experience, the Upanishadic claims and all thing linguistic and dualistic may be abeyance, but after the experience the "great sayings" are affirmed — i.e., the insight (*prajna*) occurs *outside* an absorptive experience devoid of phenomenal content.[44]

Thus, for Shankara *anubhava* is not a *pramana* for Vedic knowledge. Nor does it need any *pramana* since it is self-authenticating (4.1.15).[45] Nor is it an alternative to the Vedas as a means to gain correct knowledge or for validating the Vedic knowledge. Nor is it an independent source of knowledge. The Vedas validate the *anubhava* experience, not vice versa — the experience is not taken as confirming the doctrine of Brahman or providing empirical evidence for it. Rather, the Vedas provide the correct understanding for the experience. The liberating knowledge of the oneness of reality that cannot be subrated by any experience is in the Vedas. Direct awareness of Brahman is

---

[43] *"Anubhava"* literally means *"coming to be"* or *"coming after,"* and so it may be construed to incorporate both the experience of Brahman and the resulting continuing enlightened *state of consciousness* after that experience is over when Ishvara's phenomenal world has returned to awareness. But Shankara appears to use the term in the context of enlightenment to mean only the transient experience of the awareness of Brahman before the phenomenal world rushes back into the mind. The knowledge is eternal but not the *anubhava* experience. Later Advaitins concur.

[44] For Advaita's Vivarana school, the enlightening insight comes from the full grasp of the Upanishadic great sayings. For the Bhamati school, the insight comes through mental training that follows the grasp of the Upanishadic doctrines.

[45] There was a debate in the 1990's over whether *anubhava* was a *pramana* (see Preti 2014). *"Anubhava"* is an instance of Shankara not being very careful with his use of terms, and so there are ambiguous passages that may be taken to suggest that *anubhava* was considered a *pramana*. But his position is clear: *anubhava* did not validate the Vedas. The Vedas are the final word on what is Brahman-knowledge. The "object" (here, Brahman) determines the knowledge, but the Vedas state the proper understanding of the object. The experience also obliterates the dualism of knower and object known so there is no need for a *pramana*— the experience is self-validating. Being independent of the scope of the *pramanas* does not make *anubhava* a new *pramana*, but if some scholars want to claim that the *anubhava* experience is a *pramana* in "a different sense," no one can stop them.

not dualistic and thus falls outside the domain of distinctions in which the *pramanas* operate — the *pramanas* only operate in the realm of root-ignorance, and *anubhava* is beyond that.

Shankara never mentioned his own experiences nor appealed to others' for proving the oneness of reality. (Nor do the Upanishads.) Did he have an *anubhava* experience? Was that the source of his system? He never mentioned that he had it, but classical mystical texts in any tradition seldom mention an author's own experiences. One passage in which he asked how anyone can question the conviction felt in the heart of another (4.1.15) is sometimes taken to be an indirect reference to his own experience, but that is a stretch. Nevertheless, if enlightenment is not merely a matter of the intellectual acceptance of the claim "All is Brahman" but a matter of "drinking the water," then Advaita is a mystical tradition since by definition experiencing free of a sense of a phenomenal self is mystical. (My opinion is that the BSB does exhibit that the author had such an experience and he is not merely a "mystical theorist" whose ideas were influenced by others who had such an experience. But nothing conclusive can be demonstrated one way or the other on the issue.)

Can one be enlightened without an *anubhava* experience? Or does understanding the Upanishadic great sayings only bring us to the brink of enlightenment? Asking this is a faulty dualistic way of looking at the situation. Rather, the nondual knowledge gained in understanding the Upanishadic claims in a way that cracks dualistic thinking automatically culminates in the experience. To use the language of causation, enlightening knowledge produces the *anubhava* experience, but they are really two parts of the same transitional event from a dualistic mind to the enlightened nondual state of mind. Only Shankara's opposition to action as a means to enlightenment would make him see it as a separate event occurring subsequent to attaining the enlightening knowledge. The last act of an unenlightened is letting go of a sense of an individuated self, and the jarring rise of Brahman-knowledge that is enlightenment. This gives *anubhava* a unique status. But this means that studying the Upanishads is only part of the path to enlightenment and that understanding its claims is only part of the enlightening process.

The Path to Enlightenment

If enlightenment were merely a matter of adopting a new metaphysics, no mental preparation would be required, but if one must "drink the water" then yogic training is needed. By definition, seeing the world without a sense of "I" involve altering our ordinary root-ignorance-infected state of mind. If so, gaining the requisite knowledge of the Upanishadic claims and gaining a direct experience of Brahman, yogic training of the mind (*manas*) is required.

Shankara wrote little on this training. Since he saw enlightenment solely in terms of the knowledge that is Brahman, actions and experiences are not equivalent to enlightenment. Nor can any *action* (including ascetic ones such as fasting) or experience (including the yogic *nirvikalpa samadhi*) force the switch in the state of mind from root-ignorance to the enlightened state. Thus, he denied that any meditative practices or yogic practices could produce the requisite knowledge. But Shankara lists four prerequisite conditions for undertaking an inquiry into Brahman and thus the path to enlightenment: (1) the discrimination (*viveka*) of what is eternal from what is not; (2) nonattachment (*vairagya*) to the fruit of one's own actions, both in this life and the next; (3) the attainment of mental tranquility (*sama*), control of one's senses (*dama*), and the other means of mental preparation for attaining knowledge of Brahman; and (4) the desire for liberation from rebirth (*moksha*)(1.1.1).[46] The second and third requirements certainly indicate more is involved than the mere acceptance of a knowledge-claim in a dualistic frame of mind since no mental training is needed for merely accepting ordinary claims, although some self-discipline may be needed to accept a counterintuitive claim even without altering one's state of consciousness.

The Mimamsa school takes the Upanishadic knowledge-claims as only connected to how the rituals should be properly performed and thus subordinate to the ritual injunction portion of the Vedas which leads to liberation (3.4.2). But for Shankara, those injunctions are unconnected to knowledge of Brahman, and so the role of ritual practice is downplayed (1.1.2) — injunctions do not enjoin knowledge but only direct attention toward it (3.2.21). He never discussed the nature of *dharma* and ritual (except with regard to the renouncer stage of life), but the unenlightened are expected to follow the rituals (*karma*) and rules (*dharma*) of the orthodox Hindu way of life, even though for Shankara doing that only led to the heavens and not to

---

[46] The first prerequisite would seem to indicate one must already be enlightened. It must mean an understanding the distinction of what is eternal and what is not that is still grounded in root-ignorance or the ability to apply the distinction to one's new experiences. The later standard list of mental virtues under (3) include the two mentioned and four others: ending enjoyment of worldly things (*uparati*), patience and forbearance (*titiksha*), fixing the mind on Brahman without letting it stray (*samadhana*), and trust (*shradda*) in one's teacher and the doctrines.

the ultimate goal of liberation from rebirth, since actions and experiences are based on root-ignorance and have only temporary results. Actions presuppose a difference between an actor and something to be acquired — but reality is only one, and enlightenment is not a thing to be acquired since we are already Brahman. Any action leads to only an embodied existence. One can become enlightened before the karmic effects of all of one's past actions have played out. Actions are actually performed by Ishvara but are based on the desires of the illusory individual (*jiva*) and so involve nothing real. (It is not always clear whether Shankara is referring to ritual actions or all actions, but what he said often would apply to all actions.) But for Shankara performing rituals and following the *dharma* does have a positive effect for the unenlightened on the path: it helps to purify the mind when performed without regard to any possible reward. So too, ethical conduct can lead us away from a sense of an individuated "self" even though it is only a matter of events within the phenomenal world generated by root-ignorance.

If one can become enlightened by merely hearing the doctrine from a qualified teacher, then no mental training is necessary. The "yoga" to be practiced is the threefold "discipline of knowledge" (*jnana-yoga*) from the Upanishads: Brahman should be heard, reflected upon (*manana*), and concentrated upon (*nididhyasana*) (1.4.19; BU 2.4.5).[47] Hearing the doctrine of the oneness of Brahman explained by a qualified teacher may be enough to touch off Brahman-knowledge (as with simply being informed that you are the tenth boy in the example given above). For those who are not quick-witted, repeated hearings are required (4.1.2). So too, one may have to reflect on the doctrine, but reasoning (*yukti*) and the operations of the mind (*manas*) alone cannot lead to enlightenment but produce only dualistic knowledge generated by root-ignorance. At most, reflection can only remove obstacles to enlightenment. Concentration is unrelenting meditation focused exclusively on the meaning of the doctrine of the oneness of reality, chipping away all dualities. It is the "highest Brahman," not its form as Ishavara, that is to be meditated upon to attain liberation (1.4.19). The result is a state of mind filled only with Brahman.

But reflection and meditation are actions, and knowledge of Brahman does not depend on any act (1.1.1). Actions are simply different in nature from knowledge (1.1.4). Brahman-knowledge is eternal — if it were something to

---

[47] When Shankara states that Brahman is to be "seen" and "heard" (1.4.19), he must mean in meditation where there is a direct experience (*pratyaksha*) since Brahman is not an object of the senses (e.g., 1.1.1, 1.1.4, 2.1.27, 3.2.23).

be accomplished, it would not be eternal but dependent on the meditator. Indeed, Brahman-knowledge cannot be attained since it is always already present. But one intent on "attaining" enlightenment must possess calmness, control of the senses, and so on, since they are enjoined as subsidiaries for attaining that knowledge and thus necessarily must be practiced; they are a more direct means to knowledge, while rituals are only indirect means (3.4.27, 4.1.16-18). But meditation is like rituals in that both are actions. Similarly, asceticism or renunciation of actions may help purify the mind, but they are still actions and so cannot produce enlightening knowledge or the *anubhava* experience. So too, with the path of action (*karma-yoga*) in the *Bhagavad-gita* (BGB 5.1). All activity must cease for the clarity of the *anubhava* experience to burst forth, but that cessation is possible while we are still in the phenomenal world. Enlightenment is not action, just as Brahman does not act in the world. When the dualizing mind (*manas*) is inactive, there is no phenomenal knower to engage in an action.

Meditation is related to the concentration (*nididhyasana*) stage of the three-fold yoga. By "meditation" (*dhyana, upasana*) Shankara meant the steadfast focusing upon a single apprehension (4.1.7).[48] But *nididhyasana* may not encompass all the meditative practices in the Upanishads that are utilized to prepare the person for accepting "All is Brahman" by controlling and purifying the mind. But while Shankara vigorously attacked the metaphysics of Samkhya-Yoga, he may have implicitly accepted the meditative practices of the Yoga school for those who could not immediately realize Brahman-knowledge. However, he rejected these practices as a means to Brahman-knowledge if practiced without reference to the Vedas (2.1.3), and thus they are not an alternate means to enlightenment. Rather, they are a way to clear and stabilize the mind (*manas*) by stilling its modifications (*vrittis*). Yoga is the direct means to knowledge in the sense that it is more direct than rituals (3.4.27). Thus, yoga practices of calmness, equanimity, self-control, and so forth (3.4.27) are actions, but they prepare the mind for Brahman-knowledge, even if they are not a guaranteed means to liberation (BUB 1.4.7). Meditation on the qualified Brahman produces different results, but meditation on the unqualified Brahman leads only to liberation (3.4.52).

---

[48] The concepts of meditation, veneration, adoration, worship and serving are all covered by the term "*upasana*," but in Advaita works the meditative dimension is always present — hence, the translation "meditation" or "meditative adoration." It carries a dimension of surrender to Ishvara or reaching the form of a deity that *dhyana* does not.

Moreover, Shankara was adamant that the one-pointed concentration without a meditative object (*nirvikalpa samadhi*) is not the *anubhava* experience since that experience may be attained without studying the Upanishads. Shankara accepts that practitioners in the Yoga school in a complete meditative concentration of mind (*samadhi*) do see the unmanifested Brahman free from all plurality (3.2.24), but they erroneously understand the experience to be filled with the presence of an individuated transcendent consciousness (a *purusha*) (2.1.9).[49] For Shankara, *samadhi* is an "experience" and thus something that to be achieved while *anubhava* reflects the reality (Brahman) that is already always present. No *action* by an individual (*jiva*) including attaining *samadhi* can realize Brahman-knowledge. That experience can even be a hindrance if one thinks that is the ultimate state to be attained or if one concludes that consciousness is separate from matter or if one is attached to the bliss resulting from emptying the mind of all dualistic content. What is needed is a direct insight into the illusory nature of the phenomenal realm. Both *anubhava* and *nirvikalpa samadhi* may involve emptying the mind of all differentiated content, but the Yoga school misinterprets the resulting experience — the person is actually filled with the awareness of the one reality (Brahman), not with an individuated center of consciousness (*purusha*) that is disconnected from other centers of consciousness and from matter (*prakriti*). Enlightenment is realizing that there is one ontic essence to all things, not separating consciousness from matter, as in Yoga theory. And again, knowledge is taken to be distinct from the experience: the experience of pure consciousness is not enlightening knowledge — the insight of realizing what is real and what is not must be distinguished from the experiential event. After *samadhi*, one returns to a world of differentiated entities (2.1.9); after *anubhava*, one sees that such differentiations are unreal. Later Advaitins equated *anubhava* and *samadhi*. The Bhamati school placed more emphasis on reflection and meditation, while the Vivarana placed more on mere hearing. But the role of experience became central to both schools.

---

[49] Some scholars argue that Advaita's distinction between Brahman with attributes or qualities (*saguna*) and without (*nirguna*) derives from the Yogic distinction between concentration with objects (*savikalpa*) and without (*nirvikalpa*). As noted above, whether the two forms of Brahman are objectifications of different mystical experiences is also debated.

The Enlightened Way of Life

With the dawning of Brahman-knowledge, the delusion generated by *avidya* ends, and this ends the cycle of rebirths driven by unenlightened actions and desires — the final goal (*moksha, murti*) is attained. The true final result of the inquiry into Brahman is the enlightened state in which one no longer generates karmic actions and so is not reborn (4.1.14), not the realization of Brahman-knowledge that "You are that" or the direct experience (*pratyaksha*) of Brahman (*anubhava*).[50] Thus, Shankara's metaphysics, philosophical analysis, and quest for knowledge are tied to this soteriological goal.[51]

In this state, the knowledge, the reality that is known, and who knows are all Brahman (1.1.5, 4.4.52). One realizes the nondual nature of reality. One's essence (atman) is not changed in any way since it is changeless. (Our state within the "dream" realm does change with the end of rebirth, but change and rebirth are illusory from the ontologically correct point of view — they only look real when we still identify with a character in the dream.) Nothing is really "attained" or "achieved" since we already are Brahman. Only the error (*bhranti, ajnana, mithya*) generated by *avidya* is ended — nothing real (*sat*) changes since *avidya* is not a reality. We no longer identify with a character in the "dream," and so how we experience the world then changes. Again, this selflessness would necessarily alter one's consciousness from a state in which the imaginary ego is a driving force.[52]

Some Indian traditions deny that "liberation in life" (*jivan-mukti*) is possible: being tied to a body and a mind with subconscious functions keeps

---

[50] Those who realize only Brahman "with attributes" (*saguna*) do gain many of Ishvara's powers but remain in the Brahma-world until the end of the world-cycle (4.3.10) and are then released.

[51] Shankara used the Samkhya-Yoga term referring to the enlightened as isolated from matter — *kaivalya* — to refer to the enlightened being isolated from karma and rebirth (4.1.19). Hindus also used the Buddhist term "*nirvana*" (4.4.22; BG 2.72, 5.24).

[52] It is possible to interpret the enlightened state for Shankara as not an altered state of consciousness but as only our normal dualistic state — i.e., the *anubhava* experience involve an ASC (since no sense of "I" is involved), but the subsequent enlightened then return to our ordinary dualistic consciousness simply free of the belief in a real ego despite our experiences. This would be consistent with Shankara's claim that enlightenment is only a matter of knowledge and his downplaying meditation. But if after an *anubhava* experience one *sees* the world *dualistically and with a sense of a phenomenal self*, despite's one's newly found knowledge, it is hard to say that person is *enlightened*. Later Advaitins made the enlightened state more clearly a matter of an ASC, and yogic practices became explicitly incorporated into Advaita.

us from ever becoming truly selfless in this world. Even some later Advaitins reject it (Nelson 1996: 24). But Shankara (who only used a form of the term once [BGB 6.27]) and most Advaitins affirm such liberation since enlightenment is solely a matter of one's *knowledge* regardless of whether one is embodied or not — and how can anyone dispute others who claim to have that knowledge (since it is an internal matter of others) and yet retain a body (4.1.15)? Thus, being in the "dream" realm does not present a problem as long as one can maintain the enlightened state of consciousness and thereby realizes that this is only a dream. The Vivarana school sees the enlightened as flipping back and forth between enlightened and unenlightened states of consciousness, but there is no justification for this in Shankara's texts. For Shankara, enlightenment is a matter of knowledge and is permanent, and the enlightened experience Brahman only in the *anubhava* state.

Ishvara's world of phenomena is once again present after the *anubhava* experience, not Brahman — as noted above, since Brahman is not an object of the senses (1.1.4), the enlightened never observe Brahman with the senses. Rather, in the enlightened state they still see the phenomenal realm, but they know that the apparent distinctions are all illusory and that it is not a reality (*sat*). They see Ishvara's world as the illusion that it always has been — free of any true reality or real plurality or diversity. All that vanishes is a sense of duality and division — the illusion continues. The enlightened may or may not have a Gestalt-like shift in perception away from seeing the phenomenal world as a collection of distinct entities to a "dream" free of such artificial realities (as in Buddhism), but even without such a mental shift the enlightened realize the distinctions are in fact illusory.

In sum, enlightenment is simply a matter of knowing correctly: the inquiry into Brahman culminates in nondual knowledge, and the enlightened will now view the phenomenal world from the correct ontological point of view. They do not have the dualities set up in the state of normal *avidya*-driven awareness — they see this world of apparent reality and multiplicity and at the same time know that the nondual Brahman is the only reality. That is, the enlightening insight is applied to experiences of the "dream" realm once the enlightened are outside the *anubhava* experience: the enlightened know that only Brahman is real and all sense of diverse objects and subjects and change is illusory despite the presence of Ishvara's creation. The delusion that the phenomenal realm is a reality other than Brahman and populated with multiple distinct perceivers and entities has ended — i.e., it is the *idea* of multiple realities and atmans that is subrated by the enlightening knowledge, not the *phenomenal realm*. The "illusory" world does not disappear just because one person (*jiva*) becomes enlightened. After the enlightening experience, the phenomenal realm remains exactly as before: Ishvara's creation is not eliminated or cancelled when we wake up from the "dream" — only the superimpositions are (3.2.21). But after enlightenment, the sense of diversity returns (2.1.9). Outside the samadhic nondual state of consciousness, the enlightened see diverse phenomena in the world of Ishvara's creation, just as persons with defective eyes continue to see two moons even though they know there is only one (BSB intro., 4.1.15).[53] Thus, seeing the phenomenal world is not dropping out of the enlightened state of consciousness but a matter of *lucid dreaming* — the "dream" is still occurring as before, but the enlightened now know that they are dreaming. There is no ontological change in one's state since one has been Brahman all along. All that changes is one's knowledge: one realizes that one's phenomenal individuality and all of the diffuse world are not Brahman. "Names and forms" are seen as illusions. Thus, one's relation to the content of the "dream" has changed.

The enlightened are free of desire, sorrow, fear, and anger, and their actions produce no new karmic effects because the enlightened have no desires for things that they now see are illusions. The enlightened see the "dream" for what it is and are at peace with whatever happens to the *jiva* in the dream — they know their real "self" (the Atman) cannot be affected. But they are still fully in the dream — they move, talk, suffer physical pains, feel hunger, and so on, even if they remain emotionally unattached because these things are not part of what one really is. The differentiating mind (*manas*) is said to be no longer functioning — the enlightened are without mind (MunU 2.1.2) — and yet the enlightened can still use language (assuming Shankara was enlightened) to lead others to enlightenment. Thus, the differentiating mind must in fact still be active. The enlightened state is not a contentless state of one-pointed concentration (*samadhi*) — the enlightened are out of that state of consciousness and aware of phenomena, but they are in a state that integrates one's *anubhava* awareness of the nonduality of reality with sense-experience and a conceptualizing mind.[54]

---

[53] Enlightening knowledge may alter our *perception* of the world as in Buddhist mindfulness: our sensory-input remains the same, but the world is no longer perceived as being made of independent entities — conceptual divisions are no longer imposed.

[54] After death, the body falls away and so does any individuality of the enlightened. Individuality is a matter of the individuated mind (*manas*) within the illusory realm, not our essence. When the enlightened die, all mental functions merge into the

Shankara stated that actions and perceptions are possible only before enlightenment since they are based on the duality of experiencer and something done or experienced, like characters acting in a dream (4.3.14). But the enlightened are still in Ishvara's "creation" — only the delusion that there are multiple realities has ended, not movement in the phenomenal realm. The enlightened know that all action (*karma*) is illusory and that they are not doers — only Ishvara enacts our movements, not them for *jivas* have no real agency (3.3.32), and even that is an illusion since Brahman in reality does not change at all. Unenlightened actions are based on dualities and superimposed ideas. Brahman-knowledge destroys the entire world of actions, actors, and karmic effects (3.4.16). When Shankara spoke of the cessation of all *actions* (1.1.4) he may have meant only that knowledge of Brahman ends all actions by the enlightened that could *produce karmic effects* since movements by the enlightened and events still occur in Ishvara's "creation." (Nor did he discuss only *ritual* actions in this regard but all the acts of the enlightened.) Indeed, Shankara himself taught and wrote as his past karma worked itself out.

But one no longer thinks of oneself as the actor — the events of the dream simply occur. The characters in the dream do not own the actions, and so they perform their acts with detachment from any concern for consequences for one's *jiva* and with no sense of agency, and so no karmic effects binding the person to the cycle of rebirths are produced. There is an inner renunciation of the fruits of one's actions, but the actions still occur. (This renunciation for Shankara is an effect of Brahman-knowledge, not a cause of it.) One is at peace and becomes child-like (3.4.50). In fact, actions may not change at all — it is the inner life that matters.

The enlightened are not immediately disembodied upon gaining enlightening knowledge (4.2.7). They remain in this world until the karmic effects of earlier deeds that had begun to take effect before enlightenment (*prarabdha-karma*) are exhausted (4.1.19), just as a potter's wheel continues to spin after the potter's hand is removed (4.1.15) or an arrow once shot continues in flight until it lands. In fact, the enlightened may be *reborn* in this world if they have a specific assignment (*adhikara*) from Ishvara that has not been completed in this life (3.3.32). Other karmic effects are utterly burned up by knowledge — actions cannot destroy karmic effects. Although the

---

manas and the *manas* merges into the Atman, but then all of the mental functions dissolve (2.3.17, 4.2.12, 4.3.15) leaving no individuality or distinguishing features to be incorporated into Brahman. The Atman has no senses or mind (BSB 1.3.12). Other Vedanta schools hold that persons retain individuality in this world and after death.

enlightened produce no actions with karmic effects since they do not identify with the character in the "dream" that is the basis for desires producing actions with karmic effects, the mind and other limiting adjuncts nonetheless remain connected to the individual embodied atman as long as the individual person exists in the cycle of rebirths (3.3.30) despite the enlightened person's knowledge.[55] Thus, the actions of the enlightened are constrained by their embodiment and the effects of some past actions.

Enlightenment and Morality

For Shankara, only knowledge can produce enlightenment: *actions* are confined to the realm of *root-ignorance*. Even action combined with knowledge does not produce enlightenment. Actions can prepare the unenlightened mind but can do no more (1.1.1). In fact, he goes so far as to say that action (*karma*) is actually *incompatible* with enlightenment (Upad 1.1.8-15). Nevertheless, the enlightened must act — even if they are silent or choose not move a muscle, these are still actions. It may be that by "*karma*" Shankara in these discussions means only *ritual action* or actions that have *karmic effects*, not *all actions*. (Otherwise, Shankara is just plain inconsistent which, as discussed below, may not have bothered him.) He applied the depictions of a Hindu renouncer (*sannyasin*) to the enlightened life in which Vedic ritual injunctions and dharmic requirements no longer apply (3.4.25; Potter 1981: 35) since there is no individual person upon whom injunctions could be laid and so no room for injunctions (3.2.21).[56] No value-prescriptions apply (2.3.48).

But even if their actions have no karmic effects and ritual injunctions do not apply to them, how do the enlightened decide what to do? They have no desires to fulfill and see everything as a dream. Or do they in fact make no decisions as they move about while their *prarabdha-karma* works itself out? Are they simply mechanically propelled by lingering impressions (*samskaras*,

---

[55] Shankara stated that the enlightened are "disembodied" while in this world (1.1.4), but that can only be meant figuratively, not literally. The enlightened no longer associate their true essence with the phenomenal body and mind, and so from the highest point of view, they are "disembodied."

[56] Shankara was orthodox and conservative in his requirements for the *unenlightened* with regard to ritual and dharmic duties, but not for the enlightened. Low caste persons were not permitted to study the Vedas (BSB 1.3.38) even though caste is just another superimposed duality. The rest of orthodoxy would be of the same nature. (But see Marcaurelle 2000 for a strong argument that for Shankara enlightenment is an inner renunciation of agency available to all regardless of caste or sex.)

vasanas) left by their actions performed before they were enlightened? Or do they walk around exclaiming "It's all a dream! It doesn't matter what we do!" Or "All this world is but a game (*lila*) — be a joyful player!" But this does not jibe with Shankara bothering to teach.

This brings up the problem of a *moral concern* for other people: Shankara gave no reason why the enlightened should act in any particular way. Shankara took dharmic virtues and ritual practices as applying to the unenlightened on the path, but they have no place once we see that all this is a dream (2.1.14). Moral concern is at most a prerequisite for enlightenment: the unenlightened lessen a sense of an independent sense that way. But moral actions do not bring about enlightenment and have no basis once we see that all persons are only part of a dream. Thus, Shankara had little to say about ethics or morality for the enlightened. In commenting on the *Bhagavad-gita*, Shankara pays lip service to its position that the enlightened should fulfill duties to "hold together the world (*loka-samgraha*)" for the welfare of others (BGB 3.25, 4.20), but he does not expand on it. Indeed, why the enlightened should do this is not at all clear since the world is just a dream — there is nothing to maintain or any beings whose welfare matters.[57] Nor is the dream realm maintained by individuals but by Ishvara. Once one realizes what our true essence (atman) is, one realizes that there are no real persons to help or harm. One has no desires concerning the world — how can one care about the welfare of characters in a dream? Enlightened Advaitins are not like Mahayana Buddhist Bodhisattvas who see a reality in "persons" to guide toward the end of worldly suffering. But there is little in classical Advaita on the enlightened helping others. Nor is there much on social action in classical Advaita (Fort 1997). All in all, any concern for the welfare of others does not fit with his metaphysics of illusionism concerning the phenomenal realm — why bother to maintain even the social world if the entire realm has no reality whatsoever? Any actions that occur due to karma will do just fine.

In sum, with Shankara's version of nondual metaphysics, morality is radically undercut: there are no obligations to the *illusory characters* (*jivas*) in a dream, and without some reality to be morally concerned about morality cannot operate — the basic presupposition for morality of something to be concerned about is absent. The enlightened have no more concern for *jivas*

---

[57] "World" (*loka*) may mean *the social world* since the enlightened do not have the power to conserve (or destroy) the "physical" universe. That power is reserved for Ishvara. Still, for Shankara there is no real world to maintain — all is only an illusion. But the pull of "illusory" society may have caused him to defy his own metaphysics.

than for the "snake" once we know there is only the rope. Thus, there are no realities that would benefit from moral action: Brahman is unaffectable and changeless, and the *jivas* are mere fictions. Brahman is seen as all-knowing, all-powerful, and omnipresent (e.g., 1.1.1), as God is in the West, but not as omnibenevolent. Even when misperceived as the creator and ruler Ishvara, Brahman is never depicted as moral or as loving the characters in the dream (e.g., 2.2.3) — there is no second reality for it to be concerned with.

Thus, ethics is only part of the dualistic illusion and has no place in reality. Showing concern for others (including our loved ones) only reveals that we are deluded. The conclusion is not to be immoral toward others or antinomian or to withdraw from society: one no longer identifies with the body, and there is simply no motive or reason to do anything but let whatever events occur occur. Seeing someone killed is a matter of indifference since no one is really killed and what is actually real is unaffected (BGB 2.19; KaU II.18-19). Indeed, indifference to one's own or others' suffering (including those close to us) is the only proper respond. If all that matters is the oneness of reality (*sat*), then nothing differentiated matters. Other characters in a dream do not warrant our concern. What happens to objects in the dream is simply irrelevant and would leave the enlightened emotionally cold. Nothing that happens in our illusory world matters. To respond as if something did matter would give the phenomenal realm or *jivas* some reality. Thus, *not* caring or responding would show other (nonexistent) persons the unreality of it all.

In short, the enlightened can have no reason to be moral. Even the unenlightened should emulate the enlightened point of view by treating others as no more than dream characters. The devastating effect of his metaphysics on morality was recognized by later Advaitins. They explained why the enlightened could act in the phenomenal world in one of three ways: there is no true enlightenment in life, and so the enlightened point of view is never activated; the enlightened overcome duality and have the enlightened state only during periods of *nirvikalpa samadhi*, and so they have the enlightened knowledge outside that altered state of consciousness but still experience duality when sense-experience returns and so must take morality seriously; or even the enlightened still have a trace (*lesha*) of root-ignorance, i.e., wrong knowledge (*mithya-jnana, ajnana*) persists in the awakened state (4.1.15).[58] Advaitins also changed Shankara's metaphysics and gave the world

---

[58] But Shankara said that enlightenment could not be lost even in a waking state, and so by "*mithya-jnana*" here he may have meant only that the perception of the phenomenal *world* persists for the enlightened, not that erroneous *knowledge* is

at least a semblance of reality: the phenomenal may not be real (*sat*) but it is not totally unreal (*asat*) either — it has an "undefinable (*anirvachaniya*)" status. Thus, what is not real (*sat*) is not necessarily unreal (*asat*) — what is illusory is "nonreal" but not totally nonexistent. But for Shankara there is no middle category between being eternally real (*sat*) and being utterly unreal (*asat*) like the child of a barren woman (2.1.18) or the horns of a hare (2.2.26).

Those today who see the importance of a moral concern for others impose it on Shankara by ignoring his basic teachings (e.g., Todd 2013). Some commentators say to simply forget the true metaphysics and pretend other persons are "real" (e.g., Prasad 2009). That is intellectually dishonest about one's fundamental beliefs. Nor is it obvious how the enlightened could do that concerning their basic beliefs — how could one backslide and see the "snake" again? Such a move would also be an admission that something is wrong with their basic beliefs. But Advaitins have continued to wrestle with whether the enlightened while in the world had limitations and whether holding knowledge of Brahman in the mind was compatible with sense-experience (see Nelson 1996). Shankara would see giving morality any importance for the enlightened as a product of root-ignorance — it would be giving the dream world reality. For him, ethics is only about actions within the illusory dream and so cannot be taken seriously.[59] (But again, bothering to write or teach at all was not consistent with his metaphysics.)

* * *

---

present in him — *vidya* and *avidya* cannot coexist in the same person (BU 3.5.1).

[59] For more on Shankara's ethical problem, see Jones 2004: chap. 6 and Rao 2009: 206-209. Modern Neo-Vedanta, influenced by Western religion and philosophy, has shaped our view of ethics in Advaita (Fort 1997).

~ *Shankara's Arguments* ~

Throughout Shankara's commentary, opponents raise issues that modern Westerners would recognize as philosophical objections, and he responded with reasons.[1] (Yes, mystics do reason [see Jones 2016: chap. 7].) He implicitly employs the most basic logical principle: the law of noncontradiction — in this context, that conflicting properties cannot exist together (e.g., something cannot be both active and inactive at the same time [2.2.13], or exist and not exist [2.2.33]). Opponents are constantly pointing out apparent contradictions (*badhitas*) in Advaita claims, and Shankara is constantly showing that the apparent contradictions are the products of root-ignorance and that there is in fact no contradiction.[2] In turn, Shankara tries to show contradictions or a conflict with the Vedas in other schools' claims. He is trying to show what can be reasonably justified (*upapatti*), established (*siddha*), or inferred (*tarka*) by reasoning (*yukti*) or by scripture (*shruti, shabda*). He appeals to the Vedas, reasoning, and also to everyday experiences — what is seen in the world — to establish problems with his opponents' positions. He also appeals to everyday experiences to establish principles — e.g., nothing arises from nothing since that is never seen in the world (2.2.26). His positions and his opponents' positions may have been products of debates, which were common in classical India. But if we examine Shankara's reasoning in his commentary, we can see that Shankara's thought is very frustrating.

A Theological Framework

As discussed, Brahman is knowable (1.1.1), but it is not an object observable in the elements or space (2.3.7) and thus is not open to the senses or knowable by our conceptualizing mind (*manas*) (1.1.3, 2.1.31). It is directly experienceable as the inner consciousness that is our essence (atman) (1.3.13). For

---

[1] The *Brahma Sutra* also relies on reasoning, especially in its second book.

[2] Shankara employed the "four options" approach of Madhyamaka Buddhism (see Jones 2015: 160-62) once (2.2.14) to show that all logical possibilities are exhausted: atoms (*paramanus*) by their nature must be active, inactive, both, or neither — there is no fifth option. Also see his rejection of the Jainas' seven points of view (2.2.33).

Shankara the revealed Vedas are the only means to correct knowledge (*pramana*) for knowledge of Brahman (1.1.1-2), not our experiences or inferences. Reasoning can be utilized on the path to enlightenment to help understand the Upanishads, but it is not a means of attaining Brahman-knowledge — the highest Atman can be fathomed only by scripture (2.1.31). Nor can we know Brahman by the *pramana* of sense-experience or reasoning that applies within the phenomenal world since Brahman is not an object of observation (1.1.1, 1.1.3, 1.1.4, 2.1.6, 2.1.27, 2.3.7, 3.2.23). The standard of knowledge is certainty and only revealed texts provide that. Shankara says that this appeal to revealed authority (*shruti*) is necessary since philosophers constantly contradict each other (2.1.11). In that passage, Shankara acknowl-edges the objection that this claim is itself an instance of reasoning, but he still asserts that only the Vedas, being eternal and heard by seers, provide the necessary true knowledge.

All of Shankara's reasoning occurs in this theological framework that treats the Upanishads as the unquestioned exclusive source of authority in matters of Brahman: only reasoning (*tarka, yukti*) in conformity with this revealed scripture can be justified (2.1.11, 2.1.6). Reasoning is for worldly matters, not liberation (2.1.11). His ultimate authority for understanding Brahman is not anyone's own mystical experiences or those of mystics but the texts revealed to the ancient seers (*rishis*). Shankara explicitly criticizes reasoning that is seen as not being in accord with the scriptures: "dry reasoning (*shushka-tarka*)" unjustified by the Vedas cannot be valid, and there is no room for objections based on reasoning once the meaning of scripture is established (2.1.4). But only unfettered reasoning is rejected, not all reasoning. This does subordinate reasoning to a religious authority, but being the "handmaiden" of theology does not impair his ability to reason — thinking within first principles laid down by scripture does not disqualify thought from being philosophical in nature in India any more than it did in medieval Europe. So too, he makes arguments that do not invoke any Upanishadic passage but relies solely on reasoning. For example, in BSB 3.2.11, he explicitly relies on the principle that one thing cannot have two conflicting or contradictory characteristics — nothing can be self-contradictory.

But Shankara makes no attempt to justify the Vedas as authorities, why we should accept the testimony of the seers, or to establish Brahman's existence. The Vedas are simply accepted as eternal and their authority assumed. (It is implicitly assumed that the seers heard the texts *accurately*.) This limits the thoroughness of the rationality of his philosophy. (But then again, it is impossible to establish any first principles such as why God exists or why anything exists [see Jones 2018: chap. 5].)

Another problem is with the passages in the Upanishads: various seers apparently *contradict* each other (2.1.1). But Shankara claims that scripture cannot contradict itself and so the apparent contradictions must be *interpreted* to show the Vedas' true consistency (2.3.6).[3] For example, he reconciles the fact that in the Upanishads Brahman is called both real (*sat*) and unreal (*asat*) by claiming that *asat* refers to reality existing before the rise of the phenomenal world (1.4.15; see CU 6.2.1, TU 2.6). That is, Brahman is *asat* when in an unmanifested form (see Jones 2014a: 188–90). Thus, *asat* does not mean literal nonexistence but merely the state of *sat* before the rise of manifest names and forms (2.1.17).

Indeed, overcoming logical contradictions is a major theme of the BSB. Shankara also realizes that not all passages in the Upanishads support his nonduality, and so to create consistency, when the literal meaning of passages did not conform to his metaphysics of nondualism and illusionism, Shankara interprets them as figurative (*upachara*) and not meant literally. That is, he attempts to get around passages that clearly suggest real emanated entities or other dualities by distinguishing passages of direct meaning that express nonduality from passages of indirect meaning that reflect our unenlightened conventional (dualistic) point of view and so must be interpreted to fit with the passages of direct meaning reflecting his metaphysics. For example, when the Upanishads and the *Brahma Sutra* speak Brahman dividing itself into different forms (2.1.42) or of the individual atman being part of the Lord it is only means parts "so to speak" (*iti*) (2.3.43) since Brahman is partless.

In sum, the Upanishads, despite being eternal and heard by seers, have to be interpreted to get their proper understanding, and the proper understanding is provided by his metaphysics of only one reality and illusionism. Shankara gave no exegetical principle permitting this. (Non-Advaitins could utilize the same principle to interpret Upanishadic passages to fit their ontologies.) But in this way, he makes the revealed texts *conform to his philosophy, not vice versa*. That is, his brand of nondual metaphysics in the end controls his understanding of the Upanishads, not vice versa. But his

---

[3] Shankara might argue that the inconsistencies in the Vedas show that all the claims are products of the realm of *avidya* and that Advaita teachers are utilizing any ideas, true or false, that might help to lead the unenlightened to the end of rebirths. More on this below.

reasoning is circular: his cites the Vedas for justification of his philosophy, but his philosophy dictates how the Vedas are to be understood. In sum, Shankara claims that the Vedas are absolute on the matter of Brahman, but then he interprets the texts to fit his system. In this way, his own philosophy ends up being the final court of appeal, not allegedly revealed texts.

Consciousness and Brahman

Besides the circularity problem for authority, a major problem arises with Shankara's claim that Brahman-knowledge is self-established (*svatah-siddha*) (2.3.7) and thus is not in need of any further proof or justification. It is self-validating and not open to error. To Shankara, the "I" who knows is a timeless and unchanging consciousness (*chitta*) transcending the individual (2.3.7). This essence (atman) is our true nature and cannot be denied, just as the heat of a fire cannot be denied by the fire (2.3.7). He asserted that Brahman is known to everyone in self-awareness (1.1.1), and that this is self-evident and thus self-certifying. Thus, the denial of Brahman is self-refuting — to deny one's own existence, who would be the denier be (1.1.4, 2.3.7)?

But is Shankara's claim that a pure consciousness is the *only reality* in fact self-certifying? States of consciousness are self-certifying — if you have a headache, you have a headache and need no further certification. But claims about the headache's cause or how it is grounded in the brain or its nature as a mental phenomenon are not self-certifying. So too with all experiences qua experiences. Thus, the *anubhava* experience may be self-certifying *as an experience or state of consciousness*, but it does not follow that the enlightened *claims about its nature or causes* are self-certifying any more than for any other experience. That experience may be nonpropositional and unsubratable, but what constitutes the enlightened person's *knowledge* is still propositional in nature and is stated in the Upanishads' "great sayings" such as "I am Brahman" (BU 1.4.10) and "You are that" (CU 6.8-16)and those claims are not self-certifying but are open to question.

Establishing that we *are conscious* is one thing, but establishing that *consciousness transcends* our bodies and the phenomenal world and is the *sole reality* is quite another. Just because we know we are conscious it does not follow that we know that there is only one essence (atman) — the one reality, Brahman. We can easily question whether our essence (atman) is that reality (1.1.17, 2.3.2, 4.1.13). In the end, Shankara had to appeal to a theological argument: only the Vedas' eternal and perfect knowledge will suffice (2.1.11).

But his arguments are not compelling to those who reject the Vedas as revealed authorities or even to other Vedanta schools that do accept them as such but reject his interpretations.

René Descartes took the same experience — our *self-awareness* — that Shankara took to be of Brahman as individuated in each person and separate from material objects. That is enough to realize that Shankara's knowledge-claim about our atman being Brahman is not self-certifying or established by mere definition. Indeed, self-awareness supports claiming the reality of the *jiva*, not its denial in the face of a transcend featureless consciousness. Western philosophers following David Hume today deny there is any a self-contained center to all our mental activity — a "self." Buddhists take all consciousness to be constantly changing — a series of impermanent events. Early Buddhists claimed that we never experience an unchanging core to all our mental events. Samkhya-Yogins separate the pure transcendent, feature-less, and unmoving consciousness that constitutes a witnessing person (a *purusha*) entirely from matter (*pradana/prakriti*), thus setting up a dualism. The Vedantins Ramanuja and Madhva gave other interpretations to the same Upanishadic passages that Shankara focused upon for the oneness of consciousness in which the individual person remains distinct in some ways from Brahman. Ramanuja denied that Brahman is featureless (BSR intro. and 4.4.4). For him, consciousness is not constant and the individual self (atman) is not pure consciousness but a knower and an agent, and thus these features are not the product of root-ignorance.

In sum, Shankara's claim that the undifferentiated consciousness constitutes *all of reality* remains an metaphysical conclusion that Buddhists, Samkhya-Yogins, and many in the West do not draw from their experiences of self-consciousness or from experiences of pure consciousness empty of all differentiated phenomena. If the consciousness that is Brahman is featureless and formless, as Shankara claims, then he has to defend his interpretation of its ontological nature on other grounds — nothing is given in the *anubhava* experience itself that would attest to it being the only reality. Only after the experience can one take the experience to be a matter of being a realization of Brahman. The pure consciousness experience may seem so real and profound — more real than ordinary empirical experiences — that it may well inspire one who is trained in the Advaita tradition to adopt its metaphys-ical theory rather than Samkhya-Yoga's or another's, but endorsing that theory is still a post-experience event involving our dualistic mind. Indeed, the basic *insight* that Brahman is the only reality has to occur outside the *anubhava* experience and depends upon the experiencer's prior beliefs and theories. It remains a theory and must be defended as such — it is not self-justifying. Shankara asserted that we have a general knowledge of Brahman (*samanya jnana*) through our own consciousness (1.1.1), but he also realized that an "inquiry into Brahman" was still necessary because of conflicting opinions on the specific nature of Brahman (BSB intro.). Only Shankara's unwavering commitment to the Vedas as the sole means of correct knowl-edge on matters of Brahman (as interpreted through his particular nondual-ism) would make it seem that the metaphysical theory is self-certifying. But Shankara comes across as unable to see a very real issue. As things stand, his is metaphysical speculation and Brahman is a metaphysical posit. These must be defended by more than an apply to self-awareness and revealed texts.

Arguing by Analogy

When advancing reasons alone is inadequate, the principal means of argu-ment for Shankara, as in Western metaphysics, is to employ analogies. Since reason and ordinary experience cannot reach Brahman, Shankara offers analogies to help to us understand the relation of Brahman, the individual's atman, and the phenomenal world. The key analogies are these:

Clay and clay pot (e.g., 2.1.9, 2.1.14). The clay (Brahman) is real regardless of the shape (name-and-form) it is temporarily in and does not change when the pot is smashed. The temporary form is only imposed onto the clay by our imagination and is not real. So too with Brahman and root-ignorance.

The rope and snake (e.g., 1.1.4, 1.3.18). A rope is misperceived at dusk to be a snake. There is no snake to experience — it is totally illusory. The rope (Brahman) is real and the snake (the phenomenal world) has no reality whatsoever.[4] The rope/snake is a perceptual analog to the intellectual error.

Magician and a trick (e.g., 2.1.9, 2.1.21). The magician is real and the trick only has the appearance of reality and of being independent of the magician.

The dreamer and the dream (e.g., 1.3.18, 2.1.9). The dreamer is real (Brah-man), but the content of the dream (the phenomenal world) has no reality.

A transparent crystal and an adjacent colored object (e.g., 1.3.19, 3.2.11, 3.2.15). The crystal (Brahman) is transparent and does not change or move, but it takes on the color of the objects (limiting adjuncts) placed next to it.

---

[4] Later Advaitins who gave the world more reality as something with an "indefinable" status claimed that we *experience* an illusory snake until knowledge arises — it is the *appearance* of the real rope until knowledge arises and so is not totally unreal.

The crystal only appears permeated by color but actually remains transparent.

Space in a jar (e.g., 1.1.6, 1.2.20). Space (Brahman) is singular and continuous. The space in a jar (a phenomenon) only seems discontinuous with the rest of space. Nor does it change in the jar or when the jar is broken. Only root-ignorance makes the jar's space seem a part of the expanse of space that merges with the rest of space when the jar is broken. Just as space only appears divided, so too Brahman only appears divided into the consciousness of different individuals due to root-ignorance with its limiting adjuncts. (This is the most common analogy in the BSB.)

Two moons (e.g., Intro., 2.1.27). The moon (Brahman) is only one but seems dual to those with an eye-disease (root-ignorance). So too, there are no real differences in the phenomena of the perceived world despite appearances.

Mother-of-pearl shell (Intro.). The shell only appears to be silver — we misconstrue the shell's actual nature. So too with reality appearing diverse.

Mirage (e.g., 2.1.14, 2.2.28). Something is there but is misperceived as another reality.

However, each analogy has limitations that prevent it from being a truly effective aid to the student:

Clay and clay pot. Root-ignorance is not simply a matter of applying name-and-form (*nama-rupa*) to the phenomena of the world since the true reality (Brahman) is not objective. This makes the analogy hard to apply. Nor is Brahman a substratum to the world — there is only one reality, not layers.

The rope and snake. When we see the rope as a rope, the illusion vanishes, but with enlightening knowledge of the oneness of reality the "illusion" (the world) remains (Intro., 4.1.15). Nor is Brahman misperceived — Brahman is never an object of the senses. Nor is the illusory world a veil hiding Brahman. So too, this analogy introduces duality into Brahman.

Magician and a trick. Brahman does not project an illusion, although when Shankara speaks dualistically the world is seen as Ishvara's creation.

The dreamer and the dream. How can the pure, unchanging, and undifferentiated consciousness that constitutes the dreamer (Brahman) have any dreams in it at all since dreams must involve diversity? Does the analogy force our unenlightened mind to make Brahman into a person like us?

Space in a jar. The reality (Brahman) is not an objective, laid-out, spatial entity nor can it be divided into parts (2.1.14). It is hard to understand how to apply the idea of limited space to Brahman when Brahman is dimensionless.

A transparent crystal and an adjacent object. In what sense can Brahman come near to anything illusory? How can Brahman take on features of illusory limiting adjuncts?

Two moons. The analogy relies on a dualism of a changing perceiver and a reality perceived. In addition, the diffuse phenomenal world remains after enlightenment, and the enlightened still see it.[5]

Mother-of-pearl shell. Ishvara's "creation" remains the same even after one has gained knowledge of what it really is, but Brahman is never seen. Nor is enlightenment merely a matter of seeing the illusion properly but knowing the oneness of reality.

Mirage. This involves a dualism of something real seen improperly by a perceiver. But enlightenment is not merely seeing a mirage properly. Brahman is not seen at all since it is never an object of the senses. Nor is there a substratum underlying appearances. If there were, how could Brahman be seen improperly?

Some other analogies that Shankara employed fit his metaphysics even less well. The analogy of the sea and its differentiated foam and waves (2.1.13-14) is out of place in a strict nondualism. So too with any analogy that suggests the emanation of something real, such as fire emitting sparks (2.3.46, 3.2.25). The utter uniqueness of Brahman and the denial of any second reality makes any analogy problematic. The most basic issue is that all analogies are of necessity drawn from our experience grounded in the *dualistic* point of view of our root-ignorance — they will involve apparent diversity even though Brahman is partless and unchanging. The analogies are also limited by the fact that we cannot perceive Brahman through the senses (3.2.23). We can make Brahman into a mental object for purposes of meditation (e.g., 3.2.15), but it is not actually an object of perception or spatialized. Each analogy can convey the sense that we are deluded and give us the sense that there is a reality other than the perceived world, but that is as far as they can go — no dualistic based analogy can get us out of the root-ignorance-generated point of view. All the unenlightened will have is an idea from our deluded conceptualizing mind based in dualism. For example, thinking all this a dream still involves the dualism of a dreamer and something dreamed. Shankara himself admitted that any analogy is limited to only some common features shared by Brahman and the phenomenon utilized in the analogy

---

[5] Enlightening knowledge may alter one's *perception* of the world as in Buddhist mindfulness: the sensory input remains the same, but the enlightened no longer impose our mind's conceptual divisions. That is, the world remains but is now no longer perceived as being made up of independent entities.

(3.1.20), but Brahman is unique. Analogies rely on limiting adjuncts, which are devoid of consciousness, and Brahman participates in the properties and states of phenomenal limiting adjuncts within which it abides but only "so to speak" (*iti*) since Brahman is never modified or observed (3.2.20).

In sum, no analogy that we can make can convey the pure unchanging consciousness that is Brahman without introducing some duality and that limits their effectiveness as teaching tools or as a way to reason about Brahman's nature or to remove doubts about its existence or nature. This limits the usefulness of analogies in reasoning to justify Shankara's claims.

False Attribution and Negation

Another of Shankara's method of teaching is to affirm something of Brahman stated in the Upanishads and then to negate it — first applying an attribution (*adhyaropa*) to Brahman that is known to be false followed by its negation (*apavada*).[6] That is, even though nothing can be affirmed of Brahman as actually true, something phenomenal is temporarily superimposed onto Brahman in order to show that Brahman exists and does not have the opposite characteristic, and it is then rejected so that the student does not think that that attribute ultimately applies either.[7] Through a series of these attributions and negations, the student is led to the discrimination (*viveka*) of the real (*sat*) from the unreal (*asat*) — one realizes that Brahman is "not this, not that" (*neti neti*) but is not nonexistent either. The positive attributions in the Upanishads are then taken to be only figurative (*upachara*, *lakshana*) and not meant literally (*svartha*). Positive attributions give the student some idea of what Brahman is not (by their denial of the opposite characteristics), but they too must be denied in the end because nothing phenomenal can be affirmed of the transcendent.

Through this technique, all conceptualizations of Brahman are removed. Even the "great sayings" such as "You are that" or "Brahman is consciousness" are ultimately rejected as arising from only the conceptualizing mind (*manas*). Thinking "I am Brahman" still involves a duality. Even the words

---

[6] Gaudapada employed this method earlier.

[7] Thus, the negation of one attribute is not meant to *affirm* its opposite. Nor does the fact that something was negated mean that what was negated was real — e.g., *maya* need not be a reality to be negated. But in arguing against his opponents, Shankara stated that something must be there in the dream in order to be negated and so Brahman is affirmed in the process of negation (2.1.7).

"Atman" and "Brahman" are only superimposed onto what is real (BUB 2.3.6). In our unenlightened state, "reality (*sat*)" and "consciousness (*chitta*)" remain products of our root-ignorance and so must be rejected in the final analysis.

This teaching device means that the metaphysical affirmations concerning Brahman, the individual, and the world cannot be meant literally. But the soteriological purpose of Shankara's teachings is affirmed: to awaken the unenlightened to the fact that reality is nondual and that the diversity they see is an illusory dream. Like the *via negativa* in the West, this approach can help turn a student away from the phenomenal world and away from thinking that reason can grasp the transcendent reality, but it cannot get a student out of a dualistic point of view — from the unenlightened point of view, it only isolates one object from all other objects. No positive knowledge of Brahman can be conveyed by this method. Something more is needed, and if this method is employed by Advaitins in conjunction with meditation, trust in the Advaita theory of Brahman-knowledge may arise.

Arguing Within the Illusion: Two Points of View

The *adhyaropa/apavada* strategy can be seen as an attribution of something phenomenal from the root-ignorance point of view and a denial from the higher Brahman-knowledge point of view. This points to a broader aspect of Shankara's reasoning: he can argue from within the pluralistic "dream" and then turn around and claim that the "dream" is not ultimately real, and hence the argument is groundless.[8] He treats the embodied atman and Brahman as different and then states that they are nondifferent (e.g., 2.1.22). He speaks of the embodied atman and also claims that the Atman is not limited by adjuncts (1.2.6). He treats the embodied *atman* and Brahman as different for some arguments and then states that they are in fact nondifferent (2.1.22). That is, he treats the embodied *atman* and the transcendent *Atman* as

---

[8] The *Brahma Sutra* and Shankara may have gotten the idea of two types of "truths" from Madhyamaka Buddhism. But unlike Nagarjuna's method (see Jones 2015:158-67), he advances substantive claims about Brahman and the world and defends them with the Vedas. He shows problems with others' position based on reasoning or ordinary experiences or inconsistency with the Vedas or internal inconsistency. He shows how some positions lead to an infinite regress (2.1.18, 2.2.13, 2.39). Elsewhere he utilizes a *reductio ad absurdum* approach — i.e., he argues against an opponent "Even if we accept your premises, your position leads to a logical inconsistency," but he advances claims from the Upanishads. He did occasionally use the law of the excluded middle — i.e., everything must be *x* or *not-x* (e.g., 2.1.32).

different (e.g., 1.1.21, 1.2.8, 1.2.11) despite the fact that they are one reality. He argues extensively for the claim that the individual inner atman is infinitesimal in size (2.3.19-28) and then turns around and denies that and asserts that that claim is only a matter of limiting adjuncts since the inner atman is actually the nonfinite supreme Brahman (2.3.29).

To refute a claim Shankara treats limiting adjuncts as real and states that Brahman enters into them but then claims from the ultimately correct point of view that Brahman does not change (3.2.20) and is untouched by events in the body (2.3.46) or by limiting adjuncts (3.2.22) or by enlightenment (1.1.4). He treats the atman as distinct from the body to establish that consciousness is not material (3.3.54) and still claims that consciousness is the only reality.[9] He states that Brahman is all-pervading and then claims the world is an illusion that Brahman has no contact with (1.1.4, 1.1.20). He speaks of Brahman transforming itself to create the world (1.4.26, 2.1.14, 2.1.24) and then turns around and claims that any transformation or any other alleged change in Brahman is unreal and only imagined due to root-ignorance (2.1.27) — Brahman is not a creator, sustainer, or destroyer of anything since the Upanishads deny Brahman has any distinctive attributes (4.3.14). So too, the "atman of bliss (ananda)" is said to be the innermost atman (1.1.12, 1.1.15), but then he says that is only meant figuratively (1.1.19). So too, he can assert that there are different things "in" Brahman (2.1.28) and yet Brahman is one and featureless. He speaks as if "Brahman with attributes" (saguna) is different from "Brahman without attributes" (nirguna) (e.g., 4.3.9) and then claims and there is no dualism of saguna and nirguna Brahmans and that Brahman is spoken of as having attributes only from the point of view of root-ignorance for the sake of meditation (4.3.14). He interprets different verses as referring to one form (rupa) or another of Brahman even though from the highest point of view Brahman's true nature (svarupa) is a reality without form (arupa) (1.1.20, 1.3.19, 2.1.6, 3.2.14). He treats the world as a creation or an emanation that is dependent upon a transcendent source and then claims that this dualistic point of view is ultimately false.

Thus, the paradox is that Shankara can both take the phenomenal realm very seriously and still turn around and dismiss it as an illusion that is not real since what is actually real (Brahman) is not observable. He explicitly acknowledges that a refutation is based on distinctions in ordinary experiences but that in reality such distinctions do not exist (2.1.14). It is as if a

---

[9] The argument against materialism warrants only one aphorism (3.3.54) while such topics as rituals and the path of rebirth after death earn extensive discussions.

character within a dream utilizes elements from within the dream itself to convince other characters that they are in a dream — the enlightened are fighting fire with fire. (Of course, from what Shankara sees as the ontologically correct point of view, an illusory character is arguing to other illusory characters.) The enlightened can take advantage of Shankara claiming that phenomenal activities should be treated as real by the unenlightened prior to enlightenment (2.1.14). They can utilize dualities in their arguments and yet reject all dualities from the higher point of view.

Thus, an enlightened character can both utilize aspects of the dream and present arguments based on dualisms and yet still ultimately reject all dualisms and claim that the dream is actually only an illusion and that something else is real. Moreover, Shankara can present contradicting arguments from the root-ignorance point of view since they do not reflect reality, and so whatever argument helps a listener to gain knowledge of the oneness of reality can be advanced. To give more examples, he states that the concept of "cause" does not apply to Brahman and yet he speaks of Brahman as the material and efficient cause of the phenomenal world. So too, Shankara claims that the individual (*jiva-atman*) is distinct from Ishvara due to the limiting adjuncts and that the highest Atman is something other than the individual (e.g., 1.1.7, 3.2.5) — the embodied atman is the actor and the highest Atman is the observer (1.1.17, 1.2.9; MuU 3.1.1) — while still asserting that they are identical and not really distinct (e.g., 1.1.5, 1.1.19, 1.3.19, 3.2.6), and that the apparent embodiment of the Atman is only a product of root-ignorance (1.1.17). So too, with the atman entering the Atman in deep sleep (2.3.40) while claiming that the atman is always identical to the partless Atman. With two points of view, he can treat phenomena within the world as differentiated and yet still treat everything as nondifferent (*ananya*) from Brahman (2.3.6) although he does not care to demonstrate how the apparent differentiations are possible in a metaphysics of absolute nondualism.[10]

In sum, in this way of arguing Shankara utilizes arguments against other schools based on dualistic illusions arising from root-ignorance but then rejects all dualistic ideas. He advances arguments based on something that seems to exist or occur in the phenomenal realm and then turns around and rejects it as an illusion — he utilizes it and then denies it actually exists.

---

[10] Shankara accepts that difference and nondifference cannot exist together since they are contradictory and tries to explain the appearance in terms of the space within a jar not really being different from all of space (2.1.22). But this does not explain why there is differentiation that persists for the enlightened.

Indeed, it is surprising how much of his BSB is about rituals, Ishvara, the individual person, causation, and other worldly phenomena presented from a dualistic point of view — of course, all dualisms are then denied by his non-dualistic metaphysics.

But Shankara's approach gives him great freedom in his arguments, even though they look like inconsistencies. He can argue a position (for characters within the dream) and then reject it (from the enlightened point of view). This means that Brahman is an entity with features and Atman is multiple only "so to speak" (*iva*), but this way of speaking is permissible. He then can speak of Brahman as a person or a witnessing consciousness even though he ultimately rejects the subject and object as dualistic since it turns Brahman into consciousness and an object. He argues for a theistic creator (Ishvara) to refute Samkhya's position and then turns around and asserts that creation is an illusion and that Ishvara is merely the inactive and nonpersonal Brahman misconstrued through dualistic root-ignorance. He can utilize analogies and then immediate reject them (3.2.27-29). He utilizes the language of merging with Brahman (e.g., 4.2.15) and then says there is only one reality and so merger is only "so to speak." He adopts an emanationist cosmology for the dualistic picture (2.2.17) but dismisses it in his ontology as only a claim made from the point of view of root-ignorance. He can utilize talk of causation as appropriate from the dualistic point of view of root-ignorance and then deny that there is in fact any causation. He treats limiting adjuncts as objective parts of Ishvara's "creation" (*maya*) independent of our control and still denies their reality. He says Brahman enters into the limiting adjuncts but from the highest point of view Brahman does not change (3.2.20) and so does not really enter the "illusory" limiting adjuncts. He speaks of "external objects" in Ishvara's creation as being real to refute the alleged "idealism" of the Buddhist Yogacharins (Vijnanavadins) in which such objects are merely mental projections (2.2.28-31), but he then claims that the external realm is all an illusion and that only the consciousness of Brahman is real. He can utilize the phenomenal world to refute the reality of dreams but then utilize Brahman to refute the reality of our waking "dream" — sense-experience is utilized only within arguments on the conventional dualistic level. He speaks of "unity" with Brahman and absorption of our essence (atman) (3.2.26) and then claims that our essence is already Brahman and changeless and so there is nothing to be absorbed or to do any absorbing — no *action* is involved in gaining Brahman-knowledge.

Shankara claims that the Vedas are the sole means of correct knowledge (*pramana*) for matters of Brahman, and the other means of correct knowledge that he mentions in the BSB (sense-experience and inferential reasoning) are confined to the phenomenal realm. But those means can be utilized in that context since all reasoning is a matter of root-ignorance. The Vedas are eternal and its "perfect knowledge" cannot be denied (2.1.11). But all explanations and verifications are only for the unenlightened. Even the Vedas are products of the realm of root-ignorance and only of value for the unenlightened (4.1.3) — the enlightened have no need for an explanation or justification of Brahman-knowledge. Thus, like everything else phenomenal, the Vedas in the end are products of root-ignorance and function only until one is enlightened. They are provisional in nature — only aids for the unenlightened. This would also help him ground the claim that some claims in the Upanishads are only meant figuratively and not literally and are meant only for the unenlightened. Some false statements are more helpful than others, but ultimately they still are all false. Even the non-figurative statements are ultimately "figurative" in that sense.[11]

This way of reasoning mixes the higher (nondualistic) and conventional (dualistic) points of view, but it can be done consistently if Shankara keeps the contexts of the claims clear. That is, the character in the dream realm can utilize either point of view (the root-ignorance-generated reasons and the ultimately correct point of view) without contradiction if the context of each claim remains clear. If so, Shankara can maintain his metaphysics of absolute oneness and illusionism while still utilizing dualistic arguments. It defeats the charge of inconsistency often leveled against Shankara — he has no problem advancing conflicting claims on the conventional level since ultimately they are all just made within an illusory dream. That is, he is trying to show characters in a dream that they are dreaming and so anything that works is acceptable. "Anything goes" since nothing we say within the dream applies to Brahman. Nevertheless, for Shankara arguments pointing toward the oneness of a transcendent reality are still better than arguments that do not.

Unfortunately, it is not always clear from which point of view a statement is being made. For example, when Shankara says that Brahman has diverse powers (2.1.24) which would mean Brahman has one being but is not simple structurally, but is this about Ishvara or about Brahman as seen from the higher point of view? So too, Shankara is not always clear that two points

---

[11] Any statement will be dualistic because language necessarily makes distinctions. But mystical statements may still reflect what is allegedly experienced (see Jones 2016: chap. 7).

of view are involved or we often must infer which point of view is involved. Indeed, in his commentary on a single aphorism he may claim contradictory things from the lower point of view. It is disconcerting that he sometimes toggles between points of view within one paragraph without clearly demarcating the switch. For example, he can claim that Vedantic texts teach both Brahman as connected to limiting conditions as an object of devout meditation (*upasana*) and Brahman as free of such connections as the object of knowledge (1.1.11). So too, the highest Atman can uniquely be characterized both by the nonaction that is inherent to its nature (*svarupa*) and at the same time by its active power of illusion (*maya*) (2.2.7). That is an inconsistency if inaction is not the Atman's true nature and *maya* a product of root-ignorance. He asserts, as does the *Brahma Sutra*, that an individual is a part (*amsha*) of Brahman (2.1.26) to counter his opponent and then turns around and asserts that this is only "so to speak" (*iti*) since Brahman is partless — but then returns to treating individuals as parts of Brahman again (2.3.43-45).

Shankara does not expound on juxtaposing two points of view, but his reasoning can be seen as consistent only if one characterization of the Atman is from the higher point of view and one from root-ignorance's perspective — if both claims are from a single point of view (either enlightened or arising from root-ignorance), contradictions would arise that are politely called a "paradoxes." But Shankara affirms that Brahman cannot having contradictory properties (3.2.11). (This is not say that Shankara was always consistent — he did not stick to precise definitions for all terms.) Nevertheless, the higher point of view is not the only one that Shankara utilizes, and he does not eliminate the lower point of view generated by root-ignorance but only changes its status: the lower point of view still has validity in our unenlightened life even if the higher is more ontologically correct. But, as discussed below, his system cannot adequately explain why this is possible if the phenomenal realm is only an illusion.

Thus, Shankara still talks about substrata, multiple essences (atmans), lords, persons, and so forth while advocating a metaphysics of absolute oneness that denies these. But it does look as if Shankara is trying to have things both ways: phenomenal events are not actually real and yet our experiences can be utilized to defeat opponents, and this seems to require that the phenomena within the "dream" in fact have some reality. How can we accept that any reasoning within the dream is legitimate if the dream realm has no reality? How can these things be argued about or utilized in arguments if they are illusory and void of being (*sat*)? If everything in the world is an illusion, then the Vedas are also illusionary, as are all distinctions drawn in language, which contradicts Shankara's claim that the Vedas validate truth for the unenlightened. Indeed, his appeal to arguments proves that differentiations are valid — no means of correct knowledge apply in what is truly a dream. Adding "so to speak" does not change this. His response to his opponents who made this charge — that the Vedas only apply within the "dream" (2.1.14, 4.3.14) — does not account for why the dream is there. So too, sense-experience and inferences for the phenomenal realm proves that differentiations are real. And yet Ishvara's creation has fixed structures such as karma and the inherent nature of things (such as heat in fire). In sum, if the content of the dream world is without reality, how can any of it be the basis for an argument? Even if he is fighting fire with fire, doesn't that mean that the fire is real in some sense?

In short, Shankara's "two points of view" approach to reasoning gives *the point of view of root-ignorance* some legitimacy, and that is something Shankara ultimately rejects. It leads to a problem with his metaphysics: the sense of a manifest world introduces the appearance of duality when reality in fact is nondual. His ontology of the oneness of reality combined with illusionism that dismisses the reality of the world of apparent change and multiplicity *in toto* cannot adequately explain the presence of the realm of root-ignorance or the very appearance of an illusory realm that apparently has its own reality or why that realm persists for the enlightened after knowledge of Brahman arises (4.1.15) or why the enlightened are not immediately disembodied upon gaining enlightening knowledge (4.2.7).[12]

The Problem of Root-Ignorance

Shankara did not analyze the concept of "root-ignorance" (*avidya*) and problems arise with the concept. In particular, there are four basic questions. First, why is *avidya* even there if all that is real is one consciousness? How can we not be aware of Brahman if it is the only reality and our essence (atman) is Brahman? How is obstruction or a contaminated consciousness possible? How is delusion or superimposition possible? How can we think we are not liberated if we are Brahman and eternally free? Why do we have a sense of diversity and a sense of change if Brahman is one, unchanging, and the only

---

[12] Stating that the phenomenal realm persists because it is Ishvara's creation does not help because for Shankara Ishvara is illusion, a mere *avidya*-induced error since Brahman is actually changeless (*kutastha*).

reality and we are that reality? How can any ignorance arise from a distinc-tionless consciousness that is pure knowledge? Why is there any diversity in our consciousness at all? How can a sense of diversity enter the picture when the only reality is a pure, featureless, and undifferentiated consciousness? How do the characters in the dream have a deluded consciousness of diverse independent realities? So too, how is it possible to misconstrue Brahman as a personal creator god in the first place? Even if *avidya* were eternal (and so we always have prior ideas to superimpose on Brahman), we can still legitimately ask why it is there, why there are any ideas to superimpose, and why it has no cause. Where could it possibly come from? As Ramanuja stated in one of his objections to Shankara's notion of *avidya*, if *avidya* is part of Brahman, it is real and cannot be removed; if it is not part of Brahman, then Shankara's nondualism fails since there would then be something other than Brahman.[13] As Daniel Ingalls (1953) put the dilemma: if *avidya* is real, then Shankara's doctrine of the nonduality of reality collapses since there is another reality besides Brahman; but if *avidya* is not real, then what is central to his philosophy is merely a figment of our imagination. Whether *avidya* is a stand-alone entity or a property of someone, the problem remains.

Second, what is the object (*vashaya*) seen through *avidya*? That is, what is its field of operation? It cannot be Brahman for how could pure nondual self-luminous consciousness be obscured by what is not real? Nor can it the phenomenal world that is itself the product of *avidya*. Even if the phenom-enal world is a projection by Ishvara, it is still not real but is itself illusory. That this projection can be misperceived seems to give *avidya* some ontological status. And if we and Ishvara are really Brahman, then how can we misperceive our projection?

Third, Shankara had no answer to the question "Who has *avidya*?" As Ramanuja pointed out, the real (Brahman) cannot have what is not real (i.e., *avidya*) — the real cannot have any duality or error within it — nor can individuals (*jivas*) have it since they are a *product* of it. So who has *avidya*? In what is it based? From the root-ignorance point of view, it is the *jivas*, but they are already products of *avidya* — products of superimposition cannot be its source even if they also superimpose. They can have neither *avidya* nor Brahman-knowledge since they are nothing. So from the higher point of view, who has *avidya*? Shankara seems to be committed to *avidya* resting in the highest Lord that contains the unmanifested seed of everything whose nature

---

[13] For a discussion of all of Ramanuja's objections, see Grimes 1990.

is root-ignorance (1.4.3). But this cannot be so since Brahman cannot have any ignorance or anything that is not real (*sat*) — in short, Brahman cannot be deluded. But, again, it cannot be individuals in the dream since they are not real and are in fact products of root-ignorance. Thus, Shankara can offer no answer here any more here than with what is the object of *avidya*.

Fourth, how can *avidya* have power over *vidya*? The enlightened remain in this world until the karmic effects of earlier meritorious and demeritorious deeds that had begun to take effect before enlightenment (*prarabdha-karma*) are exhausted (3.3.27, 4.1.19), just as a potter's wheel continues to spin after the potter's hand is removed (4.1.15). But this gives karma power over even knowledge of Brahman. The inner atman cannot even destroy its own body (2.1.21). That the enlightened still see Ishvara's created phenomenal world is one thing, but they also must remain in the dream realm until the karmic effects of their *avidya*-driven *prarabdha-karma* actions are expiated.[14] If the world is only a magical illusion (*maya*), how is that possible? Knowledge is *equivalent* to Brahman itself (1.1.5, 1.3.19), and *avidya* supposedly is an illusion. So how is it that Brahman-knowledge, although the only reality, does not have the power to destroy an illusion? Why can it destroy some types of karmic effects and not others? These actions are stronger than Brahman-knowledge (BUB 1.4.7), but how can what is utterly an illusion have such power over the only reality? Even though the phenomenal world is Ishvara's "creation," it is still not real — so why must the enlightened remain in it at all? But the "illusion" may last even after the last illusory person attains illusory liberation (2.2.41).

But Shankara dismissed all such questions as pointless. For him, they are not well-formed questions — *avidya* is not real, and so the question is like asking "Who is the son of a barren woman?" As Karl Potter puts it, Shankara "conspicuously avoids [such] issues by simply denying that *avidya* belongs to anything. It is never really connected to either the *jiva* or Brahman or God [Ishvara]. And he drops the matter there" (1981: 80). He believed the same result occurred whether Brahman or the individual *jiva* had *avidya* (3.2.21). Even his answer to the direct question of to whom does root-ignorance

---

[14] In BUB 1.4.7, Shankara notes "the weakness of the operation of knowledge" and adds that the knower of Brahman must maintain a "continuous stream of recollection of knowledge of the Atman by having recourse to the strength of disciplines (*sadhanas*) such as renunciation and detachment." As Lance Nelson notes, this is an uncharacteristic reference to yogic practice by Shankara (1996: 28). But such practices may be needed to maintain the enlightened state of mind.

belong — "It is yours who is asking the question!" (4.1.3) — evades the issue
with an ambiguous answer: is it "you" Atman or "you" the *jiva*?[15] For
Shankara, any answer will reflect only an unenlightened point of view and
make *avidya* seem to be a reality of some kind — but for him *avidya* is not a
reality, and so no one "has" it any more than a rope or a perceiver has the
"snake." Only because we have a term for it does *avidya* makes us think it is
a reality and gets us caught up in the question of what its referent is. *Avidya*
simply cannot be connected to either Brahman or a *jiva*.

Nevertheless, for Shankara *avidya* is still there, coloring our unenlightened experience and preventing knowledge of Brahman. But, as discussed
below, Shankara's sole objective is evoking knowledge of the oneness of
reality in his students, not investigating *avidya's* nature or advancing
metaphysical systems — *avidya's* inexplicability is simply inconsequential and
irrelevant to him, and so he offers no explanation even if that move adversely
impacts the credibility of his philosophy.[16]

The Phenomenal World and Individuals

The ontological counterpart to the epistemological problems related to root-
ignorance is the illusion of a world that is apparently created by Ishvara
(Brahman misseen as having attributes) through his creative power (*maya*).
As discussed, the phenomenal world is not an illusion in the sense of being
a figment of our individual minds — it is Ishvara's "creation." Rather, we are
deluded in seeing the realm as independent of Brahman and as consisting of
a plurality of separate real subjects and objects. Ishvara's creation persists for
the enlightened even after their delusion vanishes by their knowledge (4.1.15).
That is, Brahman-knowledge subrates an *idea* — the delusion that the
phenomenal realm is a reality independent of Brahman and pluralistic — but
the world remains as it is (Intro., 4.1.15). The world vanishes during the
anubhava experience, but it returns to the consciousness of the enlightened

---

[15] In his commentary on the *Bhagavad-gita* 13.2, Shankara stated that the question is
meaningless, i.e., "without sense (*nirarthakah*)."

[16] Advaitins diverged after Shankara on this point. According to his older contemporary, Mandana Mishra, the locus of root-ignorance is the individual *jiva*, not
Brahman, but Brahman is its object. On the other hand, according to Shankara's students Padmapada and Sureshvara, Brahman is the only reality and so root-ignorance
must reside in it. These two positions became the basis for the Bhamati and Vivarana
branches of Advaita. For the former, each individual had his or her own *avidya*.

afterwards and they see it as such — no one can annihilate Ishvara's creation (3.2.21). Thus, the enlightened see the same realm as before attaining the liberating knowledge, but now they know that it is not a reality independent of Brahman or consisting of independent objects and subjects.

Gaudapada treated the phenomenal realm as the radiance of Brahman and thus as part of Brahman and thus as real (*sat*) (see vol. 1: 123-30). But Shankara rejected that option: for him, Brahman is consciousness and is never an object but eternally a subject. Brahman is unmanifested and not observable by the senses (1.1.1, 1.1.3, 1.1.4, 2.1.6, 2.1.27, 2.3.7, 3.2.23).[17] Thus, the observable phenomenal world is not in any way Brahman. What is seen is not Brahman and thus not real (*sat*) — it is like an illusion or dream. Again, "nonduality" (*a-dvaita*) does not mean a oneness of the phenomenal world and Brahman but simply that there no second reality to Brahman (2.1.26), and nothing real for Brahman to be connected to.

But this metaphysics leaves important questions unanswered. Even if this realm is not real (*sat*) but is also not totally unreal (*asat*) like the son of a barren woman (2.1.18), why is there an illusion of a realm at all? Even if the phenomenal world is nothing but Ishvara's dream-like projection, how can that possibility exist at all? An illusion has no place in a metaphysics with only those two all-or-nothing options — there is no intermediate option. So how could something that is not Brahman be manifested in any sense what-soever? How did these appearances or any diversity enter into Brahman's attribute-free pure consciousness? How can something apparently "objective" as the world even appear if only an eternal subject is real? How is any appear-ance possible, and why is it diverse? How could that enter the imagination if all that is real is a featureless pure consciousness? How can a featureless and unchanging Brahman have any such "dream"? Where would the content come from? In short, how is the illusion of a "snake" even possible?

But although Brahman is aspatial, atemporal, one, and changeless, there is an apparently "objective" world of space and time. The appearance is beginningless (2.1.36). Somehow limiting adjuncts like the body and mind and names and forms became associated with a formless and featureless con-sciousness to make the consciousness appear finite and formed. Brahman seems to enter things (e.g., 3.2.20) and to conform to the adjuncts (3.2.20). Where did the adjuncts and "name-and-form" (*nama-rupa*) come from? Even

---

[17] BSB 1.3.13 states that Brahman is the object of perception, but this means it is *the object to be meditated upon* (cf. 3.2.23). Shankara also states that there is no percep-tion when one is one with Brahman (citing BU 4.4.15) in a depth-mystical experience.

if *maya* is eternal, we can still ask why it is there and where it came from. How did it become part of the picture? So too, why are some parts of the dream conscious and some not (e.g., 1.1.6)? Moreover, that the phenomenal realm is a projection of Ishvara gives it an "objectivity" that limits the actions even of the enlightened — indeed, even Ishvara is constrained in his creation by the past karmic acts of the individuals (*jiva-atmans*) in the realm (2.1.24). The fixed structures regulating Ishvara's "creation" (e.g., the law of karma) existed from eternity in the past and are only deemed not real because they will cease to exist in the future when his "creation" expires. Again, what is subrated by Brahman-knowledge is the *delusion* of realities separate from Brahman, not the phenomenal realm itself or its content (4.1.15): Shankara admitted that the objects of ordinary consciousness are *never negated* in any circumstance (2.2.29) — the enlightening knowledge and the *anubhava* experience of Brahman only affect our deluded *ideas*, not *what is there*.[18]

In sum, why there is even the possibility of a phenomenal realm in the first place is not explained. Treating it as Ishvara's creation does not suffice as a final explanation since Shankara argues that Ishvara is a misperception of the one, formless, nonpersonal, actionless, and unchanging consciousness (Brahman) — he is no more real than any of our other dualistic conceptions. In short, Ishvara is part of the illusion. Thus, the ideas of a "creator" and a "creation" are only matters of root-ignorance. That delusion is not imagined for those with Brahman-knowledge, and yet the world remains. But how Brahman can be misperceived as a personal creator being is not explained. How can what is featureless and does not move or change in any way be seen as acting? How does that possibility even exist? What is it in Brahman that we see dualistically as Ishvara's nature to unfold a phenomenal world? What is real (Brahman) could not start what is not real (*avidya*, *maya*, superimposition, name-and-form), so how did the whole shebang get going?

And where did individual centers of consciousness within the phenomenal realm — persons (*jivas*) — come from? There is only one consciousness and one essence (Atman), so how do multiple *jivas* with diverse individual

---

[18] Shankara claimed limiting adjuncts are necessary for us to have cognition (3.2.7). This may mean that they are necessary to experience Brahman, not only for knowing phenomenal objects within the realm of root-ignorance. But the adjuncts also lead us incorrectly to identify the Atman with our dualizing mind and the body in the way that a translucent crystal appears colored when near a colored object (1.3.19, 3.2.11, 3.2.15), thereby leading us to confuse the real and the not real. And why we would need illusory adjuncts to experience what we really are is not explained — it is not as if Atman becomes an object distinct from itself in the *anubhava* experience.

sense-experiences and thoughts arise? Why do *jivas* have different mental states and not just pure consciousness? How can the one featureless essence relate to those *jivas*? Why are there different characters in the dream if they are not real in some sense even if they do not meet the Advaita criterion of a "reality" (i.e., being eternal and unchanging)? That is, how can individual atmans have different properties than the Atman and also different properties from each other if *jivas* are illusions? Or why can I not experience what you are experiencing if there is only one consciousness? Or how can individuals reemerge from being "absorbed" into Brahman in sleep or after an *anubhava* experience with their individuality and our memories (and those of other persons) intact? How can we forget and need reminding what we are? How could we fall out of knowledge if all is one?

This leads to the counterpart of the "who has *avidya*?" issue: who attains liberation from rebirth and suffering? It cannot be Brahman since it is already enlightened, free of rebirth, and cannot change. The embodiment of the Atman is only apparent — an illusion generated by root-ignorance. In reality, the Atman has no relation to the body or rebirth. Nor can the illusory *jivas* be what attains liberation since they are not real. So, what then? Again Shankara is not clear: "The same result occurs either way. Once it is realized that Brahman is the true being of the individual and that the individual is an illusion due only to root-ignorance, there remains no being upon whom injunctions (to know Brahman) could be laid" (3.2.21).

So too, how do rebirths arise if they are not real and neither is *avidya*? The apparent activity of individual persons in this world also is no more real than the empty activity of characters in a dream. What is reborn? What transmigrates cannot be the transcendent Atman (which never changes) nor the inner essence (atman) (1.1.5) (which is Atman) nor the *jiva* (which is not a separate reality but an illusion). Shankara has ultimately has to say its Atman "as it were" (Upad 1.18.45). But still a bundle of karmic potentialities moves on. For dualistic conventional purposes, this can be called the transmigrating person who is the size of a thumb (1.3.25, 2.3.30), but the size of the Atman is only figurative (2.3.29). And Shankara, like the *Brahma Sutra*, did distinguish the transmigrating person (*jiva-atman*) from the highest Atman (2.3.17-23). This individual atman has no beginning (2.3.16), but no real thing is actually reborn. Thinking we are in a cycle of rebirths is a delusion (*bhranti*) (2.1.22). That is, there never was any real *jiva* in any real chain of rebirths, and thus there never is any real liberation from rebirth, and so for Shankara there is no issue of who is reborn (Atman or the *jiva*) — for him, all this is only part of Ishvara's illusory creation. But the whole show is present and Shankara also states that Brahman constitutes the reality of the transmigrating person and is the embodied atman's real nature (3.2.4).

Moreover, Brahman is constituted by bliss (*ananda*) or is its source (1.1.12-19). So where did the possibility of *suffering* come from? How can there be pleasure and pain for the *jivas* within the "dream" realm while the Atman does not experience them if the phenomenal world is merely an illusion? How is the pain of a broken leg only "figurative" or a product of *avidya* even if it does not affect pure undifferentiated consciousness? Ending the delusion that the Atman suffers (2.2.10, 2.3.46, 4.1.2) and realizing that pain is only a matter of the limiting adjuncts generated by root-ignorance does not end our pain (although it may lessen the pain's emotional impact) — it is no less real because it is not part of pure consciousness. That these involve changes in the "dream" realm seems irrelevant to that question of whether it is real or not. The problem is generated by Shankara's overly restrictive criterion of what is real — what is eternal and unchanging is no doubt real, but this is does not mean that other things might not also be real.

From the point of view of Brahman-knowledge, nothing changes and no new knowledge can be gained — there never was bondage or rebirth but only changeless Brahman. From the root-ignorance point of view, there does appear to be change: first there is a process of rebirth, and then that is ended with the liberating Brahman-knowledge. How does gaining knowledge of Brahman cause a change within a part of Ishvara's creation? What is different between the enlightened in life (*jivan-mukta*) and after their final death? We cannot say that nothing is different: the loss of the *avidya* that propels rebirth is a change — there is the end of suffering for a *jiva*. Dismissing all that as not real does not seem plausible as even a stopgap explanation. Claiming "Nothing happens. I have already always been liberated, and enlightenment only removes of ignorance of that fact" does not help to explain anything. A change still occurs in the stream of a *jiva* even if change is disallowed on metaphysical grounds and the *jiva* is deemed illusory. The problem mentioned above that *prarabdha-karma* prevails over Brahman-knowledge for the enlightened only makes the realm of *avidya* seem more real.

The Inadequacy of Shankara's Metaphysics

From what was presented in the last sections, it is clear that Shankara treated the phenomenal world with enough "reality" that he cannot adequately explain it simply in terms of a metaphysics of one reality and illusionism. The most basic problem is not how to explain how enlightenment is possible or how the phenomenal realm (*jagat*) came to be. Rather, the very presence of any phenomenal world cannot be adequately accounted for if Brahman is one and unchanging. It is not only that the dualizing mind that is infested with root-ignorance cannot get around the problem of how dualism is possible at all. The problem is that the world with fixed structures remains for the enlightened. This gives Ishvara's creation a reality that is hard to see as only the result of *avidya* (either our or Ishvara's). It gives the phenomenal realm too much reality for Shankara's facile dismissal of it — the *oneness* of Brahman's reality simply cannot explain why there is the presence of an apparently diverse realm. Something more than a featureless consciousness must account for that presence, and without that component Shankara's arguments and metaphysical system collapse.

Again, all that is subrated by Brahman-knowledge is not the phenomenal world itself since the world is still there for the enlightened after the *anubhava* experience but only the *idea of a second reality* — the phenomenal world does not vanish when we realize the knowledge the way that the "snake" does when we see the rope properly. The phenomenal world itself is never subrated even if it is not present during an *anubhava* experiences — only its *status* is altered as dictated by Shankara's metaphysics. Nor does the transient *anubhava* experience require that ordinary experiences cannot be cognitive — the *anubhava* experience in itself does not show that other experiences must be grounded in root-ignorance and not disclose reality.

Shankara's defense comes down to his metaphysics of absolute oneness: a criterion for "reality" (*sat*) being eternal existence and changelessness leaves no room for diversity or change in the world, and the only alternative to something being real is being completely unreal (*asat*). A doctrine of illusionism naturally follows, as it did for the Greek Parmenides. However, Shankara must justify why we should accept such a stark criterion, especially since it leads to dismissing so much of our experience and has no place for Ishvara's changing "creation" as "real" or "unreal" even though he accepts that it is there. His justification for that metaphysics is not an experience or philosophical reasoning but only the Vedas *as interpreted by his philosophy*. Thus, as noted above, there is a fundamental circularity at the foundation of his philosophy. As noted above, Vedantins who are not Advaitins interpret the same texts in a way that accepts the oneness of the source of the being of phenomena (Brahman) while not dismissing the diversity and change in the phenomenal realm as not real. For them, worldly phenomena are real but dependent upon Brahman: Brahman is the cosmic essence, the "*Real of the real*" (*satyasya satya*) (BU 2.1.20, 2.3.6; see also BU 4.4.18, KeU 1.2).

Shankara may want to argue that only the unenlightened require such explanations in terms of creation and *maya*, and that the enlightened with their knowledge need none because they realize that there is only one reality. But again this is only from adopting the knowledge-claims given in the Upanishads under his interpretation. The enlightened may no longer be interested in explanations, but the world and *jivas* are still there, and the enlightened will have internalized a metaphysics of illusionism that will affect how they see the world and how they live. They will dismiss the suffering of others as only events in a groundless dream.

All Shankara can advance for why the enlightened should adopt the oneness of reality and illusionism are only his own intellectual ideas. He cannot cite mystical experiences as justification for his negative valuation of the world since the empty *anubhava* experience can be accommodated to different metaphysics (see Jones 2016: chap. 5). So too, one can accept that the universe is all one substance without endorsing his illusionism — today materialists in the West think all phenomena are of one nature (matter). He could have claimed that substance is necessary for anything to be real without dismissing structures and the divisions of things and claiming that substance is all there is to the reality of things. He could have claimed that Brahman is transformed into the universe (the *parinama* theory). He could have adopted Gaudapada's emanationist position that the one transcendent reality (Brahman) projects a diverse realm that is also real (*sat*). He could have accepted a oneness of being (*sat*) complemented by a diversity of powers, but he denied all such diversity from the higher point of view (2.1.24). Instead, he adopted illusionism apparently because he thought that the phenomenal realm introduced diversity into the oneness of reality.

Shankara's arguments are based on the premise that what is real must be eternal, permanent, and changeless. Thus, being (*sat*) is the only criterion. But limiting what is real to only a changeless eternal substance, as Shankara does, distorts any picture of the world — the mere presence of the phenomenal realm shows that there is more to reality than just substance. The "illusion" would not be here if undifferentiated being were all there is to reality. Indeed, there is an inherent tension between nondualism and illusionism: the presence of even an illusion cannot be explained by a changeless and undifferentiated reality. The picture seems unavoidably dualistic (see White

1981). More generally, focusing only on substance to the exclusion of other aspects of the experienced world cannot give a full picture of reality. Structures organizing substance and causal activity have to be accepted (see Jones 2013) to give a full picture of what we experience.

To dismiss the structural dimension as merely part of an illusion because what is real must be eternal and changeless must be justified by more than simple philosophical or theological declarations. One can accept that all clay objects are made of clay without claiming that clay is all there is to their reality: clay pots *do* something different than clay plates, and so focusing only on the common clay misses something real. Thus, their "form" is as real as their substance, and this makes the pot or dish more than simply a lump of clay whose structure can be dismissed as nonreal "modifications." The distinguishing features that lead to diversity among clay objects are not unreal even though they share a common substance. The forms are not merely "figurative" or mere "names" that we impose on clay through root-ignorance. So too for all of reality: the being (*sat*) of the natural world will always be in one state or another, and those states must be taken into account for any adequate picture of reality. Waves are a state of water and what they can do cannot be ignored or treated as not real when compared to the more featureless condition of water in the depths of an ocean — waves are as much a part of the ocean as still water, and why they are there must be accounted for. We certainly can adopt a point of view that focuses on substance rather than structure and actions, but we cannot treat the latter as an illusion without a very strong argument. Otherwise, the position only exhibits a strong bias against our usual experiences.

Shankara's metaphysics has no category for the phenomenal realm. Later Advaitins, starting with Shankara's immediate students, recognized that his metaphysics could not account for our experiences and accepted some degree of reality to the phenomenal realm. But they too have no category for the phenomenal realm that appears to exist. They described its ontological status as "indefinable" or "indescribable" (*anirvachaniya*) — it is a falsity (*mithya*) that is neither "real" nor "unreal."[19] But even that does not give a

---

[19] Shankara did state that the *unmanifested name-and-form* (e.g., 2.1.14; Hacker 1995: 71-73) is "inexpressible as 'that' or as 'other' (*tattvanyatvabhyam anirvachaniya*)"—i.e., it is impossible to say if name-and-form is the same or different from Brahman (1.1.5). But he did not use the phrase for the status of the manifested realm. For Shankara, there is a transcendent unmanifested name-and-form that has a role in the rise of the phenomenal realm. Later Advaitins made the ontological status of the phenomenal world "undefinable (*anirvachaniya*)." He rejected the claim that the phenomenal

positive place for the phenomenal world. As it stands, that is simply an admission that their ontology of a strict monism is inadequate or even incoherent — the world does not fit their categories. Their metaphysics still stresses being or its source to the exclusion of any other dimensions of reality. But until the diversity that we experience is accommodated in some positive fashion, any form of Advaita metaphysics will be inadequate — its cavalier dismissal of our "conventional" experiences does not explain all that needs explaining, especially after Shankara took it so seriously.

In sum, Shankara's reductive metaphysics is not simple but simplistic in not taking the diversity of the phenomenal realm into consideration. We can claim that there is only one source to all phenomena or that all phenomena are made of one substance without making substance the sole criterion for what is real or endorsing an illusionism. So too, his argument is simplistic — merely a dogmatic declaration of metaphysics that dismisses all of our experiences except *anubhava* as delusory, even ordinary experiences occurring after Brahman-knowledge dawns. He must offer some reason since illusionism dissolves all the content of our lives while leaving the basic elements of our experiences and our life as a person within the phenomenal world as more mysterious than without it. But the only reason Shankara advances is that it is backed by the Upanishads — as interpreted by his metaphysics. Why adopt his metaphysics when he has to dismiss so much of our experience as a groundless illusion in the same class as the "snake" when the rope is misperceived? The intricacies of an elaborate metaphysics are not required, but he offers precious little reason to accept a metaphysics that requires illusionism.

Shankara's One-Track Mind

Later Advaitins and Westerners generally prefer to see Shankara's ontology as two-tiered: ultimate reality and an indeterminate reality that is neither ultimately real (*sat*) nor nonexistent (*asat*). Such an ontology is simpler and easier to visualize. But the better way to look at Shankara's own philosophy is not as advancing a two-tiered ontology (since there is only one reality and a totally baseless illusion), but as advancing two perspectives — the enlightened and unenlightened points of view. Shankara stringently rejected an *ontological* dualism but had to advance an *epistemic or experiential* dualism to deal with what we see. For him, there are no "degrees of reality"

---

world can be neither real (*sat*) nor unreal (*asat*) as a contradiction (2.2.33).

Early Advaita Vedanta Philosophy, Volume 2 ~

nor is Brahman "more real" than the world — there is only Brahman. But an epistemic or experiential dualism is plausible even if there is only one reality and so no ontological dualism: we can see reality from either an enlightened (*brahma-vidya*) or deluded (*avidya*) point of view — not that he had any explanation for why that dualism can exist. Nor are the two epistemic points of view equal, as with seeing a duck or a rabbit in the Gestalt figure — the point of view of *vidya* always ultimately prevails. (But there are always complications for Shankara: here, an epistemic dualism is complicated by the fact that for Shankara Brahman and knowledge of Brahman are the same reality [1.1.5, 1.3.19].)

All of this shows that Shankara's arguments are frustrating. He defended only one basic claim — the oneness of being (*sat*) — against schools such as Samkhya and Buddhism that rejected it. But he blithely utilized the the faulty point of view generated by root-ignorance to argue with his opponents and then claims that that realm is all an illusion with no reality whatsoever. Indeed, at the root of his life, there is a blatant inconsistency: his metaphysics denies that individuals within the dream (the *jivas*) exist in any way, and yet he wrote treatises for the unenlightened and taught "illusory" students. He acted like a "real" dream character helping other dream characters.[20]

He sidestepped many philosophical issues and relegated them to the root-ignorance perspective. Perhaps he thought that answering subordinate philosophical issues would only distract students from the quest to end suffering or would present obstacles to realizing the liberating knowledge by increasing the conceptual mind's activity. Shankara apparently did not find these philosophical questions to be edifying for the quest of ending suffering, any more than did the Buddha on questions about the age of the universe, and so forth (*Majjhima Nikaya* I.140, IV.431). He dealt more with epistemological topics related to knowledge and false knowledge than ontological ones (Potter 1963:166). As Karl Potter states, Shankara, like the Buddha, apparently was more interested in teaching his pupils how to end suffering by overcoming ignorance than in discovering the proper account of the relation between Brahman, the self or selves, and the phenomenal world; he philosophizes not so much by propounding a satisfactory theory of his own as by

---

[20] It may be objected that if I see such an obvious contradiction at the very foundations of Shankara's life that perhaps I am badly misreading him. But his stress on the oneness of Brahman leads me to think that he did not seriously try to account for the phenomenal realm except to dismiss it all as a dream and not real — he simply does not care enough about the appearance of an expansive realm to bother explaining it.

criticizing what he saw as the inadequate theories of other schools (1963:165). Daniel Ingalls agrees that Shankara's center of attention was religious and his interest in metaphysics and logic was always subordinated to that (1953:72). But his single-mindedness led Shankara to being sloppy with terminology and logical consistency. As Paul Hacker put it, "we must consider an aversion for definitions and a cavalier attitude toward conceptual systematization as a general distinguishing feature" of Shankara's thought (1995: 95). Shankara is "not philosophically exact," even if he is "pedagogically impressive" (Potter 1963:166). It was left to his followers who were deeply attracted to Shankara's attitude to gradually construct a logically coherent metaphysical system (Ingalls 1953: 72). But for Shankara all philosophical speculations would be only part of the realm of nescience.

In sum, Shankara had only one objective: to lead students to the realization that there is only one reality (Brahman) in order to end their suffering through a final release (*moksha*) from being the cycle of rebirths in our world — even though in his metaphysics suffering, persons, rebirth, and liberation are all illusory. This soteriological goal appears to be more basic to him than metaphysics. Intricacies of his philosophy did not interest him. He had no place for multiplicity in his metaphysics of oneness, and so all he did was dismiss the phenomenal world of diversity and change with little more than a wave of his hand even though illusionism is hard to maintain. Such a monastic ontology would certainly calm our desires (since we then could ignore all the problems of everyday life) and thus end any rebirth driven by karma, even if the metaphysics do not actually reflect all of reality.

However, Shankara's approach does not illuminate our predicament in the world but dismisses it. His basic attitude toward these questions was "I don't know why the phenomenal world is there, and I don't care. We don't need to know the details of how root-ignorance and an illusory 'creation' are possible, and the fineries for the rest of my metaphysics aren't my concern. We just have to accept that the phenomenal 'dream' realm and that individuated conscious beings are there and get on with what really matters: there is only one unchanging, attributeless reality, and the only way to get out of the realm of suffering is to realize that." He did not so much deny the existence of the phenomenal world as affirmed only that there is only one reality. His doctrines were only teaching devices to evoke that realization. How much of his metaphysics other than the oneness of reality he was actually committed to is a moot point — for him, only if a doctrine helps to lead a student to the enlightening knowledge that ends suffering matters.

~ References and Further Reading ~

Adams, George C., Jr. 1993. *The Structure and Meaning of Badarayana's Brahma Sutras: A Translation and Analysis of Adhyaya I*. Delhi: Motilal Banarsidass.

Alston, A. J. trans. 1980-1989. *A Samkara Source-Book*. London: Shanti Sadan.

___. 2000. "Samkara in East and West Today." In Bradley J. Malkovsky ed. *New Perspectives on Advaita Vedanta: Essays in Commemoration of Professor Richard De Smet, S.J.*, pp. 84-108. Boston: Brill.

Apte, Vasudeo Mahadeo, trans. 1960. *Brahma-Sutra-Shankara-Bhashya*. Bombay: Popular Book Depot.

Bader, Jonathan. 1990. *Meditation in Sankara's Vedanta*. Delhi: Motilal Banarsidass.

Comans, Michael. 2000. *The Method of Early Advaita Vedanta: A study of Gaudapada, Shankara, Sureshvara, and Padmapada*. Delhi: Motilal Banarsidass.

Dalal, Neil. 2020. "Contemplating Nonduality: The Method of Nididhyasana in Sankara's Advaita Vedanta." In Ayon Maharaj, ed., *The Bloomsbury Research Handbook of Vedanta*, pp. 45-74. New York: Bloomsbury Academic.

Dasgupta, Surendranath. 1922-23. *A History of Indian Philosophy*, vols. 1-2. Cambridge: Cambridge Univ. Press.

Deutsch, Eliot. 1969. *Advaita Vedanta: A Philosophical Reconstruction*. Honolulu: Univ. Press of Hawaii.

___ and Rohit Dalvi. 2004. *The Essential Vedanta: A New Source Book of Advaita Vedanta*. Bloomington: World Wisdom.

Forsthoeffel, Thomas A. 2002. *Knowing Beyond Knowledge: Epistemologies of Religious Experience in Classical and Modern Advaita*. London: Ashgate.

Fort, Andrew O. 1990. *The Self and Its States*. Delhi: Motilal Banarsidass.

___. "Knowing Brahman While Embodied: Sankara on Ivanmukti." *Journal of Indian Philosophy* 19: 369-89.

___. 1997. "*Jivanmukti* and Social Service in Advaita and Neo-Vedanta." *Poznan Studies in the Philosophy of the Sciences and the Humanities* 59: 489-504.

Frauwallner, Erich. 1973. *History of Indian Philosophy*, vol. 1. Trans. by V. M. Bedekar. Delhi: Motilal Banarsidass.

Gambhirananda, Swami. 1965. *Brahma-Sutra-Bhashya of Sri Sankaracarya.* Calcutta: Advaita Ashrama.

Ghate, V. S. 1981. *The Vedanta: A Study of the Brahma-Sutras with the Bhashyas of Samkara, Ramanuja, Nimbarka, Madhva, and Vallabba.* 3rd ed. Poona: Bhan-darkar Oriental Research Institute.

Grant, Sara. 2000. "The Contemporary Relevance of the Advaita of Sam-karacarya." In Bradley J. Malkovsky, ed. *New Perspectives on Advaita Vedanta: Essays in Commemoration of Professor Richard De Smet, S.J.*, pp. 148-63. Boston: Brill.

Grimes, John A. 1990. *The Seven Great Untenables (Sapta-Vidha Anupapatti).* Dehli: Motilal Banarsidass.

Hacker, Paul. 1995. "Distinctive Features in the Doctrine and Terminology of Sankara: Avidya, Namarupa, Maya, Isvara." In Wilhelm Halbfass, ed., *Philology and Confrontation: Paul Hacker on Traditional and Modern Vedanta*, pp. 72-100. Albany: SUNY Press.

Halbfass, Wilhelm. 1988. "The Concept of Experience in the Encounter Between India and the West." In his *India and Europe: An Essay in Understanding*, pp. 378-402. Albany: SUNY Press.

____. 1991. *Tradition and Reflection: Explorations in Indian Thought.* Albany: SUNY Press.

____, ed. 1995. *Philology and Confrontation: Paul Hacker on Traditional and Modern Vedanta.* Albany: SUNY Press.

Ingalls, Daniel H. H. 1952. "The Study of Samkaracarya." *Annals of the Bhandarkar Oriental Research Institute* (Poona) 33: 1-14.

____. 1953. "Samkara on the Question: Whose is *Avidya?*" *Philosophy East and West* 3 (no. 1): 69-72.

Jones, Richard H. 2004. "Shankara's Advaita Vedanta." In *Mysticism and Morality: A New Look at Old Questions*, pp. 95-114. Lanham, Md.: Lexington Books.

____. 2013. *Analysis and the Fullness of Reality: Reductionism and Emergence Today.* New York: Jackson Square Books / Createspace.

____. 2014a. *Early Indian Philosophy.* New York: Jackson Square Books / Createspace.

____. 2014b. *Early Advaita Vedanta Philosophy*, vol. 1. New York: Jackson Square Books / Createspace.

____. 2015. *Nagarjuna: Buddhism's Most Important Philosopher.* Rev. and expanded ed. New York: Jackson Square Books/Createspace.

____. 2016. *Philosophy of Mysticism: Raids on the Ineffable.* Albany: SUNY

Press.

___. 2018. *Mystery 101: Introduction to the Big Questions and the Limits of Human Knowledge*. Albany: SUNY Press

___. 2020. "On What is Real in Nagarjuna's 'Middle Way.'" *Comparative Philosophy* 11 no.1 (January): 3-31.

Mahadevan, T. M. P. 1985. *Superimposition in Advaita Vedanta*. New Delhi: Sterling.

Maharaj, Ayon, ed. 2020. *The Bloomsbury Research Handbook of Vedanta*. New York: Bloomsbury Academic.

Malkovsky, Bradley J. 2000. "Samkara on Divine Grace." In Bradley J. Malkovsky ed. *New Perspectives on Advaita Vedanta: Essays in Commemoration of Professor Richard De Smet, S.J.*, pp. 70-83. Boston: Brill.

Marcaurelle, Roger. 2000. *Freedom Through Inner Renunciation: Sankara's Philosophy in a New Light*. Albany: SUNY Press.

Mayeda, Sengaku. 1992. *A Thousand Teachings: The Upadesasahasri of Sankara*. Albany: SUNY Press.

Nakamura, Hajime. 1983. *A History of Early Vedanta Philosophy*. 2 vols. Delhi: Motilal Banarsidass.

Nayak, G. C. 1995. "Understanding Sankara Vedanta." *Journal of the Indian Council of Philosophical Research* 13: 71-82.

Nelson, Lance E. 1996. "Living Liberation in Sankara and Classical Advaita: Sharing the Holy Waiting of God." In Andrew O. Fort and Patricia Y. Mumme, eds., *Living Liberation in Hindu Thought*, pp. 17-62. Albany: SUNY Press.

Nicholson, Andrew. n.d. "Bhedabheda Vedanta." *Internet Encyclopedia of Philosophy*.

Potter, Karl H. 1963. *Presuppositions of India's Philosophy*. Englewood Cliffs, N.J.: Prentice-Hall.

___, ed. 1981. *Encyclopedia of Indian Philosophies, vol. 3: Advaita Vedanta up to Samkara and his Pupils*. Delhi: Motilal Banarsidass.

Prasad, Rajendra. 2009. "Problem Posed by Ethics to Advaitism: The Advaitin's Attempt to Solve it Examined." In Rajendra Prasad, ed., *A Historical-Developmental Study of Classical Indian Philosophy of Morals*, pp. 333-37. New Delhi: Concept Publishing.

Preti, Alan A. 2009. "Mysticism and Brahman-Realization." *Journal of Indian Philosophy and Religion* 14 (October): 21-37.

___. 2014. "*Brahmanubhava* as *Uberpramana* in Advaita Vedanta: Revisiting an Old Debate." *Philosophy East and West* 64 (July): 718-39.

Radhakrishnan, Sarvepalli. 1960. *The Brahma Sutra: The Philosophy of Spiritual Life*. New York: Harper & Row.

Ram-Prasad, Chakravarthi. 2002. *Advaita Epistemology and Metaphysics: An Outline of Indian Non-Realism*. New York: Routledge.

Rao, Srinivasa. 2012. *Advaita Vedanta: A Contemporary Critique*. New Delhi: Oxford Univ. Press.

Sharma, Arvind. 1997. *The Rope and the Snake: A Metaphorical Exploration of Advaita Vedanta*. New Delhi: Manohar.

___. 2004. *Sleep as a State of Consciousness in Advaita Vedanta*. Albany: State Univ. of New York Press.

Stroud, Scott R. 2011. "Sankara and the Challenges of Interpretation: Advaita Vedanta and the Ethical Dilemmas of the *Bhagavad Gita*." *Journal of Indian Philosophy and Religion* 42 (no. 1): 116-37.

Suthren Hirst, Jacqueline G. 2005. *Samkara's Advaita Vedanta: A Way of Teaching*. New York: Routledge.

Thibaut, George, trans. 1962 [1896]. *The Vedanta Sutras of Badarayana with the Commentary of Shankara*, 2 vols. New York: New York: Dover Publications.

Todd, Warren Lee. 2013. *The Ethics of Sankara and Santideva: A Selfless Response to an Illusory World*. New York: Routledge.

White, John D. 1981. "God and the World from the Standpoint of Advaita Vedanta: A Critical Assessment." *International Philosophical Quarterly* 21 (no. 2): 185-93.

* * *

Printed in Great Britain
by Amazon